AUNT AGONY ADVISES

Aunt Agony Advises

PROBLEM PAGES
THROUGH THE AGES

Robin Kent

W. H. ALLEN · LONDON
A Howard & Wyndham Company
1979

Printed and bound in Great Britain by
Billing & Sons Ltd, Guildford, London & Worcester
for the Publishers W. H. Allen & Co. Ltd,
44 Hill Street, London W1X 8LB

ISBN 0 491 02476 2

Contents

Acknowledgements

This book was researched with the help of the staff of The British Library in Great Russell Street and Colindale; The Bodleian Library, Oxford; and The Picton Library, Liverpool. It was typed, sometimes under conditions of considerable urgency, by my mother, Mrs Hedda Kent, Alyss Shrimpton, Mrs Grainge, Irene McGlashan, Tina Bradshaw and Mandy Singleton. To all these, my thanks.

Kitty Warnock and John Thompson kindly found and lent me material. Julian Browne and Chris Reid read and commented on some early drafts. Nick Shrimpton read every word and commented on most of them. Such mistakes as remain are, of course, the consequence of my own obduracy.

To Nick
who has given me more good advice than any auntie.

1

A practical and wise assistance
THE HISTORY OF THE PROBLEM PAGE

The problem page was invented by John Dunton, a thirty-two year old printer and bookseller, who spoke of morality but knew more about sin. In 1691, as winter was shading into spring, his thoughts turned obsessively on a young man's fancy. He had, it would seem, been conducting an extra-marital affair and his conscience was troubled. He even, at one point, flirted with confessing all 'to some divine'. But his wish to unburden his soul, and his need to seek advice, continued to be over-ridden by a desire for anonymity – 'how to conceal myself and the wretch was the difficulty'.

As he rambled in St George's Fields, Lambeth, the Speakers' Corner of seventeenth century dissent, he suddenly realised that he could not be alone in his dilemma. He immediately stopped and announced to his startled companions, with a characteristic mixture of emotional relief and financial acumen, 'Well, Sirs, I have a thought I will not exchange for fifty guineas.' At this stage he had no more than 'a confused idea of concealing the querist and answering the question'. But the consequence was the birth, on 10 March 1691, of *The Athenian Gazette*, the first device for audience participation in the history of publishing.

The idea was novel, but not entirely without precedent. L'Estrange, Charles II's censor, had employed the question and answer format in the 1680s in *The Observer* and *Hereditus Redens*, commenting on the news through the mouths of

'The Trimmer' and 'The Observer'. But Dunton made
two important innovations. Firstly, he genuinely opened his
pages to the reader. And, secondly, he very rarely used his
question and answer technique to comment on political
matters.

The range of subjects in Dunton's problem pages was,
nonetheless, far broader than that of a twentieth century
agony column. Less than half the questions were from
readers racked by personal difficulties with love, family
loyalty or sex. The majority delved into such topics as the
mysteries of the Creation, the morality of slave-trading,
the probability of perpetual motion, what caused a
rainbow, the reasons for dizziness and why one hour's
sermon seemed longer than two hours' conversation. That
diversity   explains   Dunton's   choice   of   title.   A
contemporary history of the project, by a 'Gentleman who
got secret intelligence of their whole proceedings', reveals
that Dunton had been struck by Verse 21, Chapter 17 of
The Acts of the Apostles. The Athenians, according to St Paul,
'spent their time in nothing else, but either to tell, or to
hear some new thing'. The telling and hearing of new
things, conducted in both prose and verse, proved
popular. After one issue *The Athenian Gazette* became *The
Athenian Mercury*, under which name it ran for nearly six
years. Even then public enthusiasm was not exhausted and
highlights were reprinted by Dunton as *The Athenian Oracle*.

As a scholar Dunton had his peers. As a salesman,
however, he had none. He marketed his new idea with
typical panache. To help him do the actual writing he
enlisted his friend Richard Sault, the mathematician, and
his future brother-in-law Samuel Wesley (father of the
founders of Methodism). The agreement signed by the
three men in the April of 1691 stated that Sault and Wesley
would each week prepare enough material, by Friday
afternoon, to fill half a printed sheet of the *Gazette* or
Mercury. Failure to meet this deadline would be penalised
by the fine of one shilling, to be spent on liquid
refreshment during the editorial meeting. This modest
team of three clearly produced the bulk of *The Athenian
Mercury*'s output. It was, however, deemed insufficiently

impressive for purposes of publicity. Instead Dunton invented The Athenian Society, a team of scholarly gentlemen who supposedly paused in their scientific experiments, or laid aside their Sunday sermons, to offer advice to the readers of the new magazine.

Dr Johnson would later dismiss the Society as 'a knot of obscure men who published a periodical pamphlet of answers to questions sent, or supposed to be sent, by letters'. The great lexicographer was, however, not entirely fair. Both Sault and Wesley could lay claim to genuine intellectual achievements, and Dunton did make occasional use of other distinguished minds. John Norris, vicar of Bemerton and former Fellow of All Souls, apparently gave the benefit of his considerable knowledge without payment. The diplomat and statesman Sir William Temple, architect of the Triple Alliance, was also said to be a contributor and his secretary, Jonathan Swift, though later rather scathing about his publisher in *A Tale of a Tub*, certainly wrote a poem for the fifth issue of *The Athenian Mercury*. Defoe, Tait, Mottheux and Richardson also contributed verse to Dunton's pages.

Quite clearly the role of auntie was not yet a feminine preserve. Women were, however, involved in the problem page from a very early date. Dunton's autobiography contains a long list of distinguished female contributors to *The Athenian Mercury*. This includes 'the divine Astell' and 'the refined Lady Masham', both known for their virtuous lives, elegant phraseology and noble thoughts (Mary Astell wished to found a women's college to 'stock the kingdom with pious and prudent ladies'). By the mid 1690s it was clearly fashionable for literary ladies to write for Dunton. One of the Augustan age's most fêted poets, Mrs Rowe (née Elizabeth Singer), appears in his list as 'Madame Singer, The Pindaric Lady of the West'. Her volume of 1696, *Poems on Several Occasions*, confirms his claim. In a poem written as a 'zealous tribute' to the Athenian Society she makes specific reference to her own part in its activities:

A friendship so exalted and immense
A female breast did ne'er before commence.

Dr Johnson's other charge, that Dunton's letters were not
genuine, is once again only partly true. 'We were,' Dunton
writes, 'immediately overladen with letters and sometimes
I have found several hundreds for me at Mr Smith's coffee-
house in Stocks Market where we usually met to consult
matters.' The agreement with Sault and Wesley similarly
specifies that the editorial meeting at three o'clock each
Friday afternoon would be devoted to receiving 'new
questions for the next week'. By the tenth issue of *The
Athenian Mercury* Dunton was publicly quarrelling with his
correspondents:

> *There are some persons who have lately been very angry with us
> because we have printed their letters verbatim: we can assure them
> that we have disoblig'd none of them knowingly. It has always been
> our custom to commit all queries and cases to the press without any
> alteration unless we are desired to the contrary, or unless they are so
> very silly that they are intolerable; therefore the fault is not ours, but the
> inadvertency of those who complain that they are disobliged.*

Dr Johnson's suspicion is, of course, a perennial one which
survives to this day. Its first appearance in print, in *The
British Apollo* (a successor of *The Athenian Mercury* in the first
decade of the eighteenth century), was interestingly also
the occasion of its most definitive rebuttal:

> *Hark ye, you Apollo, don't you make questions and answers?*

> Not at present, really Sir; but should soon take that method
> if other people's questions were of no more consequence
> than yours.

The real reason for believing Dunton's letters to have been
mostly authentic is a practical one. *The Athenian Mercury* was
planned as a weekly, became bi-weekly and briefly was
published four days a week, only reverting to a bi-weekly
schedule (timed to coincide with the departure of mail
coaches for the provinces on Tuesdays and Saturdays)
when Dunton decided his staff were heading for a brain-
storm. All those involved were busy men. Like Defoe and

Steele after them, they welcomed free contributions from readers to fill up the blank pages.

For the readers, too, there were sound reasons for writing to the editor. The 'several hundreds' of letters at Mr Smith's coffee-house may have been a slight exaggeration, in an age when a long-running magazine like Defoe's *Review* had a circulation of only three hundred copies and even *The Spectator* and *The Tatler* could rarely manage more than three thousand. But the prospect of skilled legal or medical advice for 2d (1d for postage, 1d for the *Mercury*) must have been an almost irresistible bargain when a doctor's fee was already a guinea.

Dunton's correspondents seem, moreover, to have come from very diverse social backgrounds, stretching from aristocrats with an income of £1000 a year to inmates of debtor's prisons, from punctilious clergymen to lowly apprentices. In another of his publications, *The Post-Angel*, Dunton printed in 1701 a poem celebrating this variety. The verses detail the ladies who wish to know whether their lovers are being faithful, and how to attract men; the seekers of astrological advice; the parsons who wish for preferment; mathematicians who need help with their sums; 'noisie fools' with impertinent queries, and seamen who want forecasts of the outcome of the war. Meanwhile, helping them all:

Behind the scenes sit mighty we,
Nor are we known, nor will we be,
The world and we exchanging thus,
While we find chat for them, they work for us.

The Post-Angel was the prototype of the modern popular newspaper, lacking only the bosoms on page three. After some brisk coverage of the domestic and foreign news, it concentrated on crime and punishment, the sensational, and the occult. Here, for the first time, the problem page became a subordinate part of a publication with other contents. Dunton righteously included a list of the topics which would not be admitted to the correspondence column – no obscene questions, none from Jacobites or

atheists, no riddles and no personal abuse. In fact he sailed
very close to the wind, especially where the first category
was concerned. Within a year he sold out to a group of
clergymen who did indeed run it as a moral, responsible
newspaper. The consequence, inevitably, was its almost
immediate closure.

The movement of the problem page from the treatment
of abstruse and learned topics to a concentration upon
more personal and more entertaining matters was not,
however, Dunton's innovation. The glory here must go to
another Grub Street hack, Tom Browne. His agony
column first appeared in February 1692 in *The
Lacedaemonian Mercury*, a paper co-edited by William Pate
and Charles Gildon (one of Pope's dunces in *The Dunciad*).
Browne freely admitted his debt to *The Athenian Mercury*
which, he declared, he regularly read in bed when, 'being
destitute of either opium or poppy water', he needed
something to put him to sleep. Dunton took neither the
satire nor the piracy kindly and all-out warfare developed,
which descended to personal abuse and threats before
Browne agreed to stop publication. Another short-lived
publication with the same format was *The Ladies' Mercury*,
the first ever women's magazine, which appeared in 1693.
Theological and mathematical enquiries were here
unknown. The characteristic mixture of topics would be a
letter from a deflowered virgin now contemplating
marriage with someone other than her seducer, another
from a virgin wife whose husband was backward in his
attentions, and a third from a husband whose spouse had
been unfaithful to him.

Though the questions became more lurid, the advice
remained highly moral. The early aunties counselled
chastity, faithfulness within marriage, probity in financial
affairs and a dutiful submission to authority. Very rarely,
however, did they manage to live up to their own strict
standards. Browne found most profligacy attractive.
Dunton had a strong sense of morals but a very weak will.
Sault, who died mad and starving in Cambridgeshire in
1702, was accused by his wife of being 'guilty of those
unlawful freedoms' which, according to Dunton, 'might

very well sink him into Melancholy Trouble of Mind'.
Wesley, a parson as well as a problem page writer, led a
respectable life but failed signally to inspire the love of his
parishioners, who were suspected of committing arson at
the vicarage on no fewer than three occasions. Steele,
editor of *The Tatler*, mis-spent two dowries and was in
constant financial difficulty. Defoe, editor of *The Review*,
was twice bankrupted and sold his pen without scruple to
the highest bidder.

Perhaps the least suitable among them to offer advice,
was Dunton. Around the period when he began his second
great series of problem pages in *The British Apollo*
(1708–1711) he is supposed to have become insane, possibly
as a consequence of the official whipping which he
received for profanely cursing Queen Anne in April 1708.
Certainly after 1710 his writing becomes progressively
more rambling, incoherent and self-pitying.

In spite of this, *The Athenian Mercury* and *The British Apollo*
have been acclaimed as the supreme record of early
eighteenth century middle-class life and values. The
nineteenth century historian Walter Besant declared that
this class:

> ... *had no prophet unless it was* The Athenian Oracle *and its*
> *successor,* The British Apollo ... *they help the reader reconstruct an*
> *English family entirely, with its daily life, its daily ceremonies, its*
> *prejudices, its ignorances, its honesty, its narrow religion, its dignity,*
> *and its self-respect* ...

The judgements jointly formulated by the buccaneering
Dunton, by poor, eccentric Sault and by the rigidly
moralistic Wesley seem somehow to have struck a deep
chord in the men and women of their time.

To claim that Dunton's team was the sole voice of the
middle-classes, however, is too sweeping. Daniel Defoe had
equally impressive qualifications for this role. Born in the
Grub Street parish of St Giles, Cripplegate, in 1660, the
son of a tallow merchant, he became a highly successful
businessman while still in his twenties. His family had
followed the local vicar, Dr Annersley, into dissent when
he lost his living in 1662. This religious affiliation gave him

early links with Dunton and Wesley, who were both married to daughters of Dr Annersley. Certainly in the early 1690s Defore was writing question and answer verses for *The Athenian Mercury*.

His main interests at this date were still commercial ones – the whore which he claimed to dote upon was trade. But in 1692 he went bankrupt for the enormous sum of £17,000, and a subsequent attempt to revive his fortunes with a tile factory collapsed in 1703. Thereafter he would earn his living entirely from his pen.

His independent entry into problem page journalism was, nonetheless, largely accidental. In 1704 he launched a magazine called *The Review* which was, under various guises, to continue until 1713. He realised that his didactic articles on trade and foreign affairs would not by themselves appeal to a large readership. Accordingly he leavened the mixture with 'Advice from the Scandalous Club', a pot-pourri of gossip treating 'vice and villainous actions with the utmost severity'. By September 1704 Defoe found this section rapidly filling up with unsolicited questions, and felt obliged to answer them.

Unlike his less candid predecessor John Dunton, Defoe confessed the limitations of his counselling in advance. 'Here is not,' he declared, 'as was pretended in *The Athenian Mercury*, a Professor in all the Heads which the inquisitive world can propose.' The fictitious nature of the Scandalous Club was also discreetly indicated. This society of gentlemen, which supposedly held its frequent meetings in Paris, was 'allegorically, rather than significantly, called a Society'. With a bankruptcy and eight charges of fraud only a year behind him, Defoe made quite sure that the readers knew precisely what they were getting:

> ... *for sundry reasons the hand that operates this work ... may be incapable of performance in so vast a variety as is like to come before him: so he thinks no injury to the undertaking to let the world know they must be content to be answered in the best manner he can.*

The apologies appear to have been superfluous. Writing on behalf of the 'Society', in answer to a complaint, on 4 November 1704, Defoe declared:

*They are sorry if they do not please, but are not convinced of the fact;
first because they are not sensible of the reason, and second they do not
find it in consequence since more of the paper is bought than ever, and
more letters and cases sent than ever, insomuch that even the
supplement and all have hardly room to crowd in their own
observations.*

A supplement entitled *The Little Review or Inquisition of
Scandal* ran throughout the summer of 1705. Defoe then
reverted to making the problem page an occasional
feature of *The Review*. Even after that magazine had closed,
Defoe retained the role of auntie, contributing columns of
letters and advice to *Applebee's Weekly Journal* and *Mist's
Weekly Journal* in the 1720s.

In all these publications Defoe resolutely preached the
message of middle-class morality. He opposed pre-marital
sex, abortion, sex after the menopause, divorce and,
despite his own appalling record, advocated the strictest
financial rectitude. His great shortcoming as a counsellor
was a very simple one – he felt superior to his readership.
His purpose, as he condescendingly described it in *The
Review*, was 'To enlighten the stupid understandings of the
meaner and more thoughtless of the freeholders and
electors'.

Richard Steele, by contrast, was preaching to the gentry,
whose problems tended to be more frivolous than those
presented to Defoe. Both *The Tatler* and *The Spectator*
included elegant questions and answers, some of which
were clearly faked. But when pressure was such that Steele
could be reduced to printing letters he'd written to his wife
to fill up the pages, it is likely that he also made frequent
use of what he found in his post-bag.

In *The Tatler*, Steele gave his advice as 'Isaac Bickerstaff', a
name originally invented to satirise the astrologer John
Partridge. The use of such a pseudonym may well have
been comforting on those frequent occasions when
Steele's advice and Steele's private life came into collision.
He was, for example, an active campaigner against
arranged marriages in his replies to correspondents. He
had himself, however, made two singularly fortunate
matches, the first to an older widow with an estate worth

£850 who died soon after the marriage, and the second to a minor heiress whom he met at his first wife's funeral. These circumstances may, in turn, have inspired a letter which he published on 22 August 1710, supposedly from one 'Rebecca Midriffe'. Her sister had been seduced by a gentleman attending her husband's funeral, and now wished to know to whom she should attribute the parentage of her future child. Freud would have found plenty to say about that.

In both *The Tatler* and *The Spectator* Steele chose to incorporate his advice into the main body of the magazine, instead of isolating it on a separate problem page. The function of his replies was no longer primarily to educate, or even to moralise. Instead they were written essentially as elegant literary exercises, and this change was to produce many other, less talented, agony essayists.

One of the first imitators of Steele's new manner was *The Female Tatler*. The editor of this publication was a 'Mrs Crackenthorpe', whose illustrious family had come over with William the Conqueror:

> *Our being taken notice of proceeding not from immense riches, gotten by sinister practices, encouraging petty factions, or flattering the vanity of the Luxurious Great, but from religious probity, and true politicks, we were always firm in the church, loyal to our Princes and entire in the interest of our country ...*
>
> (The Female Tatler, *14 October 1709*)

Behind this unlikely mask lurked either the actress and playwright, Mrs Centlivre or, more probably, the notorious Mrs Manley.

Mary de la Riviere Manley was the daughter of the governor of Guernsey. Left an orphan in her teens, she was seduced and bigamously married by her guardian John Manley, a Member of Parliament, who soon deserted her. She then had a series of wealthy lovers, was involved in a scandal over a forged entry of marriage in a church register, wrote three plays and was arrested for libel. She was not, in short, a woman whom society hostesses admitted to their drawing rooms. Her correspondents appear to have remained unconscious of her reputation.

'Timothy Doubtful' wrote to 'Mrs Crackenthorpe' to complain that 'my learn'd wife made me an ignorant coxcomb and soon grafted such a pair of horns upon my fore-head that I could not enter her bed-chamber till she pleased to let me in'. In reply, he was told he had nothing to fear, his wife being 'as honest as the day, as chaste as my own body; and I hope, Sir, you will not call in question a matron of my character, who have withstood all temptation …'. One can only hope that Mr Doubtful found this reassuring.

In a letter to Addison, Swift expressed a damning opinion of Mrs Manley's prose style. She wrote, he claimed, 'as if she had about 2,000 Epithets and fine Words packed up in a Bag … she pulled them out by Handfuls, and strewed them on her Paper, where about once in 500 times they happen to be right'. He was not, however, above employing her to write pamphlets for him, and when she was gravely ill in 1711 he described her, in a letter to Stella, in terms which suggest her potential as an auntie:

> … *she had very generous Principles for one of her sort; and a great deal of good Sense and Invention; she is about forty, very homely and very fat.*

She survived her illness and succeeded Swift as the editor of *The Examiner.* The man who had replaced her on *The Female Tatler* in the November of 1709 was an equally interesting figure, Bernard Mandeville. Famous in his own day as a psychiatric doctor, he is better known in ours as the author of *The Fable of the Bees.* Unfortunately his revolutionary demonstration, in that book, of the way in which private selfishnesses promote the public good was not the sort of matter with which 'Lucinda' and 'Artesia', his mouthpieces in *The Female Tatler,* were allowed to concern themselves.

In 1712 journalism received a set-back with the imposition of Stamp Duty on all newspapers. Many moderately successful publications disappeared altogether, others cut back on such frivolities as the solving of readers'

problems. The question and answer device continued to
be used occasionally – in *The Censor* in 1717 and *The Visiter* in
1723, for example – but the only magazine to devote
substantial space to a problem page was *The Weekly Oracle*
of 1734–6. Taking very much the same tone as Dunton
before him, the editor wrote on 11 January, 1735:

> *We must here desire our readers to take notice that they are not to
> expect any questions answered by us, which have no meaning, are
> trifling or indecent ... We have many hundred questions sent to us, for
> which we think ourselves highly oblig'd to our correspondents, and to
> which we shall pay a proper regard.*

The Weekly Oracle was also marketed along the lines of *The
British Apollo*. Those readers who could contain their
impatience until the end of the month received a bound
version of the four weekly parts for 6d, compared with a
weekly price of 2d a copy.

The next decade witnessed the arrival of the second
major female auntie. This was Mrs Eliza Haywood, editor
of *The Female Spectator* from 1744–6 and authoress of
numerous romantic (though highly moral) novels. Like
many other early aunties, she came from a lower middle-
class background and was unfortunate in her marriage
and her lovers. After a brief career as an actress she turned
to journalism, a pattern repeated in our own day by Anna
Raeburn. To advise her readers, the fifty year old editor
recruited an admirable staff. 'Mira' came from a clever
family and was married to a gentleman 'every way worthy
of so excellent a wife, and with whom she lives in perfect
harmony'. Her second colleague was a widow of quality
'who, not having buried her vivacity in the tomb of her
lord continues to make one in all the modish diversions of
the times, so far, I mean, as she finds them consistent with
innocence and honour'. The youngest member of the staff
was 'Euphrosine', a wealthy merchant's daughter. Despite
an engraving which depicts Mrs Haywood surrounded by
this trio of writing helpers, it is hard to imagine them as
anything other than a figment of the editorial
imagination.

Mrs Haywood also suggested that she had innumerable spies in the fashionable towns of England so that 'simply by tumbling over a few papers from my emissaries I have all the secrets of Europe, at least such of them as are proper for my purpose, laid open at one view'. This claim was contested by some correspondents, one of whom had the temerity to call Mrs Haywood an 'idle, prating, gossiping old woman'. Her defence was a wish 'to check the enormous growth of luxury, to reform the morals and improve the manners of an Age, by all confess'd degenerate and sunk'. These aims were shared by another female adviser, Miss Frances Moore, who edited *The Old Maid* from November 1755 to April 1756 under the pseudonym of 'Mary Singleton, Spinster'. This magazine, as its name suggests, was an ardent advocate of celibacy, a campaign spoiled only when Miss Moore left to get married.

Mrs Haywood and Miss Moore seem to have been jointly responsible for making the public expect a problem page adviser to be female. Thereafter it was common for a male editor to take on the persona of a woman when writing his agony column. Hugh Kelly, for instance, became 'Mrs Wentworth' for the problem page of *The Court Miscellany* in the 1760s. A failed stay-maker and equally unsuccessful dramatist, he introduced his short-lived problem page in July 1765:

> *Mrs Wentworth having had several queries proposed to her, which she has undertaken to resolve in the clearest manner her abilities will permit, now offers both questions and answers to the candid public and also begs leave to inform them that all questions which come within the scope of female understanding shall be answered to the satisfaction of the querist, provided they are received early in the month.*

In fact the 'several queries' appear to have been as bogus as the sex of the adviser, since the page was initially filled with straightforward borrowings from *The British Apollo* of nearly sixty years before. That this was possible, with only the barest sub-editing, suggests that manners and morals were relatively static in the eighteenth century – at least until the last two decades, when Evangelicism began to make the lives of problem page editors extremely hard.

The new 'prim and highly proper' school was headed by *The Ladies' Magazine*, which ran from 1770 to 1832. Here, once again, the editor was clearly a man, though he preferred on his problem page to appear as an 'auntie'. Pressure of editorial business being what it is, however, he sometimes forgot his disguise. One set of parents, having written to a figure whom they clearly believed to be a respectable, elderly lady about their attempts to force a daughter into a distasteful marriage, suddenly found themselves urged to be 'advised by a man who has whisked through the giddy circles of pride and vanity'. Chastened by such slip-ups, he subsequently appointed Mrs Martha Grey, as 'The Matron', to run this column in the late 1770s and 1780s. After a lapse of some years, the magazine's problem page was revived in 1817, supposedly by Mrs Grey's granddaughter Sophie.

In keeping with the spirit of the age, both Martha and Sophie confined themselves to polite subjects. Neither could ever have advised, as Dunton had once done, a correspondent fearful of becoming an old maid to go down to the docks when the fleet was in to entrap a sex-starved sailor. Faced with such a problem, these aunties would at best have advised Christian resignation. In an attempt to create at least a modicum of excitement, Mrs Martha Grey took to printing the question one month and answering it the next. It is hard, however, to believe that the suspense ever became intolerable.

The principle competitor of *The Ladies' Magazine* was *The Lady's Monthly Museum*, which ran a short-lived advice column in 1811. Its auntie wrote under the title of 'The Busy Body' – a common name for correspondence editors in the eighteenth century. The sentiments expressed by both these Regency magazines were those that are habitually, though mistakenly, dubbed Victorian. The aunties preached propriety and piety in equal measure. Their tone was invariably improving, their style prolix. A single case-history could, on occasion, run into two thousand words. But though the space available was almost unlimited, many subjects which had previously been the mainstay of such columns were now forbidden. Most medical problems were unmentionable, and no religious heresies were aired. If the auntie was daring she might discuss a few peccadillos, but her outpourings of morality could never make any overt reference to such major sins as adultery, rape or incest. Possibly discouraged by these limitations, the livelier women journalists of the early nineteenth century did not attempt to become agony aunties though some, such as Caroline Norton, would have been admirably qualified for the job. It was in the end left to male writers, in general family magazines, to rescue the problem page from oblivion.

The passing of the Six Acts in 1819, and the extension of the Stamp Act, held up the development of a popular press. But in the 1840s and 1850s the problem page reappeared in such mass-circulation magazines as *The London Journal* and *Cassell's Illustrated Family Magazine*. The latter, founded by John Cassell in 1853, was a typical product of the new breed of editor and adviser. Cassell was a working-class boy who had risen in the world by thrift, hard work and the rejection of alcohol. His route into publishing lay through his work as a preacher and editor for the temperance movement. Unlike so many of the early agony columnists, he could justifiably have advised his readers to follow his own example.

But Cassell's primary objective as an auntie was not to preach. He effected, indeed, a significant change in the problem page, moving it away from the elegant moralising of the late eighteenth century towards the informative and educative function which it had originally possessed. On 26 December 1857 he explained to 'Gregory' the criteria by which he selected his problems:

In answering our correspondents we certainly give precedence to questions which possess something more than an individual interest. Our intention, in adopting this course, is to give as much information as we can to the greatest possible number of readers. For instance, if at the present moment, John Smith and James Smith write to us, the one with an enquiry about India, the other with a request for our opinion on his handwriting, we should certainly answer the former letter first, supposing our readers generally to have more interest, at this crisis, in the condition of India, than in the state of James Smith's calligraphy ...

Not all his readers, of course, shared this high-minded concern for self-improvement, as is clear from a disclaimer printed in the 19 January 1856 issue of *Cassell's* – a statement of policy which gives us a fascinating glimpse into a mid-Victorian editor's post-bag:

We do not profess the ability to decipher totally illegible manuscripts; we do not make long people short, short people tall ... cure inveterate stammering, remove freckles from ladies' cheeks, promote the growth of whiskers on beardless boys, extract grease spots from ladies' albums so that the page can be better than new; reconcile lovers which have quarrelled, supply young ladies with love philtres that shall entice their sluggish cavaliers into the net of Hymeneal bliss, as mice are enticed by toasted cheese to a trap. All this, and very much more, we have been pathetically solicited again and again to do.

Another important change which occurred at this date involved the presentation of the problem page. In order to squeeze in as much as possible, the editors dispensed with the questions and contented themselves with publishing the answer. In ninety-nine cases out of a hundred the original query is perfectly clear from the reply. The answer to 'Charlotte' in *The Home Magazine*, Volume 7, Number 167, for example, leaves little to the imagination:

The conduct of your lover is very equivocal. He professes the warmest attachment and seeks for a suitable return from you, but refuses to solicit the approbation of your parents. This is extremely suspicious and, coupled with his conduct in the drawing room, warrants us in concluding that his motives are not at all honourable.

Just occasionally we are left wondering. In 1850 *The London Journal* replied to 'Mary Pearce':

Your husband and his mother are both brutes, and you cannot be compelled to reside under the same roof as them, nor would you, under any circumstances, be justified in doing so. The parish authorities, upon application for relief, would compel your husband to contribute something towards your maintenance.

What had her husband and mother-in-law been up to? Was it incest, wife-battering or bestiality? Anything short of this would have been unlikely to elicit so firm a response in an age when aunties believed in preserving the matrimonial home at all costs.

Given that none of the letters appeared, we cannot judge their authenticity. But the evidence is that agony columns were run in response to great demand. *The Family Friend*, a popular magazine but by no means the leader in its field, claimed to have been sent sixty thousand letters in the first decade of its existence. Some editors complained of attempted bribery – often in the form of postage stamps – for inclusion on the page. Others railed against 'those incomprehensibles who think themselves privileged to inflict their verbiage on sadly-taxed editors'. The verbiage could, on occasion, consist of as much as thirty closely written pages from a single correspondent.

The 1850s witnessed an enormous expansion of magazine publishing. The growth of literacy after the 1833 Education Act was, of course, a significant factor. But so, too, was the removal of stamp duty on all magazines in 1855, a measure taken partly as a result of Cassell's campaigning. New magazines included *The Family Herald*, *The Home Magazine*, *The Home Circle*, *The Ladies' Treasury* and *The Englishwoman's Domestic Magazine*. The last was founded by the twenty-one year old Samuel Beeton (already husband to the Mrs Beeton of culinary fame) who must share with Peggy Makins, the 'Evelyn Home' of *Woman* from 1939 to 1974, the honour of being the youngest ever agony auntie. Beeton was noticeably more despotic in his early days on *The Englishwoman's Domestic Magazine* than he was to be a decade later, as editor of the up-market *Queen*. By that time the deaths of his wife and two of his sons had made him both more shrewd and more compassionate. His decision to include a problem page in the posh *Queen* was an important one. It rescued the agony column from being dismissed as an educative device for the lower classes. The problem page was on its way back to the drawing-room.

Samuel Beeton and John Cassell were, however, the last

as well as the first of their breed of magazine publishers, men who cared more about editing than about finance. In 1855 Cassell over-extended his credit and was forced to sell out to the printers Petter and Galpin. Beeton sold his bankrupted empire to Ward Lock in 1866, after the failure of the bankers Overend & Gurney left him insolvent. Increasingly, conglomerates took over the family magazines, and editors were hired and fired so swiftly that they had little chance to impose their personalities on the paper, let alone the problem page.

Victorian aunties were mostly anonymous, and were not 'personalised' by the use of engraved portraits or flowing signatures at the foot of their columns. This makes it hard for us to identify them. Very occasionally, however, we learn something about them from their advice, or from an editorial comment. Beeton's magazine, *The Young Englishwoman*, for example, was edited in the early 1870s by his old friend Mrs Matilda Browne, the surrogate mother to his two orphaned sons. In January 1875 we learn that Mrs Matilda Browne, who used the pseudonym 'Myra' in her professional life, was too ill to continue:

> *Myra is now so well-known to the readers of* The Young Englishwoman *that it will be, no doubt, with a feeling of regret that her readers will hear of her late illness, and that a stranger will in future occupy her place ... in the letters that appear in each number of the magazine.*

But in that same year – 1875 – Mrs Matilda Browne founded her own highly successful woman's magazine, *Myra's Journal*. It is hard to know whether the illness while editing *The Young Englishwoman* was genuine, or diplomatic. Myra's successor clearly recognised that her task would be difficult. She declared herself, however, eager to try:

> *... I present myself to our readers, ready and willing to tread in Myra's footsteps, anxious to be as useful as she was, and hopeful of gaining in time some portion of the regard she was so happy to inspire. If a sincere wish to be useful were any qualification for an onerous post like this, I should be fully qualified, without doubt! But I know that more than that is necessary – that the desire, however warm, must be backed up*

by earnest endeavour, and that the good will must be supplanted by the good deed ... Could any Englishwoman wish for a more congenial audience? Surely not; and I feel that the privilege of addressing them carries with it great responsibilities.

The earnest, careworn statement is signed 'Sylvia'. It is indicative of how seriously the work of an auntie was taken, even if problem pages were constantly satirised by 'funnies' such as *Punch* and *Ally Sloper's Half Holiday*.

Punch devoted a whole page to sending up the agony column on 1 January 1887:

Broken-hearted. *We cannot really undertake to advise you as to what is your best course. Yours is a peculiar case. It is rare for any one person to be simultaneously threatened with epilepsy, deserted by her affianced lover after the banns have already been published, bitten by a dog, which has been rendered insane through being led about by a string, expelled from her lodging for non-payment of rent and thrown out by an active volcano. These events do not often happen together. Do not, at any rate, return the presents your lover gave you. If we were in your place, we should convert them into cash. Then you might take out a County Court Summons against the owner of the dog, also the volcano, and have something over for a Breach of Promise action.*

An equally acidulous eye was cast on the problem page in 1884 by 'Madge', the doyenne of society commentators, who wrote a column for the otherwise rather radical *Truth*. On 27 November, a dead time of year when the Season had ended, she commented on *The Queen*'s speciality of giving household hints to their supposedly aristocratic readers:

Are not some of the letters in The Queen *amusing? It seems such an odd thing for ladies to write and ask what their butcher's bills ought to come to, or how many loaves they should have in a week, or how many tons of coal ought to be consumed in the year? Some of the answers to these curious questions must certainly be hoaxes. Don't you think so? For instance, 'Doris' replied to some queries of the sort that she pays £40 a year in wages and feeds her household of 10 people and pays for some washing, out of £3.10s. a week. That would be about 4/6d for the food of each of the ten. I leave you to imagine what sort of provisions could be bought for that sum. But 'Doris'' statement has evidently been*

*accepted by some simple-minded young house-keeper who innocently
asks in this week's* Queen *if Doris dines late and has a meat lunch?
Now don't forget to look out next week for Doris' answer. If she really
does manage to feed 10 persons on the sum mentioned, I should like to
peruse some of her bills of fare; but I don't absolutely yearn to be asked
to dinner there.*

By contrast with this bitchy frivolity, *The Girls' Own Paper*,
run by the Religious Tract Society, took itself very seriously
indeed. Its general purpose was made clear in a reply to
'Grey Hairs' in the first year of its existence:

*Servant girls communicate to us well-written letters and by their tone
we can see that our magazine has indeed helped them to an intelligent
carrying out of their humble work; that it has been a companion to
them in their isolation, and a counsellor in times of sore temptation.
There is much in our paper, we humbly believe, that will train our girls
in living a pure and honest life, and we rejoice to help them, for their
letters convince us that there is an honesty and nobility even in the
kitchen. From our daily letters from the girls, written upon coronetted
note-paper by those of noble birth and by others from the kitchens of
humble houses, we gather that there is help needed by all, and that our
paper has given a high aim to their lives and a practical and wise
assistance in their various engagements.*

(Girls' Own Paper, *2 October 1880*)

The aunties on the *Girls' Own Paper* were, like most of their
contemporaries, anonymous. The first editor was male,
but the problem page had an increasingly feminine
flavour. The advisers appear, from their replies, to have
been matronly, happily married ladies, who could draw on
a fund of appropriate experience. One young girl, who
was contemplating marriage, was told on 20 May 1903:

*... Never enter on the secret duties of a wife unless you can give to him
whose name you take, an honest, wholehearted affection. I can speak
from experience of the happiness that results from the true union of that
kind.*

No further details, however, were supplied. The same
auntie, probably Flora Klichman, a well-known authority
on etiquette, also confessed to identifying with the

behaviour of a correspondent (inaptly called 'Faith') who spent her time in church fancying a boy in the congregation:

> *This is very human and very girlish. Having been a girl myself in the far past, I realise it to the full and do not judge you hardly. Do I not remember my own temptations and, alas! my frequent failures in battling against them ...?*
>
> (Girls' Own Paper, *18 October 1902*)

No such admissions of weakness were to be expected from Gordon Stables, a contributor to the *Boys' Own Paper* and former naval doctor. On board *HMS Narcissus* he had travelled the world, policing the waters of the British Empire. After his return to dry land he became a prolific writer of boys' adventure stories with titles like *Wild Adventures in Wild Places* and *Kidnapped by Cannibals*. As an adviser, however, he concentrated on something rather nearer home and distinctly below the belt. In any other age his obsession with masturbation might have seemed strange. In Victorian and Edwardian England (he died in 1910) he was clearly a respected figure.

The closing years of the nineteenth-century saw the foundation of several publishing empires. George Newnes, Alfred Harmesworth and Cyril Pearson have all been credited with the invention of a new sort of mass journalism. In fact, their methods were far from novel. Newnes' scrappy *Titbits* approach to information had been innovatory – in the 1840s and 1850s when *The London Journal, Cassell's* and *The Family Herald* all had sections based on precisely this format. Harmesworth's *Answers to Correspondents* was overtly derived from *Titbits*, but claimed to be original in its direct involvement of the reader in the snippets of information on offer. Dunton had been doing something remarkably similar in the 1690s. Even the advertising campaigns, designed to grab a mass readership, were not entirely new. *The British Apollo* had tried to drum up subscriptions by inviting readers to a sponsored concert. Harmesworth sponsored exhibitions for precisely the same reason. The main difference lay not in the offer but in its consequence. Dunton found endless ingenious excuses for not naming the day, while Harmesworth delivered the goods.

Original or not, however, the new wave was important. It rescued popular journalism from the doldrums, revitalised it and captured a new audience. Just as the effects of the 1833 Education Act had not been seen in the publishing world until the late 1840s, so, too, the mass literacy created by the 1870 Act did not materialise until the 1880s, when Newnes found himself on *Titbits* editing the first million-seller. The correspondence columns, like the rest of the new mixture, were not startlingly original, but they did place a still stronger stress on the provision of practical information. Lofty moral pronouncements gave way to helpful advice for lower-middle, and even working-class readers, who wished to 'do the right thing'.

Harmesworth had actually started his journalistic career by contributing to the *Titbits* correspondence column as a lowly freelance. But, though his own subsequent empire was based on such 'mill-girl' magazines as *Forget-Me-Not*, *The Cosy Corner* and *The Red Rose*, he rapidly relinquished the role of auntie. Those who did conduct the lonely hearts sections for him made few concessions to the economic independence of their working-girl audience. When delicate questions were asked, the aunties offered an uneasy amalgam of escapist romance and hard-headed morality.

The problem pages of this period were satirised every week in the much-loved comic *Ally Sloper's Half Holiday*. Endless fun was poked at the love-lorn and at those who aspired to polite behaviour. They told 'Gladys' on 19 March 1911 that 'we cannot doubt that you are a "sweet little thing", but at present there are only three unmarried men on the staff, and what with one thing and another, their time is fully occupied just now'. They also refused to recommend any particular brand of whisky to 'AGF' on the grounds that 'No Scotch Whisky firm is advertising with us at present' – clearly a dig at such magazines as *Myra's Journal*, which frequently recommended the much advertised Antipon slimming treatment to readers who wrote in complaining of plumpness. An equally witty, and

more accurate parody of the style of the 'mill-girl' publications appears in P. G. Wodehouse's *Sam the Sudden*
of 1925. The hero briefly becomes 'Aunt Isobel', running
the 'Chats with My Girls' for *Pyke's Home Journal*. Knotty
problems include 'whether to blow on your tea or allow it
to cool in God's own time, or whether a gentleman could
present a lady with a pound of chocolates without
committing himself to anything unduly definite'. 'Aunt
Isobel' herself, we are assured, is 'like some wise pilot,
gently steering the storm-tossed barks of her fellow men
and women through the shoals and sunken rocks of the
ocean of life'.

The First World War killed off many long-running
magazines, which lost out in the scrabble for paper. The
immediately post-war batch of 'mill-girl' publications had
such names as *Peg's Paper*, *Polly's Paper* and *Pam's Paper*, and
their aunties signed their columns 'Peg', 'Polly' and 'Pam'
respectively. Many also boasted specialist advisers on
beauty and the occult, the latter with foreign-sounding
names like 'Madame Sunya' or 'Zara'. Unlike their pre-
war counterparts, who had been heartily maternal
towards their erring readers, and described themselves as
'mother-friends', the new crop of aunties tried to appear
as chums. In 1919, for example, 'Peg' introduced herself to
the readers of *Peg's Paper*:

> My name is Peg, and my one aim in life is to give you a really cheery
> paper like nothing you've ever read before. Not so long ago, I was a
> mill-girl too. Because I've been a worker, too, and know what girls
> like, I'm going to give you a paper you'll enjoy ... Look on me as a real
> friend and helper. I will try to advise you on any problem.

The atmosphere of the post-war women's magazines was
reminiscent of a girls' school locker-room. Secrets were
exchanged and men firmly excluded. The mere suggestion
that a man might have sneaked in was regarded as a
betrayal. On 19 April 1920 'Polly' defended herself
furiously, when answering a letter from a correspondent
whose friend had cast doubt on the auntie's femininity:

> Now I wonder whether that very sure and certain young lady has

realised what a grave breach of confidence such conduct as she describes would be. We ask readers – young girls for the most part, but indeed, women of all ages – to write freely to a sister woman who will advise and help all she can. And if these letters were opened by a man he would be a scoundrel of the worst description – horse-whipping would be too good for him. Really, it makes me wonder whether a girl who can have such thoughts is quite honest and honourable herself ...

The idea that these 'aunties' were in fact men obviously appealed to the popular imagination, however, and must have been strengthened by Nathanael West's cynical portrayal of a drunken, randy and suicidal, but very male, 'Miss Lonelyhearts' in his novel of 1933.

The new crop of magazines did not break entirely with the tradition of stern morality. *Every Girl's Paper*, for instance, on 30 June 1924 told 'Lady Mab':

You give no address and send me crying to bed because I am helpless to save you from your folly and you know all the time you mean to make off with another woman's husband. You may call it romance, but mine is a nastier name. I hope the law will catch up with you.

In the same manner *Polly's Paper* on 8 March 1920 wrote to 'Emily':

I am afraid the boy did not care for you as much as you thought he did, otherwise he would not have given in to the temptation. Had he been worthy, thought of you could have kept him on the straight path, but if he hasn't the grit to fight against wrong, knowing that his failure meant losing you, he is not worth a good woman's love.

It was presumably this sort of reply which led Richard Hoggart in *The Uses of Literacy* to comment that the 'mill-girl' press, 'uses boldly words like "sin", "shame", "guilt", "evil", with every appearance of meaningfulness which serious writers for more sophisticated audiences understandably find difficulty in using today'. In other words the aunties had firm standards of right and wrong which they applied to their readers' dilemmas. But could they apply them only to an unsophisticated audience? More 'up-market' magazines such as *Home Chats* and

Woman's Magazine certainly used the same vocabulary to castigate their erring correspondents.

One of the most famous twentieth century advisers was 'Mrs Jim', the comfortable auntie on Harmesworth's *Home Chats*. On 8 January 1927 she initiated an experiment in reader participation by asking 'What would YOU do?':

> *Some problems I deal with over and over again. And in replying I sometimes wonder would the majority agree with me? This is a case in point. A girl is in love with a young man who shows nothing beyond calm friendly interest in her. Then an elderly, comfortably-off decent man asks her to marry him. What should she do? What would you do? Tell me on a post-card in not more than 12 words. I will give 2/6d to the post-card which best expresses the opinion of the majority.*

She does not appear to have published the results of this competition, perhaps because giving twelve words of advice is not easy.

Mrs Jim's main competitor was May Marshall, editor of *Woman's Magazine*, the senior off-shoot of the long-running *Girls' Own Paper*. May Marshall came from a clerical background, married at twenty-one and worked on several improving magazines such as *Sunday At Home*. In a tribute to her, published in 1937, the assistant editor enumerated her many virtues:

> *She is youthful in outlook ... but fortunately not foolishly so, and is one of the sanest women I know – level-headed, knowing her own mind, able to give decisions quickly. Her reasoning is sound, and she gives much serious thought to the problems of those (and there are many) who write to her for advice. She told me once that she can easily be twisted round anyone's finger; this I find hard to believe, but I think her meaning is that she has a sympathetic heart and is capable of feeling other people's sorrows and sufferings. I do know that out of her own experience of life – which has not always been happy – she is ever ready to help those in need.*

Reading May Marshall's column today one feels that, had she not entered journalism, she would have made an admirable gym mistress. Her first reaction to 'Fed Up's' letter in 1935, for instance, was to 'want to spank you'. If readers didn't buck themselves up and start thinking positively after that sort of hearty encouragement, then they never would.

The magazines of the 1930s have been accused of trying to reverse the changes brought about by giving women the vote, by encouraging them to ignore the new opportunities available outside the home. Cynthia White argued in her book *Women's Magazines*, in 1970, that:

> *Editors expatiated in unison on the sacrificial joys of being a wife and mother. They elevated housewifery into a craft, gave it the status of a profession, and sold it to readers on the most attractive terms, thereby nullifying all that had been achieved by the Woman's Rights movements in securing greater social freedom for women and letting slip the opportunities opening up for them as a result of the war. In addition they created the perfect buying climate for every kind of household commodity which advertisers soon began to exploit.*

This makes it sound as if editors had sneaked off to a Fleet Street tea-shop, and devised a plot. Nothing could be further from the truth. The contents of the women's magazines of the period, unexciting though they might be, reflected rather than led the views of their readers. Most women in the 1930s preferred marriage to a career. Most stopped working immediately after the wedding, and long before the birth of the first child. And, though no auntie openly attacked such assumptions, some (working women themselves after all) did begin to question them.

The *Mab's Weekly* adviser, Mrs Raynor, for example, who was described by her editor as 'the most sympathetic and understanding of all my friends – the ideal confidante', reassured one fiancée on 10 March 1934 that 'it is not unwomanly to prefer your job to housework'. Though Mrs Raynor disapproved of married women running both a home and a job, she felt 'the day has gone when that (housework) was regarded as the only work for women'. The solution for a married career woman was, at this date, of course, a servant. The evidence of the problem pages suggests that, if anything, the home philosophy was preached more steadfastly by the aunties of the 1950s, when both Monica Dickens on *Housewife* and Denise

Robins on *She* counselled their married readers to give housewifery priority over a career.

Towards the end of the 1930s we begin to recognise some familiar names. Peggy Carn (later Peggy Makins) became the second 'Evelyn Home' of the recently founded *Woman* in 1937, at the age of twenty-one. Denise Robins, who had been writing serials for magazines such as *Peg's Paper* since the 1920s, was hauled back from a holiday in the as yet unspoilt town of Torremolinos to run a problem page for a Dundee-based women's magazine in the same year. And Dorothy Critchley began writing the 'Jane Dawson' column on the *Manchester Evening News*, a task which she would continue (doubling as a civil servant during the war) until 1974.

A new frankness, which had its roots in the 1930s but flowered during the Second World War, rescued problem pages from the polite and 'womanly' topics, towards which they had been edging. The new aunties had to be careful, however, not to go too far. For instance, when the first 'Evelyn Home', a refugee German psychiatrist, advised a married woman to go away for a weekend with her lover, Mary Grieves, editor of *Woman*, censored the copy for fear of prosecution as pornography. Evelyn Homes' summing up in favour of morality, re-spectability and loyalty to one's husband, made no difference to the decision.

Just prior to the war, there was a brief fashion for male advisers. Ramon Navarro, the film star, was the figurehead for one column. Ray Alister ran another in *Modern Woman*, and a pipe-smoking, confidence-inspiring Nigel Mansfield answered the problems in *Glamour* in 1939, before making a timely disappearance to Canada.

During the war, problem pages found a new role. For two hundred and fifty years they had counselled people who had nowhere else to turn. Exceptionally a reader might be urged to consult a solicitor, doctor or clergyman. But in general, the auntie was the sole adviser available to those who could not afford a professional fee. By the end of the war all this had changed. The Welfare State network was now widespread and aunties added the role of referral

agent to their existing function as last hope. Honeyed
sympathy still poured from their pens, but concrete advice
followed. A reader with matrimonial problems could be
encouraged to contact marriage guidance; those with
accommodation or consumer difficulties could seek help
at a local Housing or Consumer Advice Centre. For
anyone whose problem defied categorisation, there were
the new Citizens Advice Bureaux. These specialised
agencies may, in part, explain why post-war aunties have
proved willing to tackle the sort of problem neglected
since the early eighteenth century.

This new subject matter was noticed by a reader of
Woman's Own on 4 January 1946 who wrote:

> *The seriousness of the problems which young people send to Mary Grant
> astonishes me. They have become – sometimes through no fault of their
> own – involved in complicated situations which would embarrass much
> older and more experienced folk. Let's hope a return to peace will
> slacken the break-neck tempo at which we have lived for the past five
> years.*

This reader was to be disappointed. Problem pages have
not returned to their pre-war format. They still, however,
have to fight the image they earned in the 1920s and 1930s.
Women's magazines with intellectual pretensions are
today wary of including such a feature. The now defunct
(could it be connected?) *Nova*, for instance, was launched
with the promise that it would never carry a problem
page. And the editor of *Woman's World* said in 1978, in an
interview on Radio City, that problem pages 'were a bit of
a joke' (her magazine doesn't have one). She further
claimed that they were mainly read by the wrong people,
these being principally men. The evidence of IPC's
readership-surveys suggest otherwise. The problem page is
apparently the second feature to which most readers turn,
after reading the other letters page at the front of the
magazine.

Most modern aunties are better equipped as universal
advisers than their predecessors. Some, like Angela Willans
('Mary Grant'), have lengthy experience of psychoanalysis.

Others, such as Clare Rayner (an ex-nurse), have professional medical knowledge. All have a team of qualified legal, medical and financial experts on whom they can call. But each agrees that her real qualification for the job is common sense.

The problem page may, for that very reason, be said to be unduly biased towards a humdrum and commonsensical view of the world. But it is still, in my opinion, hard to think of a better glass through which to glimpse the lives of ordinary citizens in the past. The intimate confessions and conscientious advice of two hundred and ninety years are not to be dismissed lightly.

2

Qualifications in a consort
COURTSHIP, MARRIAGE AND DIVORCE
1690–1837

Two's company, three's a scenario for a letter to a problem page. Choice of a marriage partner, a wish to escape from an ill-considered engagement, and marital jealousy have figured largely in agony columns for nearly three centuries, with the financial implications of marriage and divorce not far behind.

Variations in the theme are apparent over this long period. Bigamy is more discussed than divorce in the earliest problem pages. Breach of Promise, much aired in the nineteenth century, has now completely disappeared although the pain occasioned by the desertion of a suitor – once soothed by a cash payment – is still familiar. It is now often felt by those who have gone into a trial marriage and found themselves not only tried but judged inadequate too. Violence in the home, now greeted with shock and the address of the battered wives' refuge, was regarded as commonplace in the seventeenth century.

The founder of the problem page, the ubiquitous John Dunton, was strictly pragmatic in his approach to matrimony, some might say mercenary. A 'handsome lady' who wrote to him, desiring his opinion whether she should marry a clergyman or a lawyer, both gentlemen but neither rich, was told that she might as well 'shake them in a bag and take your chance'. Had there been a difference in their financial position it would, in Dunton's estimation, have 'altered the case that way'.

Even adventurers received some encouragement. One

man, who hoped to settle his debts by contracting an advantageous marriage, wondered whether he was 'obliged to make her acquainted with his circumstances when he courts her and so run the hazard of not obtaining her?' Dunton not only discouraged his correspondent from revealing all, 'every man having to make the best of himself and his fortunes that he honestly can', he also urged caution, lest his future wife was simultaneously deceiving him. Although Dunton would discourage a father from marrying his daughter to 'one of vicious life, but of good estate, rather than to one of meaner fortune and an honest man', a suitor, in his opinion, had almost a duty not to marry for love a girl who could not discharge his obligations.

Twenty years later Daniel Defoe took a rather different view of men who married for money. A letter in *The Review*, on 27 January 1713, throws an interesting light on both fortune-hunters and the way in which middle-class marriages were arranged:

> ... *I have but an only daughter, and in proportion to my circumstances, resolv'd to do well for her, she being a very dutiful and obliging child;— An ordinary Fellow, but a Man with a Grave Aspect, and wheadling Tongue, comes to me, and tells me he had a Proposal to make to me, of a Match for my Daughter; he made use of a Man's name to excuse his abrupt coming. He told me there was a Young Merchant in very good business, newly come from —— and settled here in very good credit and a large Commission Trade, who, he knew, had taken a fancy to my Daughter, and, he believed, would gladly make her his Wife, if I would consider of it, he would use his Friendly offices between us, to bring it forward ...*

The father consented to the marriage, providing a substantial dowry. But his examination of his prospective son-in-law's background had been insufficiently thorough:

> *In less than two years my Merchant is known, by his Name being in the* Gazette, *and I have my Daughter with one Child, and big with another, brought home to me, almost naked, the Commission of Bankrupt having Seized all her Cloaths, Plate, Jewels etc – of which I*

gave her a good stock – Upon Enquiry, I find, this Grave Broker, who introduc'd this Cheat to me, had three or four treaties of the same kind, on foot for the same person; tho' to my Disaster, mine only proved successful to them; that he had 100 guineas for his Undertaking, and that he knew the Man was, at that very time, in a desperate condition in his Circumstances; that he only wanted my money to hold him up for a little while longer which he took, in the manner above, to the Ruin of my Child and Wounding my whole Family. Pray, give your opinion in this Case, what Course I ought to take.

I have made this letter Publick rather at the Gentleman's desire, as a Caveat for others, than that any Man else can propose anything to him to do – Your remedy, Sir, and all you can do, is to be patient; and as kind to the young lady as your Family circumstances will admit; it being, for ought I see, no Fault of hers.

Defoe, good businessman as he was, felt that there should be a law to provide redress in such circumstances. That nothing ever came of this scheme may perhaps have been because the legislators, particularly in the House of Lords, were themselves among the worst offenders in the marriage market.

Arranged marriages were still common in the seventeenth century, but the unhappiness caused by them – the historian Laurence Stone has estimated that between 1595 and 1620 a third of the older peerage was involved in serious matrimonial difficulties – may gradually have discouraged aristocratic fathers from forcing their children into the sort of loveless match they themselves had experienced. Increasingly children were encouraged to have a prior knowledge of their spouse's disposition and, preferably, to find their partner likeable.

By the 1690s, when Dunton was writing, matrimonial rights were in a state of flux – and he tried desperately to alienate neither age group. His view was that daughters should obey their parents, but that parents should not force their children into a detested marriage. When these two objectives conflicted, he tried prevarication:

… I am courted by two Gentlemen, the one I had been acquainted with from my Childhood, and scarce ever known him guilty of any

Extravagancy, his Person is neither Comely nor Contemptible, his Education has been liberal, his Profession honourable, our Fortunes equal, besides, I believe he entirely loves me. Our Friends on both sides were very much satisfied with the match till the second Lover came, who is a perfect Country Squire, whose conversation has been wholly amongst his Dogs or Company as Brutish; his temper is Resolute and Stubborn, and I fear he prefers a Bottle before his Mrs, but to make amends for all he is blest with a far larger Estate than the former, which has so much influenced my Father, as to order me to discharge my former lover.

Truly, Madam, 'Tis a little dangerous to interest ourselves in a case where we must otherwise disoblige Child or Parent ... Our general Advice is to consider that 'tis the Fear of God and Good Humour that are more happy Qualifications in so near a Consort than abundance of Wealth or Titles ... All that we can say is that you may not act contrary to your Father's Pleasure in disposing of yourself. Nor can any right of Nature force you to marry whoever he pleases, purely because it is his Pleasure, or where his Judgement is misguided: But there ought to be a great deal of caution in such Things; for Parents are more often in the Right than their Children and the Curse of Disobedience is a little too severe to be incurr'd for the Sake of an idle inaccountable Passion. You ought to weigh your Parent's Reasons well, and consult the Strength of them with others who are wise and pious, and if your Father be in the Wrong, there are handsome Methods enough to let him know it by Friends etc. If you are mistaken, you must endeavour to bring your Mind and Affections into their proper Channel ...

(The Athenian Oracle)

In other words, Dunton was in a muddle, trying to juggle the traditional concept of parental authority with the new, more liberal, attitude that those having to live with the marriage should determine its composition.

Dunton's fellow journalist Richard Steele was a more determined campaigner against arranged marriages, publishing the following letter as an awful warning to parents who enforced obedience from their children at the price of conjugal discord:

... I have the honour to be yoked to a young lady who is, in plain English ... a very eminent scold. She began to break her mind very freely both to me and to her servants about two months after our Nuptial, and tho' I have been accustomed to this Humour of her in three years, yet I do not know what is the matter with me, but I am no more delighted with it than I was at first. I have advised with her Relations about her and they all tell me that her Mother and Grand Mother before her were both taken after the same manner: so that since it runs in the blood, I have but small hope of her recovery ... If you will but put me in the way that I may bear it with indifference, I shall rest satisfied ...PS I must do the poor girl the justice to let you know that this match was none of her chusing (or indeed of mine either) in consideration of which I avoid giving her the least provocation and indeed we live better together than usually folks do who hate one another when they were first joined. To avoid the sin against the Parents, not least to extenuate it, my dear rails at my Father and Mother and I at hers for making the match.

(The Spectator, *6 August 1712*)

Parents, however, had some powerful weapons at their disposal. In the case of sons they could refuse to negotiate the jointure – provision for a daughter-in-law on the death of her husband. In the case of a daughter the dowry was their trump card. For a middle-class girl of this period no dowry meant, in most cases, no marriage. Dunton published a letter from someone who had the misfortune to be the heir to a wealthy misogynist. The young man made the mistake of marrying and found his uncle's doors shut against him. Dunton recommended making friends with his intimates and hoping through them to soften the old gentleman. Failing that, 'you must e'en sit down content. For if you can't get an estate to your mind, you ought to get a mind to your estate'.

How far a parent or guardian had the right to enforce obedience in the matter of marriage continued to be a much discussed topic in eighteenth century periodicals. *The Censor,* an up-market product with a penchant for using problem pages to publicise the editor's plays, published a long essay on forced and unequal marriages in 1717:

Absolute force in the Disposal of our Persons, is contrary to all the laws

both of Nature and of Reason, and supposes (we are) in the Condition of
Slaves to be sold at the Pleasure of the Owner ... To create merely to lay
the thing created under the severe Penalty of Unavoidable Calamity is
to frame the most unworthy Notions of the Supreme Being, and is so far
from being a Foundation for Obedience and Duty, that it infuses into us
rather sentiments of Horror and Aversion.

The article continued however by insisting that parents
should have the power 'to prevent their own or their
Issue's Ruin, Disgrace and Misery'. Fathers might advise
their sons to look at girls whose dowries fell within a
certain income bracket, though they should not force
them into the arms of any one girl within the group:

No one would blame a Parent that wrestled a Dagger from the hand of
his Child, that hindered him from being impos'd on by Villains, or
diverted him from Courses of inevitable Destruction; and yet the
youthful part of the World are constantly complaining of their
Interposition between them and Ruin, in the point of Wedlock.

Mammon did not, however, in the world of the problem
page always conquer Cupid, even when the pen was held
by the cynical Dunton. A man wrote to *The Athenian Oracle*
about his wish to break his engagement and marry
another, knowing that if he married the first girl 'they
would not live happily together tho' the former has the
most money'. The correspondent is reminded that he
entered the engagement voluntarily and that 'this
prohibited his liberty of making a retreat' for such a
promise was, as the subsequent marriage service put it,
'for better or for worse'. He has, according to Dunton,
only one escape route – to try to persuade his former love
that it would not be in her best interests to continue the
engagement and ask her to release him on the supposition
that, if he was to be unhappy, so should she be, 'for since a
man and his wife are no longer two, while one flesh, their
interests cannot possibly be divided'.

This exchange of letters is of especial interest because it
introduces a device common in the post-bags of
contemporary agony columnists. The problem is

attributed to a suitably anonymous friend and it is Dunton
who confronts the correspondent with his own identity.
'As we suppose yourself to be the person concern'd,' he
writes, 'so we are oblig'd to tell you that you should have
maturely examined the temper of the Lady, should have
made a strict search to the qualities of her mind, before
you had proceeded to the inviolate solemnity of a
matrimonial promise ...'

The fully romantic view of love and courtship appears in
Dunton's publications only in verse. *The British Apollo* of
25–27 February 1708, for example, contains the following
poetic enquiry and rejoinder:

> *Apollo's Sons, I have a Charming Creature*
> *Who, what she wants in Money, makes up in Feature,*
> *She sings like an Angel, which makes me love her.*
> *And thinks none that walk on two Legs above her;*
> *My Mother says, Cupid has my Heart betray'd*
> *And won't have me marry a Cook-Maid.*
> *A Prentice to a Tallow Chandler I am bound,*
> *Who can give his daughter £200.*
> *Now say which Road you wou'd have me to go,*
> *And whether I shall marry the Cook-Maid or no?*

> *Most witty Sir, Apollo bids you marry,*
> *For one who writes so fine, can ne'er miscarry.*
> *Your Cook-Maid's voice and your fine Verse together,*
> *Will calm the sea in stormy Weather.*
> *Your talk will prove so Wondrous Witty,*
> *You'll pray in Rhyme and scold in Ditty.*
> *You're joyn'd by Sympathy to one another*
> *Match then and never mind your Mother.*
> *To hate her for her place, would be the devil,*
> *And men of your Profession are more Civil.*
> *Her kitchenstuff should make you love her rather,*
> *For Grease and Grease, you know, should lye together.*

Defoe shared the hard-headed attitudes of Dunton's prose
advice. He informed a young man, whose father was
trying to force him into a distasteful match, that to refuse
to marry at all was permissible, since such a parental edict

is 'assuming a Power he has no Right to'. But if the
objection was merely to the particular woman to whom
his father was trying to yoke him, then Defoe wanted to
know the age of the correspondent before giving a
judgement.

Family friends were sometimes charged with the
weighty task of finding a husband for an eligible young
lady, and on occasion they too turned to *The British Apollo*
for help. The magazine responded at length:

> *Let him be of a suitable age and condition; of an even temper and*
> *stranger to a spleen; learned without pedantry; well-bred without*
> *affectation; abounding more in sense than in wit; well travelled thro'*
> *himself; the consciousness of his own ignorance will restrain him from a*
> *Contempt of his Wife; fully acquainted with the Town without being*
> *touched by the vices of it; slow of promise, but sudden of performance,*
> *as apt to give as to take an affront; tender and compassionate but firm*
> *to his honour; to all this let there be added a good estate, the want of*
> *which sometimes sours the best disposition. Now to acquaint you where*
> *to meet such a person – But that is without the limits of your question.*

Some of these virtues might strike a modern reader as
strange. A contemporary auntie would not, even in a
parody, be likely to include a readiness to give and take
affront. But in the seventeenth and eighteenth centuries
willingness to take up cudgels on the slightest pretext was a
necessary social attribute.

If they were wise, friends and relatives would check, not
only the character and disposition of a would-be husband,
but also his marital status. With divorce an impossibility
for all those who lacked the influence and money to obtain
a divorce by Act of Parliament, desertion was the cheap
and easy answer. With no centrally held records of
marriage, and little control over the church ceremony
until the Hardwicke Act of 1753, the chances of a married
partner who had put fifty miles between himself and his
former spouse being discovered in bigamy were slight.
Exceptionally, bigamy was uncovered and punished, often
by transportation. Sometimes it came as a Godsend to
those who had married unwisely. One girl, who had
married in the face of opposition from her relatives, was

rescued from what turned out to be an unsatisfactory marriage, by the discovery that her husband had married before. This, Dunton correctly claimed, made her own marriage illegal.

It was also quite common for people to commit bigamy unwittingly. Husbands who had disappeared on a long sea voyage, or deserted the wife and then unexpectedly returned, sometimes found that their place in the matrimonial bed had been usurped. It was usual to wait seven years before presuming death, but some wives were more precipitous. One man returned from the sea after an absence of a mere eighteen months to find his wife married to another. He wanted to know whose wife she was now. Dunton's reply was blunt. 'If the first really and effectively married her, she must be his still, if he has a mind to take her again and thinks her ne'er the worse for wearing.' Another letter in Dunton's post bag shows how chaotic personal relations could become in a world where marriages and deaths went unrecorded. Bigamy might almost seem to be catching:

> *I had the fortune to be joined in matrimony to a Man who had another Wife, and Children by her; which I discovering, brought an Indictment against him and cast him into the Old Bailie for his life; after which I begg'd that he might be transported, which was granted. Some time after I had an account of his death and was married some months after his supposed Death to another, and lived comfortably with him for above two Years, when I received a Letter from my first Husband Courting me for my company, that I may go overseas and live with him. Query, which of the two (if both alive) is my real Husband? Which ought I to follow or ought I to shun both?*

The first was not your Husband before God, he being another Woman's at the same time; for God can't be the Author of Adultery nor cou'd he be so in the Eye of the Law; being dead in the Law before his transportation, as also for that the Law had join'd him to another before that. This consider'd the last Husband is not at all concern'd in this question, no more than any other Woman's Husband; so that the Querist can't be at a loss, but must suppose it both Ingratitude and Injustice to leave her last Husband.

(*The Athenian Oracle*)

In a modern world, accustomed to convenient divorce, it seems strange that Dunton treated it as essentially no different from bigamy. He told one man who enquired whether a person divorced by law could marry again that 'The best causist that ever was, resolves the question in a few words. Fifth of St Matthew 32, "Whosoever shall marry her that is divorced commiteth adultery" – and that's enough to give the importunate Querist satisfaction, if he really wants or desires it.' Dunton was not much more sympathetic to those who argued that marriage was man-made and that therefore they should simply co-habit. Marriage was the direct result of civilisation, and of the need to codify the transferral of wealth, 'It being a Contradiction that Governments could be happy and at Peace without a Certain method and way was established for Legitimacy of Succession in Estates etc.'

Divorce was in fact possible on only two grounds, adultery on the part of the woman, and impotence on the part of the man. Annulment was normally only possible on the grounds of apparent virginity. Such abstinence within marriage was evidently a subject which fascinated Dunton, possibly because its salacious interest helped the sales. In reply to a man who asked whether it was lawful, having taken a vow of celibacy, to marry providing he keeps himself an undefiled virgin, he argued that 'He that is unmarried, careth for the things that belong to the Lord, how he may please the Lord. But he that is married, careth for the things that are of the World and how he may please his wife.' In these circumstances Dunton evidently felt it would be safer not to marry at all. 'Cohabitation with a wife may prove a snare to the person specified and (she) at last unhappily prevail upon him to violate his vow. And since he petitions his God, in his daily prayers, to deliver him from temptation, it is sure an act of high presumption to rush headlong into that temptation, which he earnestly implores to be deliver'd from.'

In the first magazine designed to appeal to women, published in 1693, such reasons for marital breakdown were discussed at greater length. In February a correspondent, who had sent a letter to the Latin Coffee

House, told of the death of a twice-married man. His first wife had died and, on burying her, he married another:

With this second venture he had not lived above three months, or thereabouts, when his wife's mother, making him a visit, she took private occasion to ask him some familiar motherly questions; among which one of them was, whether she might joy him or not or whether her daughter had a great belly yet etc. The husband modestly answered that that was a proper Question to be made to her Daughter herself as being best able to resolve her. Upon this, the Mother, changing the air of her countenance, reply'd; Come son, says she, Did I give £1500 to my daughter, to marry her to a Ridgelin; in plain English You are a Rascal, and so flung out of the Room. The poor Gentleman, strangely struck with this very severe, though indeed too just, Rebuke, went immediately upstairs, draw his ... sword ... and falling upon the point, ripp'd open his own bowels ... Now upon examination of the Matters which I leave you to guess the first wife lived and died a Virgin (pure), and the second was in very much fear of leaving the world in the same melancholy circumstances, which occasioned this reprimand from the Mother to the Son, as proceeding from some private Complaints of the Daughter against some very unpleasing Conjugal Disappointments ... I beg your sentiments in the whole case, together with your particular opinion of the two wifes.

... We confess indeed the first Wife to be a subject of universal Admiration, but not of Imitation. The resentments of the last Wife were very just and reasonable, in having sacrificed herself to a Marriage-bed where the End of her Creation was never to be answered; and probably the death of the poor Gentleman was some particular judgement from having twice prevaricated with Heaven itself before a High Altar, in so barbarous a Silence to the preliminary Nuptial Interrogatory, viz: if either of you know cause, why etc speak now etc when really he knew so notorious a negative Answer to be the forbidding of his own Banns; it being undoubtedly an unpardonable folly (to give it no worse a name) for a man to take that house upon his head, which he knows he can never furnish.

(*The Ladies' Mercury*, March 1693)

This letter, like those of current issues of *Penthouse*, has all the signs of a fecund hack's imagination and a publication which followed *The Ladies' Mercury* in spicing its pages with

intimate problems was *The Post-Angel*. This featured
sensational news, violent murders, supernatural occur-
rences and a back section of questions and answers.
Typical of its quasi-pornographic content was this letter of
September 1701:

> *I know a Gentlewoman who wept the first night she slept with her*
> *Husband, whether was it Joy, fear or modesty that caus'd the Tears?*

> I shall rather attribute it to a fearful Modesty than Joy, or
> any other Cause, because we find no Instances of Widows
> who upon their marrying again have wept in going to bed.

Girls were, of course, expected to be virgins on their
wedding night. Those who wrote revealing that they had
anticipated the marriage ceremony were usually advised to
marry their partner in crime, although it was generally
held that they would make bad spouses. Interestingly, the
majority of these letters was, or purported to be, written
by women who had fallen for the good looks of their
seducer rather than for his fortune or character, and it is
clear that women were recognised to have both passions
and a sensual nature.

The recognition of this fact did not, however, make the
advisers sympathetic to their dilemma. Most were told to
marry their partners, since they were not fit for any other.
One girl, for example, wrote to Defoe about a tempting
youth who had 'made a conquest of my prerogatives', and
could not be charged with Breach of Promise since he was
ready to marry her. But she was not keen, feeling he must
be a knave for seducing her, and wondering whether 'I
had better have a knave for a spark, or a fool for a
husband.' The Society (i.e. Defoe) encouraged her to marry
him so that 'both of you may be made an example to the
world in the worst punishment matrimony is capable of,
viz: that you, Madam, may have a fool for a husband, and
that he may have a w——e for his wife; and if you are not
both undone, the Author begs your pardon for being
mistaken.' In other words, the punishment was made to fit
the crime, and the price of pre-marital sex was invariably
marriage.

Despite the evidence on his own pages that marriage did not always channel the baser instincts into an acceptable course Dunton continued to advocate it. When asked whether the married or unmarried state was the happier, he cautiously replied, 'It is much as you order it.' But he plumped for marriage since ' 'tis more natural, for in that other state, Man cannot lawfully answer his Physical End ... he can neither do this lawfully, nor so much as agreeably to his nature, since beasts only have all Common, but Propriety is one of the most darling Prerogatives of Man.'

Many of Dunton's male correspondents had roving eyes, and sought advice as to why they found girls just as enticing after marriage as before. Was it necessarily wrong for a married man to look with pleasure at pretty women? ' 'Tis dangerous,' Dunton thought, 'the Eye being the Burning Glass of love and looking, liking, desiring, attempting and criminally obtaining, oftentides, or always follow one another.'

Most of the Grub Street journalists preached against jealousy. *The Spectator* published several elegant letters and answers on its destructive and foolish results. But what if Man's jealousy were not merely the result of dark suspicions? What if his wife's falseness were proven? Even then, according to the aunties, a man was not given the moral right to leave his deceiving wife and take up with another:

I am a man of Honour, and not a twelve months since I married a young woman, to whom, I was the most faithful and fondest of husbands, but as truths and endearments are no obligations to Lust and Shame, I had not been married half a year before I took her in the very act of Adultery. Now, (as I suppose you will grant me) being neither obliged as a Gentleman or a Christian to take Infamy and Pollution in my Embraces, and to lay open my constitution, not able to live without a Woman, I at present keep a Mistress, a Companion so dear to me that with all my soul I could marry her; but as the highest favour the straight-laced Doctors Commons will give me is a Divorce only a mensa et foro, *from my first hard bargain, that performance is above my power. Now my question to you Gentlemen is this; How far am I sinful in this last Conversation and whether Adultery or not,*

together with your opinion of the present law, that in cases of adultery
will no further untie the Marriage Knot than a Separation only from
Bed and Board?

(The Ladies' Mercury, *10 March 1693*)

The adviser agreed with the cuckolded husband that his
case was a hard one, 'but a man must neither Whore nor
Marry whilst she lives for the pulpit law pronounces it both
ways whoredom'.

Unfaithfulness, then as now, was only one cause of
marital breakdown. Violence and drunkenness were two
major causes chronicled in the problem pages. Financial
difficulties, with the husband either failing in his duty as
breadwinner or, more commonly, spending his earnings
without allowing his family a share, cropped up
frequently:

I am a woman under great trouble; my husband is a Blacksmith and a
good Workman, and might maintain his family very well, if he would
follow his work. But he spends his money in gaming, and neglects his
Business to the great loss of his Trade, and Ruin of his Family, I have
us'd the Interest of all my Friends to persuade him, but all to no
Purpose. Pray, Sir, if you can advise me, if there is any publick way to
hinder him, what I should do, it will not be only a Kindness to me, but
to many of my Neighbours in the same condition, living in St Giles's
Parish, to which the good Order of the City does not reach.

Poverty carries its own Punishment along with it, if he will
reduce himself to a Beggar, he may. Our Law has not
provided for the punishing of the Lazy etc. But if you fear
he will bring you to the Parish, upon your Oath made
before the Lord Chief Justice, the Church Wardens can
make him give Security for his Charge, and are the best
Defenders in this Case; you may employ your Servants, and
allow him what is fitting, he dare not abuse you, unless he
will lie in Gaol: For parishes are not to be charged with his
family while they can Prevent it. But women when they are
directed to this legal Cause, love to complain and say they
are ruin'd, have a bad Husband, love to be pitied, but
seldom follow the Advice to remedy it, if the Sot Promises
Amendment; and when a Beggar, the Remedy is too late.

(*The Post-Angel*, December 1701)

It was easy for Dunton to advise these precautions, and to
sneer at women who were reluctant to involve parish
officialdom. But this letter, and others of the same period,
show that a distaste for calling in Poor Law Guardians was
in existence long before the New Poor Law of 1834, which
strove to make relief as unattractive as possible. Clearly,
most women in the early 1700s would stoop to virtually
anything to retain their independence and that of their
husband, however unsatisfactory he was proving as a
provider, just as many women today refuse to go through
the courts to obtain a maintenance order, which permits
the Department of Health and Social Security to take the
money from a husband's pay packet at source. Families
are deterred from getting state, or local authority, support
in much the same way as they were 250 years ago. And the
only real difference in practical help available to a woman
married to such a husband is that her modern counterpart
would be advised to send her husband to the self-help
agency, Gamblers Anonymous.

Another cause of marital breakdown was the footloose
husband. The eighteenth century was, par excellence, the
age of friendship and shared pleasures outside the home.
The coffee shop, the inn, organised sports – be they
cock-fighting, boxing or racing – all these were essential
activities. Some women, resentful of their husbands'
pleasures, flirted with the idea of finding an alternative
escort. One such letter was addressed to 'Mrs Singleton',
the editress of *The Old Maid*, supposedly a spinster who
supported the Goddess of Celibacy but in real life the
soon-to-be-married Frances Moore:

> ... *I have the misfortune to be married to one of the honestest fellows in
> the world, that is a man who spends his life in a regular course of
> irregularity, and makes no conscience of disturbing me every night at
> the most unreasonable hours; he is always the last man in the club
> room, and when ... he comes home, reels into the room ... talks loud a
> quarter of an hour and then very quietly resigns himself to the sweetest
> of that repose which he has so effectually banished from his wife. I
> seldom see him from noon till after midnight, but am left to pass my
> evenings, unless relieved by an accidental visit, in the entertaining
> conversation of a maiden aunt who lives with us. I have proposed*

separate beds, but he will never hear of it … I remember to have heard my Father, who was a man of learning, say that amongst the Romans disagreement of temper was a sufficient reason for divorce, but as our laws are not so good natured, I beg you to know whether I may not consider myself as unmarried, and endeavour to lighten the conjugal load, as I see most of my neighbours do; and as I am deprived of my husband's company, admit that of somebody else, for positively I can bear this treatment no longer?

P.S. There is a very pretty gentleman your end of Town who wants very much to come and chat a few evenings with me. What would you advise?

Before I advise this Lady, I must beg leave to say a word to her husband, and to desire him to consider that if a sentinel will leave his post, he cannot wonder at finding it occupied by another. I sincerely pity her, and if she could punish her husband without hurting herself, should not blame her. In the meantime I think the maiden aunt being with her a happy circumstance and am glad to find we are sometimes of use. I can only recommend her a certain quality which I have observed to be of real service in conjugal life, I mean, patience, for she will certainly find the remedy she proposed much worse than the disease.

(*The Old Maid*, 21 February 1756)

'Mrs Wentworth', the pseudonym of the former stay-maker, Hugh Kelly, was similarly moral in her replies, though without being unctuous:

Having an acquaintance just run away with a young lady, without the knowledge and consent of the parents of either party, but who are not yet married, desire to know which is the most prudent step they can take in regard to their reputation and future happiness.

Signed Alex Harper

While the parties remain as they are, guilt and remorse will be continually haunting their unjustified proceedings. And they must expect no favour from the busy tongues of a censurous world. We therefore seriously, in friendship, recommend a speedy marriage, as the defence against the base shafts of slander and the surest foundation of happiness hereafter.

(*The Court Miscellany*, August 1765)

The Court Miscellany was one of the first magazines to publish
a letter from a rejected swain. Most of the earlier problem
pages had included letters from old maids, or from young
girls whose would-be lovers were proving dilatory or
insensitive to hints. But young men, too could be repulsed.
The following letter, published in 1765, is an indication of
a newly romantic, and less rumbustious, attitude to
courtship and marriage. The young man is beginning to
worship at the altar of feminine purity and goodness, the
idealization from which Victorian women would one day
struggle to escape:

> *I have for a long time, and still do, retain a most pure and ardent
> affection for the most beautiful of her sex, always endeavouring by every
> little service, to ingratiate myself into her esteem, or at least to be taken
> notice of by her. I succeeded in the latter part of my wishes, in such a
> manner as made her sensible I had more than common regard for her.
> This discovery only served to make my position worse, as it caused her to
> avoid my company (especially in private) more than anyone else; nor
> could I (though for a long time I sought all opportunity of declaring my
> passion) meet with one till very lately I was, a few moments, in her
> company alone. I made use of the time, as well as the shortness of it
> would permit, but met with a repulse; since which she has avoided me
> more than ever. I beg your opinion with regard to what I may hope for
> from the object of my wishes, and what course you would advise me to
> take under my present circumstances.*

(The Court Miscellany, *August 1765*)

Realistically, Hugh Kelly advised his correspondent to
forget her, quoting Mercutio's advice to Romeo, 'Forget to
think of her, take thou some new infection in your heart,
and the rank poison of the old will die ...'

A decade later, a young woman was writing to *The
Ladies' Magazine* to complain that she was similarly pestered
by an irrepressible suitor:

> *This, Madam, is my own misfortune, to be miserably haunted by a
> man, whose sight is odious to me: one whom no words can conceive!
> No denials can satisfy! No affronts affect! Insensible of my uneasiness,
> and indefensibly increasing it! – I would fly him; but I cannot, unless
> I would fly my friends too, and my parents, nor have I any intimates
> left ...*

The auntie sympathetically reminded her that 'the gentleman who is so unhappy to be the subject of her complaint will be the last to see the force of it', and went on to reflect that 'it would certainly be a great happiness if we who love without hope could desist without misery'.

As this letter appeared, a new moral climate was beginning to make itself felt. The problem pages became full of dire warnings against 'unguarded levity' which might give 'a bad man insolence to think of more'. The consequence, they threatened, might be 'absolute ruin before the very sense of it had reach'd the unguarded heart which had suffer'd it'. Both Mrs Eliza Haywood of *The Female Spectator*, and Mrs Grey of *The Ladies' Magazine* declared that their young readers should beware of the pleasure gardens at Ranelagh, the masked balls at Marylebone and the Vauxhall supper parties where:

> ... the lady may be prevailed upon to taste wine, though with reluctance. The dark walk has increased familiarity and an expedition to Richmond has completed the infernal purpose.

The auntie could go no further, but the message is very clear. Behind every ornamental bush in the pleasure gardens there lurked a wolf, promenading in every spa was a seducer. The only defence, apart from absolute purity and goodness, was Mama and Papa.

Fortune hunting, with which Dunton and Defoe had been so much concerned seventy years before, was still prevalent. Nor was it exclusively a male vice. The idea of marrying suitably involved putting a daughter up for discreet auction to the highest bidder. But accepting expensive presents and then refusing an offer of marriage was a different matter. In 1775 Mrs Grey, in *The Ladies' Magazine*, published a statement on the practice of girls' refusing to return engagement presents, in the form of a letter from one 'TB' who was 'the more eager for the redress of this grievance having lost considerable sums in this way'. Mrs Grey sympathised, but she 'should be sorry to have him, or any other man, united to a Lady who was prevented from breaking off a marriage, merely because she was not able to bring herself to part with what she had no right, after having refused her lover, to detain ... When a woman, upon a nearer acquaintanceship with her lover, finds out something in him, or feels something in herself, which seems to exclude happiness from their union, she not only acts a just, but a very kind part, in breaking off all further connections with him. With regard to presents she certainly ought to return everything which she received from him.'

But if women could, on occasion, be fickle that was their prerogative. For a man to break an engagement was a different matter. The only consolation that an auntie could offer was that if a man could act so basely before marriage, then the girl was fortunate indeed to have escaped years of suffering as his wife.

... It is now more than two years since a young gentleman, with most amiable person, and a good fortune, paid his addresses to me, and insinuated himself so far into my favour that the day was fixed for our matrimonial connection. Judge my surprise, when he was, on the preceding day, married to an intimate acquaintance of mine, for whom I had always the greatest friendship and regard; and little expected she could have acted so basely, so perfidiously.

... Pride is not a passion which I would, in general, recommend to my female correspondents; yet in some cases, a proper degree of it may not only prove becoming, but necessary. When a lady has lost the man to which she was on the point of being united, or when she is grossly deceived by a pretended friend of her own sex, she will appear, perhaps, void of sensibility by discovering no emotions on such occasions. I would have her feel, but I would not have her disclose all her feelings. Let Moira consider how little she makes herself when she shows so much sorrow on being left by a man, with whom she could never have been happy, and for whom she ought to feel the strongest contempt; her friend too is quite unworthy of the name: such a character could not possibly be capable of friendship. She is, therefore, in my opinion, happily rid of them both: I would only have her possess a sufficient share of spirits to regret the loss of them no longer.

(*The Ladies' Magazine*, December 1781)

Sensibility was, as we see from this letter, being assiduously cultivated as a ladylike accessory in the 1780s. And the Victorian shrinking violet did not just appear, her seeds were planted in the previous century.

The Ladies' Magazine's main competitor, until *La Belle Assemblée* appeared in 1806, was *The Lady's Monthly Museum* where letters appeared addressed to 'The Busy Body'. A letter which appeared in February, 1811, illustrates how far the virtues commonly considered Victorian were prevalent in the Regency, if not earlier. Though the friends of the Regent might be permitted a certain licence, the tentacles of middle-class respectability and Evangelical morality ensured that the successful girl was the dutiful, drooping creature who spoke, saw and thought commonplace things. 'Samuel Single' wrote to the 'Busy Body' about his choice of bride. Should it be Matilda, rich, handsome, well-mannered, and a good house-keeper but 'with a bold and authoritative manner', and capable of slapping 'any gentleman of my acquaintance upon the shoulder, as the stage coachman would the ostler at an Inn?' Or would Selinda be preferable, with her pretty, delicate figure and timid disposition? She is child-like and childish, having no will of her own, but then she has such a delicate constitution 'that I never see her without being entertained with a long catalogue of complaints, and it is, in fact, the only subject which she ventures to converse.' Then again, Eliza might be the best, as she is pretty and accomplished but her superior talents 'make me feel intimidated ... and she seems to consider herself entitled to universal attention, and appears to receive every silly compliment with eager avidity.'

The auntie was opposed to them all. 'Matilda is both a termagant and a hoyden, Selina is a compound of deceit and affectation and Eliza is vain, coquettish and extravagant.' In order to help him find a suitable bride she listed the qualities which she thought would be most likely to ensure his permanent happiness;

In the first place, the young lady should be, in company, more eager to listen than to speak.

In private to speak well of others, silent as to herself.
Abroad modestly dressed; at home, plain, clean and neat.
Complaisant, without meanness to her superiors.
Gentle and considerate to her inferiors.
Generous without prodigality; frugal without stinginess.
Accomplished according to her station in life.
Industrious according to her necessities.
Unassuming in her deportment, and modest in her conversation.
If my young correspondent can meet with these essentials in any lady of his acquaintance, I would advise him not to let want of fortune, beauty or wit, or even a few peculiarities of temper stand in his way.

3

Honour and obey

COURTSHIP, MARRIAGE AND DIVORCE
1837–1900

Marriage in the nineteenth century required, in addition to all the virtues listed by the *Lady's Monthly Magazine*, a metamorphosis on the part of the bride. From a blushing, empty-headed girl, fearful of Papa, dutiful to Mama and accomplishment-prone, an authoritarian wife was expected to emerge, modest and subservient to her husband, but otherwise mistress of a house and servants. Her empire was not large, but it required constant vigilance.

To run a middle-class household on £300 a year was not easy, particularly in so status-conscious an era. Such an income would confer only the bare necessities of genteel existence – a detached house and garden, with three servants. A dinner party once a month would require economies in the children's and servants' meals for a week afterwards to cover the cost. Important items of clothing could be purchased, but children's dresses, all underclothing and the husband's nightshirts would be sewn at home, until the 1880s, entirely by hand.

With ten children, and a total household of fifteen, the demands on three hundred pounds were considerable. But middle-class pretensions started with a clerkship and £120 a year, and by such families three servants would be regarded as the height of luxury. Many housewives ran the home with the aid of a single general-servant, untrained and unsurprisingly sulky about the amount of work expected of her. Architects did their best to make her life,

and that of her mistress, still more difficult by clever
designs which placed the coal hole as far as possible from
the kitchen fire. This was to promote a thrifty use of fuel. It
also, however, encouraged bad temper, exhaustion and, in
the servant's case, revolt.

But revolt was not possible for her mistress. Lacking
labour-saving devices, and having a large family to cater
for, many Victorian women died, literally, of over-work.
The exhaustion of child-rearing could be as dangerous as
child-bearing itself. The picture of the idle Victorian lady,
reclining with a novel in her hand while her children play
quietly in an upstairs nursery, may be seductive. It is,
however, inaccurate for all but the most upper-class of
households. The novels in which it appeared played the
same escapist role in women's lives that soap operas do
today. In reality the housewife's work-load was so over-
powering that it might not be far-fetched to attribute her
attitude to sex to total exhaustion rather than repression.

The typical Victorian girl, moreover, had little time to
achieve this difficult transformation from drawing-room
Miss to bustling housewife before motherhood arrived.
Four-fifths of all middle-class married women had a baby
within the first year of marriage. A much read book,
frequently recommended by women's magazines, called
How I Managed My House on Two Hundred Pounds drew on the
experience of the authoress, Eliza Warren. 'My children,'
she writes, 'were around me before I had devised any
certain method of managing my household affairs.'

In one sense, women's magazines were responsible for
romanticizing matrimony. It was presented as the pinnacle
of every woman's happiness and the goal of every girl's
endeavours. Certainly most serials ended at the altar. But
closer reading of the magazines, and particularly of the
problem pages, reveals a more hard-headed approach.
Both they and the much maligned home-management
books (which are regarded as a by-word for extravagance
only by those who forget the size of the average Victorian
household) give a thoroughly prosaic account of the
housewife's duties. She is pictured struggling to make ends
meet, instructing her daughters in the rudiments of

reading and writing, and keeping an eye on the cook to ensure that the weekly budget is not overspent. Such time as is left might be devoted to sewing, attending the endless sick-beds of her children and relatives, and entertaining her husband. Tatting, embroidery and poker-work all feature in the pages of women's magazines, but so do weekly recipes designed to ensure that every scrap of food is used up, and hints to cut the heating and lighting bills. The effect of an improvident foolish wife, who could not control her servants and failed to check the tradesmen's bills, was shown in *David Copperfield*. What made Dora attractive as a girl was precisely what made David's married life so unbearable. The problem pages threw their increasing influence into the struggle to save people from so dreadful a fate.

Home was all-important, and scrimping and saving behind the scenes was encouraged to support the necessary veneer of respectability and easy circumstances. But the weight of the economies was invariably expected to fall on the women and children. A woman with a straying husband was advised to make her house more attractive. That she should try to make herself more attractive was not considered:

> *A wife's duties. − A wife should endeavour to make her home as comfortable as possible, so that her husband may always look forward with pleasure to the time when he reaches home. Many husbands are driven from their homes to clubs and other places that they should shun, by the bad management of their wives or, what is worse, by their want of discretion in exposing all their little faults to neighbours. That system of gossiping that some wives indulge in is frequently the cause of much misery; when a woman exposes her husband's failings, she breaks her marriage vow, and makes her home unbearable, perhaps for ever. Whatever may be the private character of her husband, it should be defended rather than laid open to attack by the public. Your own good sense will guide you in the other domestic duties of a wife.*
>
> (The Family Friend, *1852*)

Those who failed to make their home and their husband's comfort their primary concern were shown to pay the price:

Catherine Charles A. Hogan, who tells us that during her seventeen years of married life she has looked more 'after the conduct of her neighbours' sons and daughter than her own family' and complains of her husband's bad habits and practices, asking our advice, has, we think, no one but herself to blame for the domestic misery she suffers. The only counsel, therefore, we can give her, is to stay at home and mind her own business, and make his fireside so attractive to her spouse that he will have no desire to seek society elsewhere.

(Cassell's Family Magazine, 25 April 1857)

A man who was attracted to a fluffy, mindless girl and then found her more interested in her dog than in her children, or better on the piano than in the pantry, had in the end only himself to blame. But the husband whose fluffy girl did successfully transform herself into a competent manager, with a mind and temper of her own, could on occasion be equally dissatisfied. 'Arthur Biggs', who wrote to *Cassell's* after six months of marriage in March 1859, was a surprised victim of just such a change:

He thought his 'Euphemia Ellen' would always see things as he saw them, and that his will would be her law. To his real disappointment, he finds that she has a will of her own, and often sees things from a different point of view to his own. In fact, 'Arthur Biggs' is disappointed, and perhaps 'Euphemia Ellen' is also disappointed.

Cassell's confined their advice to Arthur:

If you wish your wife to appear as amiable as she did when she was bride-elect, infuse into your own manner now you are a husband, some of the fondness of a lover. After a parting, endeavour to meet Euphemia with some of the warmth of former days. Recollect how fond was the first meeting – how tender was the last farewell – how fervent were your vows.

Euphemia, they suggested, might be equally unhappy as she contrasted this happy picture with his current discontent.

These were clearly the first sparrings of what was to be a difficult marriage. But it was a marriage which would last until death. Divorce was highly unlikely and separation a step which middle-class couples would be loath to take. They had much more to lose than their working-class equivalents if they offended the tenets of conventional morality. The man's livelihood might suffer. The woman, if she moved to a separate establishment, would not be visited by her new neighbours. The cost of two homes would require both to live in straitened circumstances. Such considerations made the middle-classes the bastion of marriage, and at times the victims of resignation or despair.

The middle-class magazines of this period reflect these realities, and most were committed to patching up a marriage at whatever cost. They were quite open about this. *The London Journal* printed a stern reply on 2 August 1862:

> *We are afraid we cannot afford you any consolation of a practical kind, for our duty as journalists is to lend our aid in preventing, not promoting the separation of husband and wife. Your case is certainly a grievous one and you are to be pitied; but we should advise you only to appeal to the law for protection in the last extremity. To obtain a judicial separation, the evidence of cruelty must be very strong, and we do not think the Court would say that vulgar taunts of a vulgar mind amounted to cruelty contemplated by the law in these painful matters.*

From the answers given by journalists it is clear that they shared the feelings of the Houses of Parliament, who decided in 1857 to liberalise the Divorce Laws only very slightly, enabling those with exceptional grounds – adultery in the case of the woman, adultery in the case of the man when coupled with cruelty or incest – to obtain a divorce without an Act of Parliament. It is also apparent that many women failed to understand either the old or the new law. A rough sample of problem page letters in the 1850s and 1860s shows that approximately as many men wrote in about their unhappy marriages as women, but a far higher proportion of women asked about divorce. For most of them the advice was to remain what it had been before 1857, when an Act of Parliament and a couple of thousand pounds in cash were necessary to dissolve a marriage. As *The London Journal* wrote to 'Punch' on 18 March 1854, 'You ought to have looked before you leaped.'

None the less, the Divorce Bill provoked a rash of hopeful queries and on 9 January 1858, *Cassell's* decided to save time and space with an all-embracing answer:

> *We have received several communications from married ladies on the subject of grievances for which they may obtain redress by the new act, when it shall come into operation on the 11th day of January 1858. We cannot undertake to answer each letter separately; but we beg to inform all deserted wives that on and after the 11th day of January next, they can, by applying to a police magistrate, if they are residing in London, or with a Justice in Petty Sessions, if residing in the country, obtain an order to protect any property they may become possessed of after desertion, against their husband and their husband's creditors. This order will, by the operation of the new act, give the deserted wife the same right and title over her earnings and her property that she would have had if she had been a single woman. Creditors of the husband continuing to retain possession of the property of the deserted wife after notice of such an order, are not only liable to a suit for the value of the property, which suit the wife is by this act entitled to bring, but also to a fine of double the value of the property thus illegally detained.*

The advice is arid but indispensable. The agony column is, once again, providing essential information for people who know of no other source of help.

The new Matrimonial and Divorce Act, largely won by the campaigning of the remarkable Caroline Norton, ameliorated the position of women to some extent. But married women who had not applied for a divorce or separation still had no separate property rights, a woman could until 1884 still be imprisoned for refusing to have sexual intercourse with her husband, and a man could detain his wife by force until 1891. Even those who did obtain a divorce could not expect encouragement from the problem pages for a wish to re-marry. *Cassell's* counselled 'Minnie' to 'close her ears at once against the voice of the charmer, and avoid a second trial of an experiment which answered so ill, that we confess we are surprised at her taking it again even into consideration'.

This assumption that one unsuccessful marriage should be quite enough was repeated to another correspondent 'EJT' just one month before the new Act came into effect in January 1858:

> *However disgraceful the bridegroom's conduct may have been in deserting his bride, it does not exonerate her from her duties and his claim. She cannot marry again; nor, unless she is a bolder woman than ordinary, would she, after past experience, wish it.*

In previous centuries those wishing to escape from an unhappy marriage had found one of the simplest and cheapest devices was to annul it by bribing a clergyman to swear that he had married one or other of the pair before. With the 1837 Act legalizing registry office marriage and the general growth of bureaucracy, such devices were less likely to succeed. They did not, however, completely disappear. The following letter from a man trying to prove his marriage bigamous is also interesting in another respect – the divorce laws, although hard on women married to bullies or philanderers, could also work the other way round. Men yoked to unsatisfactory wives were forced to continue their upkeep, unless they wished to find the money and the witnesses to prove their cuckoldry:

> *The law as it stands with respect to bigamy is … stringent enough to take care of those who know how to take care of themselves. From the lengthy statement you have sent us about yourself, you appear previous to your marriage to have made yourself acquainted with not a single passage in the history of your wife. You knew not who were her parents, her relatives, her connections, her friends. Her place of abode was a mystery to you – not less so her conduct and character. None could tell you what ties she had contracted. Well, this vagrant who comes to Birmingham you were insane enough to marry. After which she proves to be an abandoned female, elopes, you make enquiries about her, and in the course of your investigations have reason to suspect her of bigamy; but at the same time, you have doubts whether her former husband was not himself a bigamist. In that case, her marriage with him was illegal, and left her quite free to marry you. The law, therefore, can afford you no redress from the deceit she practised upon you. Nay, acknowledging her for your lawful wife, it obliges you – as long as she is not divorced from you – to support her under all*

*circumstances, even though she may be living with a paramour. You
are certainly to be commiserated, but you are much to be blamed. Had
you married with all due caution, you would have had no occasion to
make any complaints against the law.*

(The London Journal, *28 November 1846*)

This correspondent's troubles stemmed from an
ignorance of his wife's circumstances and character (could
it be there was some sense in the Victorian dictum of
shunning all those who have not been introduced by
friends?). Others suffered from too great a knowledge of
their prospective bride. Frequently they would have lived
with her for some years without a breath of scandal
touching either. The spinster sister, taken into her
brother-in-law's household out of charity, often
blossomed on her sister's death, gathered the reins of the
household into her capable hands and, finally, stepped
into her sister's side of the bed. Nothing in the prayer book
prevented such marriages, but nineteenth century
sensibility found them objectionable. A Deceased Wife's
Sisters law was passed preventing the marriage between
sister and brother-in-law.

The motives behind such legislation were various.
Family harmony was safe-guarded and the last hours of a
wife no longer clouded by suspicions that the soothing
hand on her brow might soon be soothing something else.
There was less fear that a man might be tempted to set up
a mini-harem, based on his wife's sisters, either before or
after her death. Above all, propriety was served. For if
brother and sister-in-law could marry, then it made
nonsense of the chaperonage of the brother-in-law and
turned the woman's continued existence in his house after
his wife's death into an outrage. Attitudes to the Act in the
problem pages were mixed. *The Ladies' Treasury* declared in
January 1858:

*We greatly disapprove of marriage with deceased wives' sisters, and
this is not merely on account of their illegality. We consider if English
law should ever sanction such marriage, a serious blow would be struck
at domestic affection and family confidence.*

The London Journal, however, on 8 April 1854 told 'Alice and Henry' that:

> *On the question of marriage with a deceased wife's sister we have already delivered our opinion. And we repeat, that we cannot perceive any natural, moral or religious objection to such a union.*

But the balance of opinion was with *The Ladies' Treasury* and the law was not repealed until 1907.

The mid-nineteenth century was a period when separation and divorce became marginally easier, but getting married actually began to be more difficult. In the 1840's the new family magazines started to take over from the personal columns of newspapers the publication of matrimonial advertisements. The views of the problem pages were once again mixed. *The Family Herald*, which warned its readers against answering anonymous advertisements, claimed:

> *They emanate from needy adventurers and are traps for the unwary. Deceptive advertisements are of various kinds, but, in general, they are dangerous to the purse only; medical and matrimonial begin with deception and end with destruction.*

Cassell's considered the practice of advertising for a wife 'highly objectionable'. One man, who had asked their opinion on the advisability of advertising, was told to find a suitable mate among his own friends, and to concentrate his attentions on the female members of his chapel. But he was warned that, 'if the woman must have £1000 pa of her own, it is probable that she might not consider a gentleman, middle-aged and in receipt of the same income, an eligible match'.

The Home Magazine varied its stance, one hand seeming not to know what the pen in its other was doing. They told 'Minnie' that:

> *No decent woman ever tampers with 'matrimonial advertisements'. There is no occasion for such to advertise for a husband. It is the refuse of the market which is put up at auction ...*

But they frequently carried such advertisements from girls, couched in language designed to attract. Accomplishments were listed, physical attributes catalogued, and the lure of a dowry sometimes thrown in for good measure. Sometimes the editors even allowed their own columns to be used as stepping stones to assignations. 'Tempus Fugit', for example, a clerk living in Knightsbridge who described himself as 'not particularly ugly, rather tall and my age is 16' was answered by a 'Signora Lodisky' three copies later, who was also 'not very bad-looking, of good birth and heart whole'. She suggested that if Tempus Fugit was in earnest he should meet her at the corner of Leicester Square. The editor's comment was 'Well, here's a chance for an aspiring young man. But beware, Signora, beware!'

The London Journal treated attempts to turn its columns into a matrimonial agency with jocularity. Twenty-one year old 'Maud' is described as 'pleasing in face, and figure, and thinks it's hard she should be overlooked in the crowd. Her Mama, who ought to be a judge, says she would make an excellent wife.' 'Sarah Saunders', a pretty, blue-eyed girl of nineteen years, in search of a husband admitted to one fault, biting her lip when in a passion. 'Well, we can see no very great harm in that, provided she is quite sure she would never bite anyone else,' wrote the advisers, without committing themselves to a search through their male readership for a volunteer.

Not infrequently, awful warnings were published by those magazines which refused to carry matrimonial advertisements. Beautiful, rich young ladies turned out to be brawny apprentices who took a hearty revenge on would-be suitors. These perils must have deterred some, as must the revelation, some decades later, that the Brides-in-the-Bath murderer had attracted his victims through the same medium.

But what eventually removed matrimonial advertisements from the pages of respectable family magazines was, probably, a desperate wish to insist on the principle that Mr Right should find Miss Right, and not vice-versa. We often forget the didactic purpose of the works from which we derive our view of Victorian morality, mistaking hopeful proselytizing for current practice. If all Victorian girls stayed in their fathers' drawing-rooms sewing a sampler, blowing the noses of their little brothers and perfecting their performance on the harp, what need was there of the endless stream of reminders of a young girl's duty? The burst of authoritarian etiquette books and moral tales in the mid-century may, in fact, reflect an older generation's need to protect its authority from the freedoms demanded by Victorian girls.

The problem pages of the 1850s and 1860s provide a picture of young women exceptionally ready to play an active part in courtship. Though these attempts were discouraged, the very fact that they appear so frequently suggests that, whatever the official view of flirting, Victorian girls pursued men with a single-mindedness rarely equalled before or since. *Cassell's* on 11 April 1856, conceded that girls might interest themselves in those things which clearly interest the man they have selected as a mate. 'Is he fond of reading?' Evangelina is asked. 'Talk to him about his favourite authors and listen attentively to his profound wisdom.' Though a woman should never chase a man 'there is no law that we are aware of to prevent a lady from doing her best (with all proper reserve of course) to make herself agreeable to the object of her affections, and to attract his regard.' Other magazines were more actively dissuasive. *The Ladies' Treasury* quoted seventeenth century source on courtship in leap-years:

> ... *the ladyes have the sole priveledge of making love, which they do either by wordes or lookes, as to them seemeth proper; and moreover, no man may be entitled to the benefit of the clergy who doth refuse the offers of a ladye, or who doth in any wise treat her proposal with slight or contumely.*

But it did so only to remark that 'We cannot tell you why leap-year, above all others, was fixed as the time when ladies were to lose their greatest charm by laying aside feminine restraint.' In still sterner vein, one love-lorn girl was told she must be a lunatic to love a man who conspicuously ignored her. A hundred and fifty years previously those who wrote to Dunton to ask whether they should die of love or inform their beloved of their feelings were advised to take the latter course. Their Victorian successors found *The Family Herald* and *The Ladies' Treasury* less obliging. Hearts, they were assured, only break in romantic novelettes. In real life a stiff upper lip and maidenly reticence were all that was needed to keep both a healthy body and a healthy position in local society.

But not every girl followed the advice of her favourite magazine. Young men, startled by such unexpected feminine forwardness, themselves wrote to the problem pages. *The Home Circle* replied to 'Archer Earnest' on 7 February 1852:

> *The young lady is somewhat premature in making a declaration of love to you. She should have waited until you had displayed the necessary preference. You are both, however, too young to entertain such romantic notions; and if the young lady's mother were to have a hint given to her of the initiative her daughter has taken in this matter, it would be quite as well.*

In June of that year *The Home Circle* gave a more sympathetic hearing to 'Ellen':

> *The situation must have been embarrassing for you both. The gentleman should have had a better command of language, or, at least, have been less ambiguous in his observation, so as not to have led you into the belief that he was making you an offer of marriage, and you should not have been quite to ready to suggest a positive meaning to his speech. It was no doubt very kind of you when he stumbled to give him a hand; but it was awkward for you, when you respectfully denied the honour (?) to be told by the gentleman that he never dreamt of making you such an offer.*

Neither of these letters accords with our picture of the little Victorian Miss waiting demurely for a proposal, a proposal which was only to be made after her father's permission had been granted. The polite fiction of the shrinking violet might colour the advice of the auntie, but no one can read the evidence of the problem pages without realising that every feminine wile was brought into play by girls for whom marriage provided the only passport to power and status. *The Home Magazine* published one remarkable letter from a man chased by a woman who was determined to hook him at any cost. She had hinted strongly at her love, as a result of which he stopped visiting her. She then wrote, requesting an interview, confessing her love and begging him to see her. He, wriggling desperately, announced that he intended never to marry. She then applied a strong dose of emotional blackmail:

> ... *she lived only in the hope of seeing him and ... if he entirely forsook her she should destroy herself. Overcome by her persuasions and fearful of having the blood of a human being on his soul, he consented to see her now and then, which he has done and is still doing.*

The Home Magazine gave its advice with relish:

> ... *she is an artful and immodest woman who is determined upon getting a Husband by fair means or foul, and who finds in our correspondent one of those soft, amicable irresolute persons who seem born to fall prey to such women. Whether this opinion be correct or not, we still advise our friend to drop her acquaintance. He owes it to her, as well as himself; for a marriage thus effected can not be a happy one, and the longer the acquaintance is continued without marriage, the worse it will be for both.*

In a more flippant vein, *The London Journal* advised a correspondent who wished to encourage a shy, retiring man to put him in a cage, so rare a specimen did they consider him to be. And *The Englishwoman's Domestic Magazine* answered a venturesome female who wished to know 'Now that Gretna Green is done away with, are there any means of getting married secretly and expediously?' in the affirmative but added:

> ... *it is not our business to teach persons how to evade the laws. We could imagine circumstances where we might, in confidence, impart the coveted knowledge, but we would rather not be asked.*

That women should have pursued marriage so ruthlessly is
not surprising. No alternative career presented itself, and
even this one was increasingly fraught with difficulties.
Parents who had struggled to obtain their middle-class
status (etiquette books of the era distinguished between a
gentlewoman, born to her position, and a lady, who had
to achieve hers) expected their daughters to consolidate
their advance. A potential husband had to be a man of
equal or superior class whose income was sufficient to
keep his bride in the manner to which she was
accustomed. As the century wore on, this produced a slide
into increasingly late marriages. Most girls, whose
schooling ended between the ages of sixteen and eighteen,
had to wait until they were twenty-five before taking on
the duties of a wife. That empty decade bred an increasing
anxiety about one's eventual fate and, even for those
whose self-confidence remained undiminished, flirting
must have seemed as good a way as any of passing the
celibate years. Though the problem pages may have
disapproved of forwardness they never lost their strong
sense of the importance of marriage. Those blessed with
several suitors were warned to beware of encouraging all
and winning none. And the attacks of flirting were often
based as much on pragmatism as they were on morality.
'Dark Eyes' was warned by *Every Week* on 3 January 1863
that 'we cannot altogether acquit you of imprudent
conduct ... It is always unwise – not to say unbecoming –
in a young lady to flirt with any man. It may endanger her
life's happiness.' Nothing, the aunties believed, would
compensate for the lost respect of a man with serious
intentions.

But though men might be encouraged to take the
leading role in courtship, they were not allowed to get
above themselves in other respects. *Cassell's* clearly did not
believe that modesty should be the exclusive preserve of
the softer sex. 'You must be a very fascinating fellow,' it
wrote on 2 January 1858, 'to bewitch young ladies into
such a disregard of propriety and decorum. How to help
you I don't really know. You would not like to part with
any of the attractions which make you so irresistible, and

unless you do, we fear there is no safety for you. Honey jars
will be beset with flies.'

Men could be unsatisfactory creatures in other ways too,
and the aunties took a pessimistic view of their potential
for improvement. Bounders were bounders, and were best
avoided:

> *A drooping lily is miserable because she is in love with a heartless rake*
> *– a man with whom she could not be happy unless he reformed, and yet*
> *she clings to him with a passion that reason cannot control. We can*
> *give her no other advice than to muster resolution and cast him off.*
> *There is a fearful amount of this folly amongst young women. The*
> *common proverb about a reformed rake making a good husband has*
> *found a free currency, and they trust to it as they do to a gipsy prophecy*
> *– many a victim that proverb has made. It goes about amongst young*
> *ladies like a roaring lion, seeking whom it may devour. We have done*
> *a little to check its course and we hope to do more ... If you marry a*
> *worthless rake before he is reformed, what will reform him? He is just*
> *the man to sicken of marriage and the dullness and monotony of*
> *domestic life. Marriage will settle a gay young man, with good*
> *principles and respect for character; but what will settle a worthless,*
> *unprincipled man who is driven by his ruling passions to perdition, like*
> *an ox to the slaughter? Without a good conscience a man is a beast;*
> *and to love such a man is itself a crime and is sure to be punished.*

> (The Family Herald, *20 May 1852*)

The punishment would, of course, at this date be to marry
a wastrel whose power extended to his wife's property,
earnings and children over the age of seven.

Unequal marriages were discouraged by most problem
page journalists. *The London Journal* explicitly warned
against adventurers whose 'addresses were rather to be
found in the *Newgate Calendar* than in the *Court Guide*'. Even
if a man's finances had declined, through no fault of his
own, during the engagement he was expected to do the
decent thing and release his fiancée from her promise.
One such was advised to work to replenish his family's
fortunes. If his sweetheart really loved him 'he would find
her waiting'. Attitudes were rather different, however, in
the case of an alliance contracted before the meteoric rise
of a successful young man. This he was expected to

honour in spite of his new wealth and status, as 'Henry S' was sternly informed:

If you are a man you will marry the girl you loved and were beloved by in your poor days. Be just and honourable, although fortune has smiled on you. Do not let the itching palm of avarice sully the new garment in which you are decked, but be a man 'for a' that' and show how proud you are of the opportunity of having your sincerity tested.

Those who were jilted, in these or other circumstances, had a legal recourse in the form of a Breach of Promise Action. Most cases were brought by girls who had become pregnant (farmers in particular believed in testing the goods before committing themselves) and these could not be mentioned in Victorian problem pages. The other major grievance, however, the lending of money to the unfaithful lover, was much discussed. Typical of such girls was 'Rose' who spent her money on household articles prior to her long-awaited marriage. 'She has now lost her place, her money and her sweetheart. The last of these is the least to be regretted. As this sweetheart was evidently cruel and faithless, we think Rose is well rid of him.' It was pointed out to her that, although she had a perfect case of Breach of Promise, she had neither knowledge of her lover's abode nor the money to bring a case. Therefore she was told to 'drive the traitor from her thoughts, and bend all her energies towards getting another place'. 'Martha', another innocent girl taken in by the advances of a man more interested in her pocket than her person, was encouraged to go to court. Her lover, a journeyman baker, had used her money to set himself up in business and had then promptly married a younger and prettier girl.

Blackmail was not, however, encouraged. 'Ada', who had been conducting a clandestine engagement with a social superior for seven years and now found that he was flirting with her best friend, wanted to know whether she should pretend she had not destroyed his love letters to her, in order to frighten him into a declaration. 'Certainly not,' said the aunties. 'Appeal to his honour and good feeling ... The result will be, we much fear, a withdrawal

on his part, but even that is better than Ada's wasting any
more years on a heartless deceiver.'

But the Breach of Promise Action was not a one-edged
weapon. It could be the man who carried the torch and
was rejected. In 1859 'AG' wished to know if he could sue a
lady for Breach of Promise:

> *Certainly he can, if he chooses, but we do not advise him to do so. Let
> him not give the lady the satisfaction of perceiving how much her
> heartless conduct has wounded him, rather let him resolve on
> conquering useless regret and on fixing his affections on a worthier
> object.*

Sadder still, perhaps, was the experience of 'Tchow-aka',
who spent four years conducting a very proper courtship.
But so circumspect was his behaviour that although he
walked with the lady, talked (on indifferent subjects) and
looked tenderly at her (when her head was turned away)
she did not realise his passion. He in turn did not realise
that she was promised to a man who was busy making a
fortune in Australia. 'Tchow-aka' was advised to find a
new object for his affections and to explain his intentions
next time in less than four years.

In the final decades of the nineteenth century difficulties
arising from the middle-class practice of delayed marriage
became more and more prominent. Late marriage had
some undoubted advantages. Medical opinion
recommended that women should preferably stop bearing
children by the age of thirty-two, and definitely by
thirty-five. If a woman married at the age of twenty-five,
therefore, she might escape with as few as six or seven
pregnancies before her husband turned his attention
exclusively to his mistresses or his work. But the ten-year
hiatus in a girl's life, between school and altar, remained a
problem. What was she expected to do?

The answer found in the magazines of the 1880s and
1890s was rarely a positive one. What she was expected not
to do, however, was writ large. Flirting, from being a
misdemeanour, became a crime. Described by the *Girls'
Own Paper* as 'one who keeps up a bantering, jesting
intercourse with men – a sort of undignified and spurious

love-making', a flirt did not hide behind the voluminous
skirts of her chaperone or sit quietly in her papa's drawing
room. Instead she sallied forth in search of amusement
provided by the opposite sex. This sort of girl was violently
attacked by Mrs Linton, in *The Girl of the Period*, for being
'A creature who dyes her hair, paints her face as first
articles of her personal religion, a creature whose sole idea
of life is fun'. Episodes that the aunties of the 1850s and
1860s had been prepared to dismiss as foolish, but not
harmful, now came under the full blast of Linton-like
judgements. In the *Girls' Own Paper* of 24 January 1884
'Bluebell' was informed, 'It is disgraceful in a little girl of
your age' – she was sixteen – 'to resist the wishes and
authority of your mother and to dream of going out alone.
Your reputation would not be worth much if you did.'
'ERMC', however, was a still worse case and the *Girls' Own
Paper* attempted to make her thoroughly ashamed of
herself:

> *To receive clandestine love-letters, when your own filial confidence to
> your mother and submission to her will and judgement forbid it, is most
> ungrateful as well as undutiful. But to take in letters of two men
> continually through the blinds of your bedroom window, encouraging
> both at the same time, is simply disgusting! 'How shall I squash them?'
> is a heartless question after so much encouragement. It would be well if
> your mother was informed of your unseemly conduct, and would
> effectually 'squash' you.*

This reply, which appeared in 1890, can be compared with
the answer given in *Cassell's*, in 1857, to 'Sabine' who asked
what he should do with his betrothed:

> *… in defiance of her pledges to him, she carries on a correspondence
> with a young man of questionable character living opposite, by means
> of the deaf and dumb alphabet. Shall he give her up at once, or require
> an explanation? Really, we don't know. We are always adverse to
> harsh measures, so long at least as there is any hope of mild ones being
> effectual; but truly the damsel herself seems to be of such questionable
> principles and possessed of such liberal ideas of propriety, that we do
> think 'Sabine' could not be happy with her as a wife, and therefore we
> incline to the former of his suggestions.*

The offence in these two cases is very similar, but the severity of the censure is very different. Both are breaking the code of acceptable behaviour, but ERMC's case is treated with no humour and a great deal of shocked disapproval. This is the tone we associate with late Victorian England and it is well represented in the problem pages. Rarely did a week go by without the *Girls' Own Paper* carrying at least one awful warning about flirting. But the very repetition of the advice suggests that the recipients took very little notice.

Many middle-class girls who did not have the talents of a Florence Nightingale or a Sylvia Pankhurst, in fact, rebelled. Such a rebellion did not necessarily take the positive form of seeking a career. Urged to fill their time with domestic chores and self-improvement, they instead giggled with their girlfriends, went visiting, played croquet or tennis and, of course, flirted. 'Verena' was sternly told by the *Girls' Own Paper* that:

> *No well principled person, thoroughly well-bred, would demean themselves to what is termed a 'flirtation'. It is a vulgar, undignified amusement and no man respects a girl who allows him to be so familiar.*

Again and again, the *Girls' Own Paper* found itself obliged to add the shocked phrase 'You have evidently been trifling shamefully with him.' One suspects that the feelings it provoked were as much triumphant as shameful.

The late Victorians were less keen on Breach of Promise since it exposed the girl's eagerness to get married, and her rejection, too clearly. But, to a much greater extent than their counterparts of the 1850s and 1860s, they liked everything to be clear cut and properly witnessed. Men who had not proposed after two years were assumed to be trifling with a girl's affection. And a change of mind about an engagement was seen, at worst as a heinous sin, at best as ill-mannered and inconsiderate. A long and detailed reply in *The British Weekly*, a Methodist magazine appealing mainly if the pseudonyms used in the correspondence column are anything to go by, to clergymen's wives, cap-

tures the general view of problem page advisers at this
date towards those who wished to reconsider:

> Private – *It is a very serious thing to marry an invalid, the
> consequences may be far reaching; but it is also a very serious thing to
> break off an engagement of long standing, the conditions being in no
> way altered since the engagement was made. You do not expect me to
> advise you to do the latter! If young men would only not be in such a
> hurry to engage themselves to the first sympathetic girl they meet, before
> they have attained to any responsible position in life, there would be a
> great deal of unnecessary pain and regret saved from both sexes.
> Having entered on the engagement you must consider how serious it is
> for the girl, and how much it must necessarily mean to her. Nothing has
> changed since the engagement except your feelings and your knowledge
> of what would be advantageous to yourself. This is, perhaps, a harsh
> way of putting the case, but it is merely a bald statement of what you
> wrote. Could you go to the girl and tell her the exact truth? say to her:
> 'I have improved my education since I asked you to marry me, my
> horizon has widened, I know more cultured people, I could marry into
> a better social circle now, and could get a wife more calculated to do me
> credit. You are very good, and very much attached to me, I know, but
> you are not very pretty, you are not very learned, your literary tastes
> have not been developed, your health is not good, and if you became a
> chronic invalid it would bother me exceedingly. I know it is hard to ask
> you to give me up, seeing that this thing has lasted a good many years,
> and that you have no other prospects for the future, and no facilities for
> beginning the battle of life single-handed and disillusioned; but that is
> only your side of the question. Women should not be selfish, and since I
> have shown you in the most considerate way that this thing should end,
> I hope you will make it quite comfortable for me by saying you wish it
> ended. Of course, you can make a fuss and cause me some annoyance,
> but I hope you will not do so, as it would result in nothing except to
> injure your place in my regard for ever.' Now this is by no means the
> worst or the most painful way in which an engagement can be broken,
> but you see for yourself it is not pretty. There are cases in which the
> breaking of an engagement is not a very serious thing, but there are
> other cases where it simply means a shipwrecked life for the person who
> has been betrayed, whichever this may be. To have a delicate wife is a
> great trial; but to be equally delicate and equally penniless and jilted in
> addition is worse still for the woman. I leave the matter to yourself. I
> decline to advise.*

(The British Weekly, 11 June 1891)

A rather different answer, however, was given when women wrote in about lovers attempting to get out of their engagements. Give them up was the advice, since it was better to accept the inevitable than to force a marriage and have a wandering husband.

Following the rash of queries about divorce in the 1850s and 1860s, it was no longer possible to maintain the polite fiction that marriage inevitably led to bliss – an attitude staunchly held by the serial writers whose contributions filled the main part of the family magazines. It also became more difficult for the problem page writers to preach the message of resignation recommended, for example, by the author of *The Wives of England, their Relative Duties, Domestic Influence and Social Obligations* in 1843: 'I have spoken of the married state as one of the trial of Principle rather than the fruition of Hope.' As late as 1871, however, aunties were still advising women, if not to grin, then at least to bear it. A woman who had borne for twenty-two years 'with all humility and gentleness of spirit all the insults of a coarse nature' revealed that, although she could put up with her husband's behaviour in so far as it affected herself, yet 'my blood boils when I see my gentle, innocent girls tremble at the sound of their father's voice'. Realistically, the editorial advice in *The Englishwoman's Domestic Magazine* was 'As he is the bread winner you must bear it with a meek and quiet spirit.' Even this was too adventurous for some of the readership, one of whom felt moved to 'send a word of remonstrance for such a violent letter against a husband.' In the face of such audience participation it is not surprising that the aunties sometimes moved rather cautiously.

The late century witnessed one important campaign for legal reform equivalent to that for new divorce laws in the 1850s, and once again the problem pages were much involved. The Married Women's Property Act had in fact originally come up in the same session as the Divorce and Matrimonial Act of 1857, and had been torpedoed by it. A divorced or separated woman could now prevent her husband from keeping her property. It was therefore argued that happily married women needed no further protection. Barbara Leigh Smith's campaign on behalf of all women was accidentally held up for twenty-five years by Caroline Norton's victory for the abused minority.

But though parliament did not recognize the need for a Married Women's Property Act, the aunties did. Sam Beeton, editor of *The Englishwoman's Domestic Magazine*, was one adviser who regarded the automatic transfer of property to the husband on marriage as a legal injustice. He, like most of his fellow journalists, insisted that, in the absence of a new law, the settlement of property, either on the wife or on her children, was indispensable. He wrote to 'Mary H' in January 1860:

> *The personal property of the wife passes to her husband absolutely on her marriage, but her real (i.e. freehold) property can only be alienated by him during her life; with her consent. If, as should be, it had been given to trustees for her sole use, he has no power over it.*
>
> (The Englishwoman's Domestic Magazine)

The London Journal, too, felt 'it is always advisable to have a settlement before marriage'. *Cassell's* went further by criticising the law as it stood and suggesting it should be changed to give wives, whose rights Caroline Norton compared unfavourably with those of the slaves in America, the same property rights as single women. Of the three Married Women's Property Acts – of 1870, 1882 and 1893 – the second was the most important, giving the majority of women control over their own property. This was the legislation which the mid-century magazines such as *Cassell's* and *The London Journal* had campaigned for, and one would expect it to have been greeted with universal enthusiasm in the correspondence columns. This was not so. *Women's Life*, and *Girls' Own Paper* and *The Family Herald* all had interesting reservations.

These advisers feared that the change in the law would make settlements redundant, with disastrous consequences. In their view the 1882 Married Women's Property Act was sufficient protection for what one journalist called the 'strong minded woman', but not for the more conventional creature who meekly believed that her husband knew best. Under the new law the wife had the right to assign her property as she thought fit, without reference to the trustees involved in a settlement. As a consequence a persuasive or violent husband could actually appropriate his wife's property more easily than before. Once again what seems, at first sight, a reactionary or blinkered attitude in fact reveals the problem page's strong sense of the real circumstances of everyday life and its remarkable understanding of ordinary, rather than exceptional, people.

Divorce continued to be a troublesome matter. By the 1880s the new powers of the 1857 Act were widely used by magistrates, and problem page writers never suggested, as they had done previously, that a cruelly used wife should seek the protection of 'some benevolent lady'. But the woman, however ill-treated, remained at a disadvantage. Proof of a husband's adultery was useless unless it was coupled with incest, rape or violence. And whatever the provocation, wives must remain good wives, at least until the separation was signed. 'Maud', for instance, was told by the *Girls' Own Paper* of 18 December 1886 to go to the Police Office and inform the inspector of the cruel treatment her husband subjected her to. He would take it to the 'proper quarters' where she would obtain a separation and an allowance. But, she was warned:

> *Do nothing rash and nothing wrong, be your trials and provocations what they may. What you have suggested would be very wrong indeed, and we think and hope that you must have done so under great excitement. If by word or act you thoughtlessly give cause for any jealousy you might not obtain the separation and allowance to which otherwise you could lay just claim.*

Such reaction to the merest hint of marital infidelity was characteristic. The auntie of *The Young Woman* in July 1895 put the view of her contemporaries succinctly when she informed 'Mortimer':

> *I have no sympathy whatever with the loves of married people for others than their legitimate partners. They may not be able to love these, that*

*is always possible, but a painful position is not bettered or rendered
more dignified by wayward desires towards what is none of theirs.*

Similarly a correspondent in *Mothers and Daughters* who
admitted to unfaithfulness was firmly told that his
willingness to 'besmirch' his own marriage did not in any
way blacken the institution of matrimony in general.

The fact that marriage was the only truly acceptable
profession for the middle-class girl in Victorian England
meant that a failure to marry or a failure at marriage was
far more disastrous than it is today. A separation or a
divorce could mark a woman for life, the usual alternative
to alimony was the workhouse. And only fortuitous death
gave a girl a second chance in the matrimony lottery. It
was for these reasons that marriage was made so binding
and such care taken over the selection of a suitable
partner. Those intrusive and domineering parents had
good cause to worry.

The temptation to impose our values on Victorian
society, and to judge it accordingly, is sometimes
overwhelming. The late Victorians especially lived, in
many outward respects, a life similar to ours. They
travelled by train and, latterly, by car. Electric light was
available in many middle-class town houses. Their
bathrooms were not only similar to ours, they are often
the ones we use today. But they did, nonetheless, live in a
different world and the moral standards and social
customs of that world constituted a system of safe-guards
which suited its circumstances. Stability was often bought
at the price of repression, and safety imposed through
stultification. But a Victorian might well claim that the
price paid, though different, was actually no greater than
that paid today when freedom has brought in its train
insecurity, numerous single-parent families and a growing
class of deserted, middle-aged women. The following reply
which appeared in *Mothers and Daughters* in 1893,
exemplifies the extreme care, both personal and financial,
with which the Victorian advisers believed marriage
should be approached:

Minnie – *It is impossible to overrate the need for caution in forming a marriage engagement. The one weakness in spite of all the virtues, would doubtless land you in sorrow. However beautifully painted and fitted up the boat, a leakage in the bottom would quickly sink it. Certainly whoever you marry, have your money settled on yourself. It is no disloyalty to a husband for a wife to do this. She is protecting his interests in the future as well as her own.*

The use of the metaphor of shipwreck for marital break-down accurately reflects the overwhelming importance of a 'good' marriage for a Victorian woman. To be a spinster was both socially and economically unfortunate. To be a deserted wife, or to have a thriftless husband, was a disaster. In the previous century marriage had seemed a comparatively light-hearted affair, with erring partners committing bigamy, or doing a disappearing act, without the disapproval of their peer group catching up with them. In the twentieth century the status of marriage would again be diminished by a permissive code of conduct and a greater willingness on the part of the state to assume the role of provider. In the century in between, however, the literate classes – and their advisers – had good reason to value the claims of married respectability above all others.

4

And so to bed

COURTSHIP, MARRIAGE AND DIVORCE IN THE TWENTIETH CENTURY

With the birth of the twentieth century, guile became less larded with seeming godliness when a girl sought a mate. An Edwardian brazen hussy could have as much fun as her male counterpart, the cad, with a better chance of getting away with it. She enjoyed the perks available to a weaker sex still unhampered by the chimera of equality, and was exempt from the unwritten code of gentlemanly behaviour. Caught in her toils, the man could only pay the price, as some correspondents of the problem pages discovered to their cost.

'Trapped', a trusting young man, was a reader of *Titbits* who wrote, in March 1901, of his entanglement with a 'fascinating young lady at a South Coast holiday resort' which resulted in an engagement. After his holiday he discovered that his intended had already been engaged four times and had secured three substantial settlements from Breach of Promise cases. 'From what I hear,' wrote 'Trapped', 'she is nothing but a professional flirt whose favourite form of wooing is law-courting.' Should he marry her, or pay the price of Breach of Promise? The editors of *Titbits* recommended the latter, since 'there can be no happiness in marrying a girl of this character'.

Titbits, Answers to Correspondents, Forget-Me-Not and the other publications produced by Newnes and Harmesworth to capture the mass market continued, nonetheless, to recommend the moral standards upheld by their predecessors, the Victorian family magazine. 'Violet', a 'lover of a very resolute type', was warned by *Titbits* on 23 March 1901 to rethink her plan to marry a disreputable fiancé, despite her impressive resolve that 'were he as evil as Satan I should consider it my duty to marry him, if only to try to reform him'. The editors felt bound to point out that 'she should not lose sight of the terrible risk she is running in allying herself to a notoriously bad man, and she ought to consider the prospect very seriously before taking the irrevocable step'. There are hints here of a gap between the moral vocabulary of the problem page and the new social reality on which it is commenting.

The novelty of the Edwardian era should not, however, be overstated. Though the period was notable for reforms in social legislation, it did not see any equivalent changes in the domestic sphere. A more equitable divorce system, a complete separation of the wife's property from that of the husband, and a reversal of the husband's prior claims of guardianship of the children over the age of seven did not come until the mid or late 1920s. An Act of 1889 allowed women who left their husbands on grounds of cruelty to claim maintenance, another of 1895 slightly liberalised grounds for separation. In other respects, the rights of the Edwardian woman were not much different from those enjoyed by her grandmother. What had changed was the attitude to unsatisfactory husbands. There was little of the 'meek and quiet spirit' formerly recommended by *The Englishwoman's Domestic Magazine* to be seen in a correspondent of *The Cosy Corner* whose question was answered on 2 June 1906:

> *Your husband may be irritating and exacting, but you should remember that he comes home weary and tired after his day's work. Naturally he expects to find a bright, smiling wife and a cosy meal waiting for him. You do very wrong to make a point of being out when he returns and leaving him to fend for himself. Mind, he does not spend his evenings away from home. Then, when it is too late, you may regret your present conduct. Take my advice and turn over a new leaf; be a true and loving wife, and I am sure you will not find your husband wanting in affection.*

On the whole, wives and husbands were encouraged to

think the best of each other – irrespective of the evidence. Aunties invariably tried to stifle jealousy with firm good sense. A persistent correspondent of *The Family Herald*, for instance, was told in January 1903 that 'we are writing in all kindness when we say that so far you have not brought forward one tittle of evidence of the wrong which you assert has been committed, and it would be a great mistake to speak of it to anyone less pledged than we are to keep your confidence sacred ...' Similarly, a mother-in-law who was determined to think the worst of her new daughter-in-law was encouraged by *The Cosy Corner* on 10 March 1906 to 'be a true woman and accord her the love and care which your son must wish to see bestowed on his wife'. They predicted 'You'll be surprised how much happier you will be if you do so'.

Class consciousness was a major bar to marriage – in the eyes of Edwardian parents at least. The new wave of down-market magazines forming the Newnes and Harmesworth empire proved as conscious of status as any middle-class magazine of the Victorian period. Social differentials had, moreover, become far more complex. The sanctimonious *Home Companion* found itself, on 13 February 1909, advising a servant girl who was in love with the son of a coachman. His parents considered her not good enough for him. The auntie advised that the parents were:

> ... to be won, and love will be the key – true, unselfish love – to unlock the door of their hearts. Don't try to beat down the wall they have raised with your own strength, turn to your Heavenly Father and ask His assistance.

A week later 'Dr Sphinx', Love Consultant (so-called) of the *Home Companion* advised another girl, who faced this situation in reverse and was struggling between her love for a social inferior and her duty to her snooty family. 'Dr Sphinx' claimed:

> We all know that poverty is no sin and that love has worked wonders – exceptionally. If you are as certain of his love as your own, if he is a hard worker and a faithful, energetic, keen man, if you tested your own feelings thoroughly and are willing to suffer for his sake, and to raise

him to your level instead of lowering yourself to his, then break the news gently to your mother and convince her that your happiness and love depend on him.

Sometimes desperate measures were taken to prevent the consequences of a mésalliance, even if the marriage could not be stopped. One mother wrote in 1903 to *The Family Herald* to obtain their support for sending her 'common' prospective daughter-in-law to a posh school to eradicate her faults of speech and deportment. The editors of *The Family Herald* were unhelpful, pointing out that any academy for young ladies would be chary of admitting an over-age, lower-class pupil. In addition, they warned against sham gentility which, they feared, would be spotted by all the neighbours. Better by far, they advised, to admit openly that her future daughter-in-law was beautiful, amiable, but not middle-class.

The Great War, rather than the death of Victoria, should be taken as the dividing line in the history of marriage. It has been said (by Viola Klein) that 'the place in which Feminist Movement was born was not the factory nor the mine, but the Victorian middle-class drawing room'. But the trenches, rather than the drawing room, were finally responsible for the franchise of women and for their freedom from restricting clothes and conventions.

The War swallowed up a generation of young men. It called all classes of women out of the home and into the munitions factories, the buses and shops, the banks and government departments. It also rudely interrupted the neat lives of countless couples whose future – a few years of engagement, then marriage and children – was changed with the arrival of call-up papers. The battles of 1914 destroyed the regular army. 1915 was the year of the territorials, the pre-war volunteers. It brought heart-ache for the girls whose sweethearts had thus enlisted. But it brought worries, too, for those girls whose escorts were showing a curious reluctance to die for them, King and Country with the new armies which Kitchener was training:

For nearly three years I have had a sweetheart whom I love deeply. He is 25 and I am 18. He is eligible for the army, but has never offered, though he is free and his post would be kept open for him. I have begged him to enlist but he says he won't go until 'the street loafers' do. On the other hand he is longing for conscription. His mother is coaxing him not to go, and I could not overcome her influence. Most of my girlfriends' sweethearts have gone, and I feel horrid when I meet them with my boy; the humiliation is dreadful. .... Shall I give him up or not? Life without him would be so awful, but I feel I am not doing the right thing to go about with him.

Your lover's argument is a weak one, my dear. If the loafer is wrong not to enlist, then so is he. And surely it is better to go without compulsion with the flower of our manhood, than to be pressed into service with less worthy ones. No mother is justified in keeping her son back while other mothers send theirs. As for the question of your going with him, do not act rashly, but let him see that to be with him now gives you little pride or pleasure compared with that of being able to show the world that he is doing his evident duty.

(Forget-Me-Not, *26 June 1915*)

The white-feather campaign, launched by girls who presented any seemingly fit male civilian with a token of cowardliness, did have its echoes in women's magazines. *The Girl's Realm* in 1915, for instance, declared:

I have heard many people who really know say that it is the girls who are keeping the young men back from serving their King and Country. The married women of the last generation let their men go with smiling faces, though at the same time their hearts were breaking. The girl who keeps a man from going to his duty is worse than selfish, she is cowardly.

But most aunties were aware of the reality, and were chary of advising their readers to drop sweethearts simply because they were laggards in volunteering. One girl, for instance, whose steady was not willing to take the shilling, flirted with transferring her affections to a more dashing Tommy. *Forget-Me-Not*'s auntie disapproved:

It is quite true that one must respect as well as love one's sweetheart, or affection is worth but little. If your feelings have really undergone a change, my dear, then you should tell this first lover so, and give him a reason. But be quite sure of yourself before you do so.

The following letter, which was published after only five months of War, makes it even clearer that, at this period at least, problem pages recognised other claims on a man besides military ones:

My sweetheart has enlisted. He did so without telling me he was going to do it. And when I reproached him, he said that his duty to his country came first, and I might have kept him back. Of course I wouldn't and he is cruel to say so. Now he is trying to make my brother go, and he is the support of my poor, old parents and my invalid sister for I can only keep myself and a very little over. He says I have no right to stop Tom from joining. Is he right? He is so good and so straight that I wonder whet :r *I am wrong, but I don't know how we shall manage without Tom.*

My poor little girl, I am sorry for you in all your perplexity. Perhaps your sweetheart was right to enlist, but he should have trusted you and told you. It was unkind to do as he did. But as regards your brother, his duty seems to be to stay at home; at any rate for the present. I hope he will see this for himself, and not be led away by a well-sounding argument. Be patient, my dear, and I think things will turn out right for you. He has probably acted impulsively and will be sorry for this mistake later.

(Forget-Me-Not, *16 January 1915*)

The weighing of the practicalities of the situation against the calls of patriotic duty prevailed throughout the War. Even the jingoistic *Betty's Weekly*, which specialised in carrying anti-German propaganda on the lines of 'Will She Divorce Him? Germany's Crown Princess and Her Profligate Husband' and 'Is Austria's Emperor Mad? The Story of a Royal Family Ruined by Illicit Love', did not encourage its readers to cold shoulder every man not in khaki. And *Forget-Me-Not* went so far as to reassure a girl whose fiancé was Austrian on his mother's side that 'If he is a good honourable man who is on the side of the allies, you run no unpleasant risks'.

The uglier face of war was largely banished from the problem page, appearing only obliquely. Just occasionally the aunties would give details of how to check with the War Office whether a loved one had fallen at Ypres, the Somme, or Salonica. But more common was the implied warning of the sort given by *Forget-Me-Not* to 'Cecilia' who was planning her trousseau, with her lover at the front with Kitchener's volunteer army and the Battle of the Somme looming. She was advised to concentrate on those things, such as personal linen, which are always useful since 'one has to think of many serious possibilities nowadays'. On an even more practical note *Forget-Me-Not* pointed out to a two-timing reader, whose first love was out in Flanders, that although she should 'count it an honour to wait patiently for the brave man who is risking his life for you over there', she should perhaps wait patiently before sending him a 'Dear John' letter since 'perhaps time and fate will settle the difficulty for you'.

Unlike the problem pages of the Second World War, which were filled with letters from girls whose patriotic farewells to departing warriors had left them, nine months later, holding a baby, the problem pages of the Great War concentrated on the uplifting and the poignant. Letters appeared from men, just off to the front, wondering whether it was caddish to keep their girls to engagements. As the Battle of the Somme commenced, in the first week of July 1916, for example, this letter appeared in *Forget-Me-Not*:

> *I have a sweetheart whom one day I hope to make my wife, but as I am under orders for the Front, do you think it is right to become engaged to her? I should be very much upset if I returned from the fray to find someone else had 'bagged' her. She is a real bargain, you know. I am not yet 19.*

I think you are so young that it could be inadvisable to have a formal engagement, but there is no reason why you should not consider one another 'best chums' and look forward to being, one day, something else even closer.

Realistically, of course, there was a very good reason. A very high proportion of the men under orders for the front at the start of the Somme would never see another leave. Those who did return found their holidays from the trenches all too brief. Some of their needs, however, had been anticipated by a grateful government. Servicemen wishing to marry during a short leave could do so without the three weekly calling of the banns, and clergymen often waived the fees. According to one auntie, 'everyone is eager to do all they can to help a brave soldier to his happiness'. For those who stayed at home, long-awaited leave could pose some delicate problems. But 'Betty' was there to help:

> *Dear Betty – My boy has been in the trenches for six months, and expects to get furlough any moment. What I want to ask is that, if you were me, would you meet him at the station, or would you wait for him at home?*

> You ask me a difficult question, little girl, and I find it hard to advise you. Were I you I'd want with all my heart and soul to be the first woman my boy would see when he arrived. And yet, dear, the meeting him after all he's been through would mean so much to me and to him, too, that I don't think I could bear to see him in public. Really and truly, were I you, I'd wait for him alone somewhere – at home, if possible. Somehow, such a meeting is too sacred to be witnessed by anybody. But be sure you go to see him off when he leaves for the Front again, and be as brave as you can, dear.
>
> (Betty's Weekly, 19 February 1916)

There was a more common reason than leave for returning home – a serious wound. During the war, no letters were published from wives or girlfriends who were horrified at the thought of sharing a bed with a maimed or disfigured man (whether this was self-censorship or auntie-censorship is not clear). Instead, a strenuously positive attitude was taken towards the possibility of a loved one's returning wounded. *The Woman's Weekly*, on 28 August 1915, told a twenty-three year old, who had been engaged for eighteen months and wished to marry against the wishes of her mother, to think carefully before leaving a comfortable home and trying to live on the separation allowance provided for wives of serving men. And yet, the auntie felt, 'I don't want to influence you against your mother's wishes, but if it were my own case, I would rather have him go away as my husband. For one reason, if he came back wounded no one could dispute your right to nurse him.' In 1919, however, the problem pages found themselves dealing with a rash of letters from women trying to cope with the aftermath of war – shell-shock victims, cripples whose limbs had been removed by shells and invalids with respiratory systems that would never recover from gassing. Some girls found that they could not bear the sight of their returning hero. But if one girl ditched a crippled, demobbed soldier there were still 'a great many girls who want to marry him'. Put crudely, even a cripple had a value in a market denuded of young men.

As usual, the aunties encouraged a hard-headed, sensible response. Readers whose men had been killed were encouraged to mourn for a socially acceptable period, and then to think about the future. 'Ada', for instance, was told by *Peg's Paper* in June 1919 that 'It is no use living in the past, my dear, and what might have been'. Her new man would fill her life as completely as the other one had done, and 'I'm sure your first boy would wish you to be happy, for life without love is very lonely for a girl.'

This many girls rapidly found out for themselves. Very soon a male escort outweighed such traditional symbols as diamonds or a fur coat. And, like those items, he could come expensive. The practice of going Dutch on a date had begun during the war. Subsequently many girls were so desperate to be seen with a man that they continued to pay for their pleasures. In *Every Girl's Paper* 'Joyce' discussed the plight of 'Mary', a working girl who for the past two years had given her man expensive presents, kept him in cigarettes, and paid for their cinema seats. In the eighteen months since he had found a good job, all Mary remembered him paying for was one tram ticket. 'Now she wants to know if I think he loves her. And seeing the matter is so easy, I answer: 'find out'.' Joyce knew only too well, however, that, given the risk of losing him, this was not an easy question to ask.

The war brought other problems as well. It had been fought, not by the British, French and Americans alone, but by the entire British Empire. The cemeteries of Flanders are filled with Canadian, Australian, New Zealand and Indian troops. Some of those who did not die for the King-Emperor spent their leaves getting to know the British slightly better. As a result, our first inter-racial (as distinct from inter-religious) marital problem appears in *The Family Herald* of November 1918. In line with its now somewhat old-fashioned editorial policy, only the answer to the question appeared:

> *Sister M – You are acting wisely in using your influence to prevent marriage between two people of widely different racial types, so long as you act and speak with great discretion. Interference in questions of marriage often has the effect of hurrying unwise youth into the very mistake that is feared. But it is your duty, placed as you are, to point out, of course, with delicacy and affection, that all the difficulties inherent in marriage are trebled in the case of men and women of different races binding themselves together.*

In other respects attitudes had grown more liberal. A man planning to ditch his girlfriend since his discovery that her parents were not married when she was born, was advised in the 24 March 1924 issue of *Every Girl's Paper* to 'Think again, my dear lad, and do not allow yourself to be guilty of such a horrible injustice. I hope you will write to me and tell me you have reconsidered the matter and cultivated a little more breadth of mind.' A more sympathetic attitude was also shown to those whose marital duties had preceded the wedding. 'Molly Brown', for instance, in *Polly's Paper* of 21 June 1920, was told 'Yours is a very sad case indeed, but as your mother knows the truth, surely she can tell your father and get him to see, under the circumstances, he ought to give way.' Failing that, Molly's sweetheart was encouraged to have a man-to-man talk with the vicar and ask him to get the consent of the father.

Flirting, a heinous offence in Victorian days, was now

regarded as a harmless amusement, a natural expression of exuberant youth. One girl who proclaimed herself a flirt was reassured in *Pam's Paper*, on 24 April 1926:

> *For your years, my dear Mary, I think you abound in sheer common sense ... You are in the heyday of your youth and it is only natural that you should long to make the most out of life and have the best possible time. And providing you don't carry this hobby too far, no harm can come to you.*

Post-war aunties also took a more liberal view of broken engagements, and rarely encouraged their readers to bring Breach of Promise actions. The auntie of *Pam's Paper*, on 4 September 1926, could see no reason at all:

> *... why either the boy or girl should not be free to change his or her mind without having a name besmirched by a law suit. I would advocate that it is better to be sporting about these things. Don't you really think that a man who has the courage to break off an engagement rather than to marry a girl whom he suddenly realises he does not care for sufficiently to go through life with, is doing a nobler thing than marrying her? I do.*

Another significant post-war change was the new attitude shown towards marrying above one's social rank. Until 1918 all aunties had, without exception, agreed that for a girl to try to catch a social superior was foolhardy and undesirable. Now it was not so much 'all's fair in love and war' as 'all's fair in love after war'. Reflecting this new attitude, *Peg's Paper* on 21 August 1919 encouraged 'RT' who loved a social superior and asked 'is it wise to continue the courtship?' Peg answered, 'If he loves you, why not? A good woman is the equal of any man, even if he is in a higher social position.'

The demolition of social barriers was not in itself, however, the answer to the dearth of men. The enterprising girl, faced with a missing generation, had recourse to one of two solutions. The first was to attract an older man, often ignoring the disadvantage of a previous engagement or marriage. This tactic was not encouraged by the aunties of the 1920s. 'Joyce', for instance, on 3 March 1924, dealt sharply with 'Florrie', who loved a married man and felt sorry for herself. 'If she doesn't pull herself together she'll be more sorry before the finish', Joyce predicted, and then castigated those like 'Florrie' whose 'sloppy desires are so much stronger than their horror of sin, which they won't agree is sin, but a Heavensent love'. The second solution was to cradle-snatch a younger man. This was hardly more acceptable in the eyes of society, but aunties did not find it quite so dreadful.

The advisers of the inter-war years did, however, firmly believe in selecting a partner with prospects. However successful a girl was at supporting herself as a clerk, or on a production line, after marriage she would be expected to give up her job and be supported by her husband. As the depression began, many girls grew tired of waiting for that job for their man which was a pre-requisite of marriage. 'Patience' from Derby, for instance, wrote to *Peg's Paper* on 24 December 1929 about her courtship, lasting over two years, with a boy who was still unemployed. Should she drop him for a man who had a good job? The aunties thought so, recommending that she should tell the former that 'as there seems no prospect of him ever going to be in a position to marry you, you think it would be better to end the friendship altogether'. They did, however, mention that the action would be rather hard on him. But then, despite the romantic serials which formed the major part of any 'mill-girl' publication, realism was never too far below the surface.

During the depression the feeling grew that women should stay at home and free the job-market for the men. Either consciously or unconsciously, the problem pages responded by dealing at greater length with the dilemmas of married women, preaching a matronly attitude to life, with an emphasis on well-tried virtues and a well-polished home. A clean-cut, all-British housewife was the ideal of the 1930s:

> Alex married the man she loved, and everything went well for a year or two, then she began to be bored with having 'Nothing to do but keep the house in order and cook food', and no money to spend while all the girls she knows who haven't married and kept their independence and

their situations, seem to be having such a good time, and so Alex thinks
I should advise all girls not to marry young.

Well, Alex, I certainly should if none of them had more
sense than you. What did you marry for? Judging from
your letter, it was to give up working and have a good time
yourself. I hardly know how to advise you because you seem
to me to need to be taken all to bits and put together again
like a watch that won't go properly ... Now pull yourself
together, and start all over again. It doesn't matter that
four years have passed since you married. Tomorrow is a
new day; start tomorrow – or today if you like – determined
to make a success of your marriage. Don't blame your
husband because you've been bored and cross with each
other for months. Get a new viewpoint and blame yourself.
After all, there is nothing very terrible in blaming yourself.
It's all rather fun really, and it's a thing that grows on one
and gives one a sense of power. Why? Because instead of
thinking, 'Oh, I'm a poor, martyred soul; everything is
against me; there's nothing but misery in my life, and I
can't help it', one thinks, 'Well, now, here's a nice mess
I've made of things; where have I gone wrong? I must have
gone astray somewhere. Now I am going to put it right ...'.
Your strength will dry up, too, if not renewed from its
inexhaustible supply, so remember your prayers. As for
envying these girls, just think how many women would
gladly give up their so-called independence to have a home
and a husband of their own, to have your chance of making
a success of a married life and a home. Women who will
never have that chance because the war took their lovers
and their husbands and made them the real tragedy and
pathos of our times – the surplus women. And don't make
a joke of them as you do at the end of your letter, for
besides the tragedy and sorrow of their fate, your petty
troubles are indeed as nought.

(Woman's Magazine, *1934*)

Peggy Makins, the second 'Evelyn Home', was less
consciously hearty in her advice to a discontented wife, but
she too counselled a realistic approach to marriage:

Nature does not, I am firmly convinced, send each man into the world
as a good mate for only one individual woman. Nature, most likely,
made us almost all inter-marriageable ... When a girl marries she
must face the fact that it is perfectly possible for her to fall in love again,

*with someone other than her husband. But now she has more than her
own heart at stake – the happiness of her family, her husband's trust,
the home she rules – these things matter infinitely more than any illicit
romance, however overwhelmingly her feelings may attempt to prove
the opposite.*

In 1923 the legal differences in the grounds for divorce for
men and for women were abandoned. Two years later the
conditions for separation and maintenance were
improved and, in 1937, the Herbert Act extended the
grounds for divorce to insanity and desertion. But equality
in the eyes of the law did little to change the attitudes of
society, which continued to censure a divorced woman,
while pitying or envying the husband. 'Evelyn Home' in
The Woman's Weekend Book, an annual compilation of the
best of her column in *Woman*, showed how destructive this
attitude could be. She described the plight of a woman
married for sixteen years to a drunken and unfaithful
husband. After a divorce:

> *Bravely she went to work to keep herself and two children – and then
> the whispering campaign began. People began to say that the boy of the
> family needed the guidance of a man and that as his father was willing
> to re-marry his former wife, and to start again, she should forget all
> about that divorce.*

Despite her misgivings, she was persuaded to re-marry her
husband and in two months he was once more unfaithful,
cruel and drunk. She left him again and this time he
divorced her for desertion. Now she had found a good
man who wished to marry her, but his relatives who 'know
of the woman's wretched past' were threatening to cast off
her fiancé if the marriage took place. Peggy Makins was emphatic – ignore the gossip for 'as long as a woman behaves
honourably, she need never fear what people say about her'.

By the mid-1930s the aunties, though still rooting for
faithfulness and the sanctity of marriage, had begun to
admit that 'certain urges' could be strong in engaged
couples, and that what had formerly been dismissed as
'wrong-doing', was their natural outlet. By the late thirties
a further advance had been made. Abandoning the view
that no nice woman enjoyed sex, the aunties now gave

lady-like hints on the joys of orgasm and discreetly counselled those who failed to get, or to give, satisfaction. This advice, however, was only for the married. The unmarried were firmly told 'After marriage you will find that more experience will set things right. I need not tell you, I hope, that you have been doing wrong, and that I trust you will not do so again.' More detailed help was promised by 'Evelyn Home' under the cover of a stamped, addressed envelope.

Marion Darke, the adviser on *Glamour*, comforted a married woman, happily married for seven years but off sex since the birth of her second child, by recommending an appropriate book or a visit to a female doctor. The woman's husband, who had been threatening to leave her, was also advised to read the book (the title was not mentioned on the printed page) because 'frigidity, as it is called, is quite often caused through ignorance on the husband's side'. She added the encouraging words, 'Cheer up. It is only a passing phase of married life, and once you understand all the reasons which cause it you can be happy again, both of you'.

For those who found it difficult to resist the 'certain urges', the aunties often suggested that the wedding should be brought forward. This, however, was not always possible. In the 1930s it was still common for employers to lay down a minimum age for marriage. Captains in the army were not supposed to marry before the age of thirty, and were not eligible for married quarters. Most bank clerks could not marry until after their twenty-fifth birthday.

The Second World War did away with these restrictions, and with much else. Its initial impact on problem pages was to increase the number of letters concerned with rapid marriage. 'Mrs Marryat', remembering her (or her namesake's?) postbag from the previous war, warned her readers against hastily contracted marriages which would be rued at leisure. 'Evelyn Home' was equally forthright. In the 7 October 1939 issue of *Woman* she wrote:

The wedding boom has affected my mailbag. I have had letters from many girls, urged by their young men to marry, who are not quite sure that a very quick wedding is a good thing, especially if separation is to come soon after the honeymoon ... She should remember that great events invariably bring out the best in people and that the man who is a hero in a national crisis may be anything but that in an ordinary every day home. But does she want a hero anyway? Will a dare-devil be happy within marriage limitations? Marriage, after all, is a life-work. It is not worth risking two people's unhappiness for years, just because circumstances and hazards seem to make the chances of permanence small. Many of the miserable couples of today are people who married at a moment's notice during the last war and discovered when they came to make a home together that they were completely unsuited.

The auntie on *Modern Woman* advised a nineteen year old girl to ask herself 'two hard, cruel questions':

First, are you sure that you care enough for him apart from the good times you have together to face years of poverty without a shilling to spare for fun? Secondly, if he came home a helpless invalid would you rather be tied to nursing him, unpleasant nursing, than be free to take whatever interest and excitement life offered? If you answer a triumphant 'yes', then I think you are right to marry him.

This answer provides an interesting comparison with that given in *Forget-Me-Not* in 1915. Then the idea of nursing a future husband was a positive spur to marriage. Now it was a deterrent. A similar contrast can be drawn between the letter of 1915 about the ethics of marrying a man with an Austrian mother and a letter printed in *Glamour* twenty-four years later:

My boyfriend is German and I'm very unhappy about it, and don't know whether to marry him or not, as I shall have to live in Germany. He's for the Nazis and I'm all against them, never having been out of England until a holiday two years ago when we met. But we love each other terribly, and it's not as if I met a lot of boys at home. To tell the truth, he's the only one I've ever had, and I'm 26 and want a home and children desperately – Very Democratic (Doncaster).

You want a home and children; that's natural, my dear. But do you want the unhappy children likely to be born into a divided home? Only you yourself can possibly know how far you could submerge your own views in those of

your husband and his country. But if – as your letter
suggests – your feelings are passionately anti-Nazi I don't
see how your home could be anything but unhappy.
Remember, you will be set in the midst of millions who
dare only think as he does. In spite of love, I'm afraid you'd
know a loneliness that might prove unbearable. Even your
children would have to be brought up young Nazis, out of
sympathy with all your beliefs. It is a lot to face, my dear, I
wouldn't face it myself. I doubt if love would last long
under such conditions. You've lots of time to find more
certain happiness.

(Glamour, 25 March 1939)

In many respects the aunties of the Second World War
were less tolerant of erring wives and sweethearts than
their First World War predecessors had been. A
correspondent who had been evacuated to a quiet village
with her twelve month old baby and had there fallen in
love with another man, while her husband slugged it out
with Rommel, was indignantly rebuked:

> *What right have you got to fall in love with another man when your
> husband is away serving his country, to say nothing of your
> responsibility to your child? Have you no idea of right and wrong – and
> of playing fair?*

Slightly stranger was the reply to a worried mother who
had written in about her daughter's modern marriage, in
which both halves were involved in partner swopping with
another couple. 'It seems,' the auntie declared, 'that they
have no responsibilities and are not even taking this war
seriously, otherwise they would not have so much time for
pleasure.'

The new strictness may have reflected the different
reasons for the availability of men. In the First World War
most young men to be found at home were injured. In the
Second World War the chief emotional danger was
presented by the large number of perfectly healthy, red-
blooded Americans. A girl didn't even have the excuse
that she was cheering up an invalid when she was caught
misbehaving. Another influence on the unexpectedly
puritanical tone of the problem pages was the realisation

that, for the first time, both sexes were caught up in conscription and had a military duty to perform. Lonely land-girls, for example, were reminded of the equally lonely outposts in Africa and the Far East manned by their sweethearts. The implication was that they too should do their duty without complaint.

The agony columns concentrated on women who, against all odds, did their bit – the mother with five children who juggled child-care, house-work and a shift at the munitions factory, or the spinster with a full-time job who also manned an evening canteen for soldiers. Not every woman, however, welcomed call-up. For those who did not, there was one foolproof escape – pregnancy. It had only one disadvantage. It required the connivance of a man, and not every husband, it seems, was willing to oblige:

> ... *I married four years ago, when she was very young, a young lady with no liking for children. I am passionately attached to youngsters and she never told me of her aversion to them until we got married. Then she was clever and, unbeknownst to me, got herself fixed up so that she could not have any. I think it did something to my feelings for her when I found out, quite by accident, through finding a doctor's bill three years later. Now conscription is here and she looks like being called up, she begs me to let her have a child whenever I am home on leave. She doesn't want the youngster any more than she ever did. She merely wants to stay at home and go on as if there wasn't any war and make the baby her excuse. I don't feel it's good enough for my child ... I feel bitter and angry and most unwilling to gratify my wife's desire.*

I don't think that a child born resentfully and to escape the responsibilities of citizenship would have much of a chance of inheriting a happy nature or a happy home ... A child is a great privilege; not, as you say, an excuse for the evasion of citizenship and its responsibilities in wartime. I think what your wife needs is to come to her senses and grow a real human heart and feelings. If she is called up, she will come into close contact with other women; their problems, troubles and worries may do it. It will certainly force home to her that she isn't so important after all, and that you and her home and her chance of peace and happiness are. Possibly she was an only child, and spoilt; I seem to feel that

at the back of all this. In a factory or the Services she will be
learning lessons she should have learnt as a little girl and
that will prepare her ... for building a happy home and a
happy family.

(*Glamour*, 14 April 1942)

The war may have provided character training for some
wives, but many servicemen came back from winning the
war to find that they had a fight on their hands on the
home front too. The most frequent problem was, of
course, unfaithfulness. Sometimes, however, the problem
was not so much another man, as another woman – the
mother-in-law. One ex-serviceman had hurriedly
married, while on embarkation leave in 1942, what he
thought was a sweet girl. On his return home he
discovered that his young wife had an awesome mother,
who insisted that her daughter shared her bedroom and
allotted the attic to the returning hero. Mother had
decreed that 'we must not have a family for many years to
come' and accordingly never left the couple alone for an
instant. 'Nurse Janet' of *Glamour*, on 6 November 1945,
suggested that his wife was 'not acting her age'. Her
mother, a spritely woman of forty-four, was influencing
her unduly and the best solution was to find alternative
accommodation, preferably at some distance from the
ogre. As a last resort, 'Nurse Janet' pointed out that he
would not be financially responsible for his wife, were she
to refuse to follow him to his new abode. 'The older
woman,' she shrewdly suspected, 'is likely to have more
sense once the matter concerns the maintenance of her
daughter.'

A more common problem involved wives who feared
that their ardour – or that of their husband – had cooled
during the years of separation. To these women, the
aunties adopted a bracing tone, 'Of course you love your
husband and you will be happy again ... you must be
ready to welcome him home and make him happy.'
Others, who had dallied during their husband's absence
but not yet broken the news to the returning hero,
worried about the most tactful method to employ. It was
especially difficult for one woman, who wrote to *Glamour*

on 4 December 1945. She had been conducting an affair, while her husband was away fighting, and 'had tried to do the decent thing and not harass a man, possibly on the eve of going into battle, by writing to him that my feelings had changed'. Her intention had been to tell him when he stepped over his threshold at home. Unfortunately, in the last weeks of the war, he was badly wounded. As a result, 'My friends tell me I must give up my lover and stand by my husband'. Marion Darke, *Glamour*'s auntie, agreed and reminded the wife of the sacred vows she had made on her wedding day:

> *I realise it may be hard on you at this moment to give up your lover, but just think what your husband must have endured in the years of gruelling fighting. Remember that he, like many other servicemen, went into battle primarily to protect his wife and children and think of your obligation to him. Also, what kind of conscience can this other man have that he can even contemplate being the cause of breaking up the marriage of a man who wasn't able to be on the spot to protect his rights? You may think you love him, but search your own heart and see if you can find it in yourself to respect him. Love without respect can never have any qualities of permanency, I assure you.*

Returning husbands posed a problem also for those girls who had married into the other allied armies. The Polish Air Force was responsible for a disproportionate number of letters. Girls had invariably married without thought of their husbands' eventual repatriation. 'Do you think,' wrote one young wife in July 1945, 'I have a right to demand my husband doesn't ask this sacrifice of me?' Marion Darke, writing before Poland's satellite status had been shown to be permanent, encouraged her correspondent to look at her husband's plans from a less selfish point of view, given that 'from a purely material point of view, he will probably find a more remunerative means of making his living there than here'. More sympathy was shown towards the widow of a Polish airman, whose child she had borne. Now she feared that the Polish authorities would insist they should live in Poland. Marion Darke, on 13 March 1945, was reassuring: 'as things are today I don't think there will be any

likelihood of your being asked to go to live in your
husband's country'.

Compulsory emigration was not the only fear of those
who had married a soldier from a distant land. Some
thought he might return home leaving them behind.
Difference in social class was sometimes the cause of this
uncertainty; an already rocky marriage was another
reason. In the face of some fairly unhopeful evidence,
problem page advisors tended to be optimistic:

> *Please tell me what to do as I am very miserable. I am only 23 but have*
> *two children. I had my first baby when I was 17, but it was a mistake,*
> *and I knew nothing about life and the man was a lot older than me.*
> *My step-father turned me out and I was put in a Home where my baby*
> *was born. They made this man pay towards expenses which he has*
> *done ever since, and I went into service. Then, when the war began, I*
> *joined the Land Army, and I met a young Canadian officer who was*
> *very nice and I fell in love with him. He was in love with me and after*
> *a bit I told him I was going to have a baby. This wasn't true, but I*
> *tricked him into marrying me. We lived together and I did start a baby*
> *which was born before he went to France. He found out about my other*
> *baby, also he said I had deceived him and he is very funny with me. I*
> *get his allowance, but he wouldn't take me back to Canada with him*
> *where he has now gone back, but I am so afraid that he wouldn't mean*
> *to live with me. I love him very much. What am I to do?*

Deceit is always wrong, as you know. You are paying for
the wrong you did. But I don't think your husband intends
to desert you or that he won't make arrangements for you
and the child to go back with him when he is out of the
Army. If, as I gather from your letter, he is from a different
station in life, probably he wants to explain to his people
and prepare them for receiving you and the child ... So
cheer up, write lovingly to him, get a picture taken of baby
and send it out and I think everything will come right in the
end.

(Glamour, September 1945)

For several years after 1945 the agony columns continued
to deal with problems rooted in war. Girls used to the
excitement and comradeship of the WRAFS or WRENS
had to settle back into marriage. Men had to put their
paratrooping exploits behind them and concentrate on

the mortgage. Indirectly the war had been responsible for
some fundamental improvements in the facilities offered
to working women. In 1946, for instance, there were more
state-run nursery schools per head of population than
there are now. Such provision rapidly produced a new
attitude to marriage. The unhappy wife was now more
tempted to brave a life outside the unsatisfactory arms of
her husband. A knowledge that escape, if only to a life of
free milk, orange juice and means-tested supplementary
benefit, was possible enabled wives to be more aggressive.
In this they were supported by the aunties, who no longer
encouraged a wife to be a doormat. In her usual flippant
vein, which masks some of the shrewdest advice in the
business, Marje Proops was a leader of this revolution:

> *What would you do with a husband like mine? He won't take me out,
> never makes so much as a cuppa, refuses to help me wash up and
> doesn't care that I haven't had a new dress in the two years we've been
> married.*

Your old man is a right selfish so-and-so. If I could resist
bashing him over the head with the teapot, I'd leave the
washing up in the sink, and clear off with a girl friend for a
weekly beano. I'd also rifle the housekeeping – or his beer
money – to buy a brand-new dress. And I wouldn't be
unduly worried if I half-starved him in the process.

On the other hand, Marje Proops did have a warning for
the girl whose husband resented the happy relationship
she had with her mother. 'I tell him,' she wrote, 'my
mother is my best friend and most girls think the same.'
According to Marje:

> *It depends on the girls. But don't make the mistake of neglecting your
> better half for Mum. This may lead him to take less notice of the girl he
> married and seek the company of his dear old Dad – or worse still, a
> poor little orphan girl.*

Curiously, this tough approach to the realities of marriage
was shared by Denise Robins, the auntie on *She* and well
known as a romantic novelist. Wearing her auntie's hat,
Denise Robins had some definitely unromantic advice for

one pregnant wife who feared that her husband was ready to comfort a poor lonely waif, stranded in a strange country, far from parents or friends – otherwise know as the au pair. This woman, who felt unable to compete with the mini-skirted beauty in her own home, was offered no bland consolations. Instead Denise Robins wrote, in the March 1969 issue of *She*, 'if you continue to feel so badly about this au pair, find some excuse to give her notice and try to find another who won't upset you.'

Modern day aunties, even the redoubtable Anna Raeburn of *Woman* who has herself been divorced, are sometimes accused of too great an attachment to marriage at whatever cost. Most advisers, be they Marriage Guidance or the neighbour hanging over the fence, do certainly prefer a happy ending and a reconciliation. The professional advisers, though they recognise that the best solution may often be what is now termed 'creative breaking up', also know the cost of divorce. This is much more than the lawyer's bills. For a childless woman it can mean utter loneliness as her married circle of friends disintegrates (who wants an extra woman at a dinner party?). For a woman with young children it can mean being trapped at home, too poor to afford a baby-sitter, without any chance of finding a new partner. For a man a divorce may mean the loss of his chance to watch his family grow up – except on alternate Sundays. For both parties, it probably means a drastic drop in income, with one wage being stretched to cover two establishments and, possibly, two families.

The higher divorce rate has been variously ascribed to a more permissive attitude to sexuality, to a general social malaise, to higher expectations on the part of the woman, and to the greater ease with which a divorce can now be obtained. What is sometimes forgotten is the massive extension of the marriage-sentence in the second half of the twentieth century. The average Victorian woman married at the age of twenty-five and was dead by the age of fifty. The average girl now marries at twenty-two and lives into her mid-seventies. So the average time spent married, taking only natural causes into account, has roughly doubled in the last hundred years. Not surprisingly, many couples quail before the prospect, and many more turn to divorce at an age when, in the Victorian era, they would have been in their dotage, or dead. The break-down in the marriage of the middle-aged couple, whose children are off their hands, is fast replacing 'the seven year itch' as the prime danger point. 'Mary Grant', like so many modern aunties, is often critical of couples who make no attempt to save their marriage at this stage:

I'm a frustrated wife chained to an impotent man, aged 50. If it were not for my children I'd leave him tomorrow. I'm not surprised that more and more women are walking out on their husbands. Obviously it's because they're unhappy in their sex lives.

Maybe that's the last straw, yes. But behind a frustrating or unhappy sex life is a much deeper reason for the breakdown of a marriage and that's the inability or unwillingness of husband and wife to sort out their sexual troubles together and recover their happiness. Your husband is unlikely to be impotent permanently at 50. It more likely stems from a feeling of inadequacy and hopelessness. And this, if you want to, is something you can help with – and be helping yourself too ... Don't you think it would be a better bet than just waiting for the day your children leave home?

Many women nowadays, of course, see marriage as a bad risk, which compares unfavourably with the rewards of a career. This idea some men still find hard to grasp:

I've seen letters on your page from women who are in love with 'confirmed bachelors' and despair of getting them to the altar. But what about men like me who are in love with 'confirmed spinsters'? I'm 36, divorced with one child in my ex-wife's custody. My girl friend is 25, a fashion buyer with her own flat and car. I want to marry her, but her answer is always 'not yet', and I'm afraid that she will never marry me. But I wonder if she realises how lonely and futile her life is going to be in about ten years time?

You're virtually saying that if your girl doesn't take this

golden opportunity to become your wife, the rest of her life
is going to be nothing – no one else to love her, no
satisfying work, no home, no personal freedom, and no
friends. But many girls nowadays prefer the rewards they
are getting now – and can continue to have – to the rewards
of marriage. Especially I might add, to a man who can't
even envisage her having any kind of fulfillment without
him. So you'll have to make your proposal sound a lot less
like rescuing her from a fate worse than death.

(*Woman's Own*, 30 March 1976)

Homosexual pair-bonding has also begun to receive at
least a limited degree of approval from the aunties,
although some, such as Denise Robins and Claire Rayner
(whose editor on *The Sun* bans all mention of the subject)
still find it hard to discuss on their pages. Until the Sexual
Offences Act of 1967 which, despite its forbidding name,
permitted homosexual relationships between consenting
adults over the age of twenty-one, male homosexuality
was a taboo subject. The only overt reference was made by
Dunton in 1701:

*How do you prove that one man may have a greater affection for
another, than for the fair sex?*

This question is not put well; for every person that indulges
in the Male amours and and those who have been executed
for Catamiting proves, that some one man may have a
greater passion for a Catamite than for a female prostitute.
Now if the question had been, how such a degeneracy
comes in the affections of Man to prefer Male Concubinage
with a greater affection than the female, it might have been
better put.

(*The Post-Angel*, November 1701)

Thereafter male homosexuality was mentioned only by
implication, in magazines such as the *Boys' Own Paper*,
which urged constant vigilance when in the company of
older lads, but never spelt out what the danger consisted
of.
  Lesbianism, by contrast, was discussed with refreshing
innocence. A series of letters in *Woman's Life*, in 1899,

suggests that Queen Victoria (whose Prime Minister was supposedly too embarrassed to explain the practice to her) was not alone in thinking that what was an illegal vice in men could be a pure and natural love when women were involved. The correspondence was sparked off by an editorial, entitled 'Girls Who Fall in Love With Each Other', which suggested that emotional involvement between women was school-girlish and silly. On 5 August an outraged reader responded:

> *Although I am a normal, healthy minded tennis-playing, cycling, athletic, studious person, I do not shudder at 'the bare idea of such foolishness'. I can claim average good looks and an average liking for the opposite sex, yet this 'love' flourishes and is in no respect a one-sided affair. Men have their great men friends (there are David and Jonathans still), and are we to have our great attachments for our girl friends ridiculed and treated with contempt? ... Is there too much love in the world as it is, that we should let our feelings be crushed by another's opinion however true in motive it may be? The article never said anything about the strength of character and influence for good the loved one exercises, the morbid disposition which it brightens, the motherless child this 'adored friend' fills the lonely heart of.*

A week later, another correspondent, the 'head of a large establishment' (a headmistress?) wrote in connection with the article:

> *I am so pleased that I get to know scores of women in their twenties very intimately ... I know many girls who love each other so fondly and truly that no lover could come between them. Such a love is more beautiful and pure in its nature than that existing between two persons of opposite sex. Women are rising, and as they rise, their petty jealousies that used to stand between them are passing away. Instead of one girl loving because she cannot get a lover, it is more often that she finds the love of another girl infinitely sweeter and purer.*
>
> (Woman's Life, *12 August 1899*)

Throughout the first half of the twentieth century there continued to be innocent (but slightly more guarded) references to adolescent lesbianism – girls who wrote of their undying love for their gym mistress, or were worried about advances made by female acquaintances. On 30

September 1939, for instance, 'Evelyn Home' told 'M':

> *The problem you have told me is a very serious one, though the emotion*
> *you have described is by no means unknown or impossible. You should*
> *avoid this girl, and tell her quite plainly if she persists, you will have*
> *nothing to do with such relationships and you refuse to be worried*
> *further. Such feelings are perhaps unavoidable, but they should not be*
> *inflicted on other people.*

Strangely enough, it was the magazines for teenagers
which were most courageous in breaking the taboo on
male homosexuality. This may be because bi-sexuality has
always been more acceptable in the young, despite the
strictures of Dr Stables in the *Boy's Own Paper*. One of the
first magazines to break the barrier was *Petticoat* where, on
6 September 1969, Dodie Wells dealt with the following
query:

> *One of my friends has told me that the boy I'm in love with was once a*
> *homosexual. I am shattered. She swears it is true as her brother went to*
> *the same college as my boyfriend, and there was a set of them. Though*
> *it appalls me it hasn't made me love him any less. Could it have been*
> *cured? – Sally.*

It's not something you catch and then cure. But on the
other hand, if it is true, is isn't necessarily as serious as all
that. Lots of boys and young men have found themselves
involved in this kind of set-up without being genuinely
inclined in a permanent way. Talk to this boy about his
behaviour now. It may turn out to be a fuss about nothing.

On the other hand, *Rave* warned one young homosexual
not to contemplate marriage:

> *I hope you don't mind receiving a letter from a boy, but I am*
> *desperately in need of help. I am 21 and engaged to marry a girl of 18*
> *I have known since we were at school together. But now I know I am*
> *in love with a man, a friend I have known for some time, and my boss*
> *in the shop I work in ... I am happier with him than I have ever been*
> *with my girl friend, but I just don't know what to do. I have told her,*
> *and she said she would try to understand and that we could get married*
> *just the same. My girl friend and I have never been lovers, but we are*
> *very close friends, and I can't hurt her. – John (Manchester)*

Dear John,
You must not, repeat not, marry this girl under these
circumstances. It would be disastrous for you and
miserable for her. She is too young to realise what life with
you would mean.
Just relax for a moment. You are in such a state that you'll
rush into anything; you need time to sort yourself out; so
tell the girl that you can't see her for six months. Don't
share a flat with your boyfriend until you are absolutely
certain that is what you want. You feel guilty. This is to be
expected in the kind of society where homosexuality has
been sneered at. But recently things have changed. The
Law has been altered and the Law does generally accept
homosexuals as ordinary members of the community.
                                              (*Rave*, March 1970)

The auntie concluded by advising a special clinic, and
offering the address of his nearest centre if he wrote to her
privately. But, however permissive the legislation, many
women, especially mothers, are shocked and distressed to
discover that the men in their lives are homosexuals. In
this situation the aunties can do little to help.

Conventional, heterosexual marriage continues, of
course, to flourish and its problems are today discussed
with an intimacy and frankness unequalled since Dunton's
era. Drawing generalized conclusions about it exclusively
from the evidence of the problem page, however, would
be rash. For one thing, the radiantly happy couple is never
likely to figure in such a column. For another, the pages
were for long periods far too proper to discuss in detail
such major causes of marital discord as adultery and
sexual incompatability. But they do at least help us to
understand the changing attitudes of our evolving society
to the delights, duties and disasters of its most central
institution.

5

Blighted lady

Our concept of beauty constantly changes, but the problems arising from it occur with remarkable frequency in the agony columns of every period. Excessive weight and spots are the all-time favourites. Blushing and facial hair (or lack of it in the case of men) have caused only slightly less anguish to generations of worried correspondents.

The advice, too, has altered only marginally. A fatty writing to Dunton wished to know how to lose weight. She, like her modern counterpart, wanted to hear of a miracle belt, a wonder cream or a grapefruit diet that would whittle away the inches without pain. Instead the callous Dunton suggested that if she ate less, she would weigh less:

> *A lady of extraordinary shape (but inclining to fat) fears her fat may grow excessive, and therefore desires your advice, what she shall do in that case? ... will you prescribe a method for obtaining her desire (viz.) stopping or rather lessening her fat ...?*

It's needless to prescribe many things where fewer will do. Therefore if the lady confines herself to make her breakfasts and suppers for a month or two of water-gruel, made only with a little oat-meal, this diuretic gruel will discharge and sensibly diminish the superfluous fatness. If it only be to prevent the increase of fat then a week now and then will be sufficient. Purging once a week with pills called Nendick's Popular Pills, bought at the Coffee-house

at Westminster Hall Gate, by this method the lady will
obtain what is desired.

(*Athenian Oracle*, Vol. VI)

Fatness is, of course, a relative matter. The fashionable
Edwardian silhouette, with burgeoning bust and bottom,
would be a candidate for a health farm today. The
eighteenth century, too, liked its women well-upholstered.
Defoe's heroines, for example, are built on noticeably
generous lines. In his magazine *The Review* their creator
actually wrote an essay on the text 'Laugh and be Fat',
claiming that the women of his generation were stouter
than their grandmothers. Having considered whether this
increasing rotundity was the consequence of men being
better husbands, or of women being more masterful in the
marital home, he settled in the end on a change in diet:

> *Some will have it be, chocolate in bed, Bohea, and bread and butter,*
> *some hot tea, some cold and the like; and these being modern drinks,*
> *which our Ancestors never had, incline me to think, there may be*
> *something in that ...*

(The Review)

Fatter or not, eighteenth century readers seemed
particularly prone to blushing. So numerous were the
queries on this subject that Dunton often referred his
readers back to earlier replies. His theory combined
reassurance with moral strenuousness, by making the
blush a straight-forward agent of the conscience. It was, he
declared in *The Post-Angel* for February 1701, designed by
nature as a 'Bridle to withhold them from all unchaste and
dishonourable actions ...'

In the seventeenth century men were often the peacocks
and women, unless they had an allowance built into their
marriage contract, dowdy hens. It is therefore not
surprising that the very first question on hair-dye should
have come from a red-headed man. His lady having 'the
greatest aversion imaginable to that colour'd hair', he
asked for a dye, proof against rain and sweat, which would
last for fifteen to sixteen days. Dunton, as usual, had a
simple solution. Writing in *The British Apollo*, he advised his

correspondent to try a Kojak hair-cut and a peruke wig:

> *However, if you are fix'd not to part with it, hoping it may be, to catch*
> *the fair one in your fine tresses, as her sex sometimes serves us, we yet*
> *fancy it can't be impossible to have your hair stain'd or dy'd by a skilful*
> *painter, with ingredients so strong, as would never out till that crop*
> *were off the ground.*

But, however skilfully he may have treated them, Dunton
was not in the end greatly interested in matters of so little
moment. In his own eyes at least he was an intellectual,
and the still slighter topic of fashion was largely ignored
except for purposes of satire. In this he was at one with his
contemporaries. The onslaught on fashionable
pretensions in *The Ladies' Mercury* of 1693, for example, was
continued by Steele in *The Tatler* and by Addison in *The
Spectator*.

Such hostility was, however, accompanied by a tolerant
approach to painting, powdering and patching. Dunton
refused to endorse the view, held by some of his
correspondents, that the Devil lurked behind every painted
visage. He agreed that a pretty face could be spoilt by the
application of paint. But he argued that it could hardly be
described as a sin, unless one extended the claim to its
logical conclusion and included all wigs, washes to remove
freckles and smallpox marks, and 'most other artificial
ornaments'. One enraged and moralistic correspondent of
The Athenian Mercury received the brisk retort 'We can't
help thinking there's more of the Devil in one
uncharitable censure than in a whole box full of Half-
moons and Lozenges'.

Later journalists strayed into the world of beauty and
fashion with more expertise to guide them. 'Mrs
Wentworth' for instance, who borrowed questions freely
from *The British Apollo* to fill her columns in *The Court
Miscellany*, was admirably qualified to probe the delicate
secrets of the lingerie department. For, although not a
woman, 'she' was, of course, a former stay-maker. Hugh
Kelly's pseudonymous answers reveal that, then as now, a
thorough knowledge of the trade and its politics could be
an indispensable part of the supposedly frivolous business

of fashion-writing. The London weavers' riots of 1765, for example, provoked this worried letter:

> *I have several yards of French silk by me, which I purchased at Messieurs Carré Ibbetson on Ludgate-Hill before the late tumult of the weavers; but as these disorders are now subsided, should be glad to know whether I may or not have it made up, and be able to wear it without any danger arising therefrom?*

As there is no law in England to restrain the subject from wearing whatever he pleases, if the lady chuses to run the hazard of the consequences which may possibly ensue, she has my leave to do it, I do assure her; but at the same time, could wish my fair country-women would show more propensity towards encouraging the artists of their own nation, than those of a foreign one and did they but know how much more admirable they appear in the eyes of a man of sense, when clothed in the manufactory of Spital-fields, they would surely blush at their past folly, and never more appear abroad in the tawdry productions of France.

(*The Court Miscellany*, July 1765)

Another auntie who began by composing both question and answer was the editor of the vastly successful *Ladies' Magazine*. It is here that we first read of a blemish that was to dog readers until the advent of electrolysis – the beard. 'Emilia', the correspondent of *The Ladies' Magazine* in 1790, could resort to nothing more effective than her tweezers but begged for a more long-lasting cure. In the following century bearded ladies seem, from the evidence of the problem pages, to have been so common that circuses must have considered dropping them from the bill. Fortitude, a razor, or the recognition of hair's 'God-given' origin was the best advice that most mid-Victorian aunties could manage. Caustically, Samuel Beeton recommended one way of coping to 'Julia' in the April, 1860 issue of *The Englishwoman's Domestic Magazine*: 'If you have a moustache upon your upper lip, you must bear it like a man ...'

Bare – but unlike a man – another correspondent wrote to *Cassell's* with the problem in reverse:

AMS is in sore trouble because he is 21 and doesn't look like a man — is, in fact, short and beardless. He wishes to go courting and is shy, on account of his juvenile appearance, and in lachrymose strains he writes to us, to ask how he is to grow taller, and what is the best way of cultivating a moustache! We cannot furnish the recipe — we do not know; but we may encourage him to act like a man — which he is not doing now, or he would not have put such silly questions — though he might be but five foot nothing and his face as smooth as a maiden's.

(Cassell's, *29 August 1863*)

Cassell's had scarcely more sympathy for a hairy 'Polly' who, like the previous correspondent, bewailed her fate rather than trying to rise above it. On 14 March 1857 *Cassell's* told 'Poor Polly' of another girl, similarly afflicted:

… who was not only extremely popular, but most successful in achieving the great object of a lady's life — a capital match. To be sure, she was very sensible, industrious, amicable and unselfish, but we do not suppose that had anything to do with her success.

Red hair was especially unfashionable in the mid-nineteenth century and at this date advisers could no longer fall back on Dunton's expedient of a shaved head and a peruke. The ideal Victorian miss had a delicate complexion, pretty but unobtrusive features and a muted colouring. Red hair (often accompanied by freckles) was considered brash:

Scarlet — The lock of hair enclosed for our inspection is, we grieve to say it, decidedly red. No mother in the world, however doting, could call it auburn. A lead comb is frequently and successfully used to darken the hues of tresses which happen to be more brilliant than pleasant.

(Cassell's, *21 January 1858*)

An alternative, and highly misleading, tip from *The Ladies' Treasury* in August, 1859 was to use henna to change red hair to brown. Failing that, they suggested a strong infusion of tea. Red hair did, however, appear to have some consolations. One reader of the *Girl's Own Paper* was told that red-heads never had dandruff and were less liable to go insane.

Then as now, dumb brunettes tried constantly to turn themselves into bottled blondes, with disastrous results in pre-peroxide days. Most aunties were opposed to any such experimentation. *The Ladies' Treasury* warned 'Lady Georgina F.' in their issue of 1 January 1869 that 'Persons of weak constitution should never use hair dyes'. 'Lily', in *The Young Ladies' Journal* on 1 June 1869, was told, rather more convincingly, that 'No sensible woman would condescend to dye her hair. It is a well-known fact that the natural colour of the hair harmonises with the complexion; whatever colour it may be.' The *Girl's Own Paper* even printed a cautionary tale to illustrate the dangers. A 'Highland Lassie', it was revealed on 8 March 1900, bought some professedly 'golden' hair-dye and 'Behold! instead of the hue of sunshine it turned her locks dark green. How very green she must have felt! Mentally as well as physically.'

In addition to the right colour of hair, a Victorian beauty required a flawless complexion. Problem page writers were endlessly solicited for miracle cures for spots, normally on behalf of some third party. Samuel Beeton, still in 1860 editing *The Englishwoman's Domestic Magazine*, commented on the concern of these 'friends':

> *Marianna Tintina is very solicitous to know 'what would render the complexion dead white, for she has a friend who is troubled with a florid, greasy-looking skin'. We never understand what it is that makes so many friends write to us on account of their friends. The virtue of unselfishness is certainly more shown in letters 'To the Editor' than under any other circumstance we ever came in contact with; and, as we go through our correspondence, we cannot help feeling what kind creatures there are in the world. It does not occur to us for a single moment, of course, when our correspondents say they wish all this information on behalf of their friends, that they themselves are in the least interested, that would be unkind ...*

(The Englishwoman's Domestic Magazine, *December 1860*)

Those who scorned to hide behind a fictitious acquaintance could use instead a nom de plume, on occasion a startlingly apt one, as *The Young Ladies' Magazine* discovered on 1 May 1869:

Blighted Lady – Eruptions on the face are seldom successfully treated by outward application. Most likely you require medical treatment. We should advise you to consult a doctor at once. Chronic eruptions in the face are a most unfortunate malady for a lady.

Quite what comfort the unhappy 'Blighted Lady' was supposed to derive from that final statement of the obvious must remain a mystery.

Spots were particularly distressing for the tiny minority of readers facing a first London season. A peer's daughter who had a 'red nose and a fearful complexion' was advised by the editor of the *Girls' Own Paper* that 'until the great entertainment at which you say you are to come out, you should bathe the face in cold rain water, to which a little toilet vinegar has been added, and use cold cream at night'. Sometimes, however, the arts employed to attract attention on special occasions repelled suitors who liked their girls to appear as Nature intended:

Clarissa says she has had a quarrel with her lover, Roland ... It seems that he strongly objects to all those arts which, professing to heighten beauty, often destroy it. 'Clarissa' says that, solely with a view to shining in his eyes and not to be eclipsed in the presence of her friend, Aurelia, she has followed that lady's example and advice, purchased some additional clustering ringlets, a packet of poudre imperatrice, *a bottle of Pear's Liquid Bloom of Roses, and a dye which has converted her light eyebrows to a jetty arch; thus 'improved', and arrayed in the newest fashion and most expensive crinoline, she met Roland at a ball and he cut her. He pretended not to know her, but she heard from Aurelia, it was only pretended. 'Clarissa' says she bore it as long as she could, and then went off, in spite of herself, into strong hysterics. Roland remained obdurate and the next day wrote to say, he loved nature in women and flowers, and the artificial had no charms for him, that such as she was when he knew her, she was his* beau idéal, *such as she appeared at the ball, she was his aversion. We advise 'Clarissa' to promise her lover to sacrifice art, cosmetics and crinoline to true love and true taste.*

(The Ladies' Treasury, *July 1859*)

Another correspondent, writing to *Cassell's* that same year, complained that his love had appeared at a party arrayed in pink (which he loathed) and ringlets (which he detested), after he had made his views on these two fashions perfectly plain. Did this, he asked, 'put a damper on his hopes?' *Cassell's* certainly thought so.

Fashion was a burden in more ways than one for the early Victorian woman. A correspondent of *The Family Mirror* on 3 January 1856 did some calculations on the amount of material used in a Parisian robe with flounces, supported by the customary five petticoats. Put end to end, he pointed out, the fifty three yards involved would stretch fifteen feet higher than the column of the Place Vendome, the statue of Napoleon included. The crinoline, however ridiculous, did at least free women from the weight of all this yardage.

· A gift to both Punch cartoonists and carpenters (employed to widen doorways and re-build narrow carriages), the crinoline met with initial resistance from the problem page aunties who were aware that a gust of wind could reveal an improper ankle. One counsellor wrote approvingly of a crinoline tax imposed in America. Another advised 'Peachblossom' not to attempt the climbing of stiles while wearing a crinoline: 'if she suffers from the comments of vulgar little boys, it would be better, in a high wind, to remain indoors.' But the crinoline actually gave rise to less sweeping criticism than its practical opposite, the bloomer costume. Only the short-lived *Every Week* published a letter in support of this attire, which most aunties regarded as unwomanly and indecent:

> *Jane H. Stall concurs with our view on the Bloomer costume, as opposed to the Eugenie crinoline and long dresses. Her life, she says, and that of thousands of her English sisters, is made a torment to her because of her insane costume. The long dresses are always wet and muddy, and in the way. They afford no warmth or comfort, and outrage all decency. Men call women weak and women render themselves more helpless by the mode in which they appear.*
>
> (Every Week, *10 January 1863*)

We tend now to think of tight-lacing as another uniquely Victorian invention, associating it perhaps with our image of a straight-laced age. The Victorians themselves, however, believed the practice to have ancient origins. Questioned by 'Rebecca' on 27 December 1856 *The Family Mirror*, in hostile mood, attributed it to the Middle Ages. It was devised, they claimed, by:

> ... *a cruel butcher of the thirteenth century as a punishment for his wife. She was very loquacious, and finding nothing would cure her, he put a pair of stays on her in order to take away her breath and so prevent her from talking.*

The century had, of course, opened with Regency girls enjoying the liberty of Empire-line dresses. But even in Victoria's childhood the fashion for constriction returned. A correspondent of *The Ladies' Magazine* in 1828 described the consequences of his daughters' habit of squeezing their waists 'until the body resembles that of an ant'. They were, he claimed, unable to move or to sit, and stooping was out of the question. 'My daughter Margaret,' he revealed, 'made the experiment the other day. Her stays gave way with a tremendous explosion, and down she fell upon the ground, and I thought she had snapped in two.'

A very similar experience was reported in *The Englishwoman's Domestic Magazine* in the late sixties, suggesting that their long-running and famous debate on the desirability of corsets was started by the use of a fake letter re-written from the *Ladies' Magazine*. So fervent was this correspondence that its high-lights were reprinted by Ward Locke (by this date the owners of *The Englishwoman's Domestic Magazine*) under the title *The Corset and the Crinoline*.

Much was endured by the Victorian girl desirous of the necessary hour-glass figure. The general rule was that a teenage girl should, by gradual stages, be able to restrict her waist to two-thirds its natural size. Corsets, made so stiff that they could stand unsupported, were worn at all times, including in bed. One correspondent of *The Englishwoman's Domestic Magazine* boasted of removing hers for only one hour every week over a six week period.

Another scorned slovenly French females who wore loose-fitting robes without a corset until the evening. Rarely has the adage 'Il faut souffrir pour être belle' been followed so whole-heartedly. The result was the 15 inch waist, as much an inspiration in its day as Jayne Mansfield's 44 inches above the belt were to be for less well endowed school-girls in the late 1950s.

Not every English girl, however, welcomed the restrictions imposed by the corset. One mother who advocated the wearing of corsets in bed was distressed to discover that her fourteen year old daughter had been reading newfangled theories and 'has become impressed with the idea that being made to wear properly laced corsets was equivalent to being condemned to death by slow torture'. When forced to don the hated garment, the daughter removed it under cover of darkness. On the following night she was knotted into a Houdini-defying corset but promptly cut the laces. Now her fond Mama proposed a complicated series of padlocks. *The Englishwoman's Domestic Magazine* warned this mother, in February 1870, to leave her daughter alone, 'and let her manage her figure for two years longer at least'.

Other readers wrote of the fearful deformities, the internal injuries, indigestion and red noses which would result from tight-lacing. *The Englishwoman's Domestic Magazine* would occasionally print, without comment, the coroners' reports on girls who had died from its effects. But the correspondence was not exclusively female. Men, too, contributed to the 'Conversazione' section, both as admirers of corsets on others, and as practitioners themselves. One gentleman argued that the members of his sex 'admire small-waisted women in the same way that they admire a hippopotamus, or tiger, or ballet dancer – as something worth the trouble of looking at, but not for our wives'. 'Allured' and 'Moralist', however, both male correspondents, believed that tight-lacing was a virtue which should be practised by every nubile girl:

Allured ... I have no hesitation in saying that I am a great admirer of a slender waist, and I admire it the more that I know it to be the result of tight-lacing. There is something to me extraordinarily fascinating in the thought that a young girl has for many years been subjected to the strictest discipline of the corset. If she has suffered, as I have no doubt she has, great pain, or at any rate inconvenience, from their extreme pressure, it must be quite made up to her by the admiration her figure excites ... High heeled boots also excite my admiration and I am very glad they are so generally worn. I dare say they are not very comfortable but that is a small matter.

(The Englishwoman's Domestic Magazine, *January 1870*)

A month later 'Moralist' also showed an interest in the corset as a restraint or, as he put it, 'an ever present monitor'. Modern readers might consider these letters showed an undue interest in sadistic fetishism. Certainly 'Moralist' advocated pain:

Because it carries with it the supposition that all the roughness, so to speak, has been subdued, or at least modified, that a valuable lesson of self-abnegation has been taught; that patience and endurance of pain and inconvenience for the sake of others has been inculcated; that the crude spirit has been, as it were, tamed and civilised ...

Tight-lacing, apart from its overtones of bondage, did achieve something that no amount of slimming could – it gave a girl a slender waist without losing her voluptuous curves above and below. The nice, polite *Girls' Own Paper* in the 1880s and 1890s predictably discouraged it. But they also attempted to dissuade their young readership from more innocuous slimming techniques such as a fad for drinking vinegar. It will, they told one correspondent, 'impoverish the blood and induce dropsy, with other complaints, and she may have to be "tapped".' This same fatty was encouraged to wear flat heels and to thank God for her good health.

When all else failed the fat, the spotty and the plain were encouraged to solace themselves with the thought that beauty was but skin-deep. Men, they were assured, were really far more interested in the inner virtues:

E. K. Hart – Certainly there are many men who would prefer a quiet, homely girl to a very pretty, fascinating one, much admired and run after. Besides many men do not know anything about physical beauty and its hard and fast rules, and regard it as a dangerous gift. But all can appreciate the beauty of a sweet and candid expression, a gentle manner and a good temper. The grace of God in the heart does much to improve the countenance; and this, we trust, is your most blessed possession. Pray for it.

(Girls' Own Paper, *26 June 1894*)

Such a message must have come as a particular relief to one reader of Harmesworth's *Forget-Me-Not* in February 1898:

Such a splendid man – one I have known for over a year – has asked me to marry him. I said 'yes', and my people consented two days ago. But I have false teeth and wear a false fringe and it seems to me I'm not the girl he thinks me. What shall I do? I can't bear to tell him, yet if he finds out after we are married, will it not be a shock to him?

If it is sufficient to alter his feelings towards you, they must have very little foundation. Tell him certainly, if you like, but as I suppose he cares for you, and not for your teeth and hair, I cannot see how the revelation will greatly affect him.

(*Forget-Me-Not*, 5 February 1898)

In spite of such pious theorising in the agony columns, many hours of suffering must have been endured for the sake of a little extra personal attractiveness. The beautiful girl clearly had a much better chance of achieving the universal object – a good match – than her spotty sister. A certain latitude was, therefore, allowed in the obscuring of defects. Frills and flounces often added inches to the bust that lacked a certain fullness. A well-cut corset could disguise those extra rolls of puppy-fat.

By the twentieth century the agony columns were even relaxing their long-running campaign against the use of powder. Their disapproval had originally had medical grounds. Many Georgian beauties had belatedly found that their liberal use of arsenic and lead-based powders left their skins permanently discoloured. But the prejudice had lasted long after more innocuous means of obtaining a perfectly white complexion had been discovered. In 1905 the aptly named *Cosy Comfort Boudoir* at last felt free to tell 'Engaged Girl' that 'to powder or not to powder is a question every woman must decide for herself, since no hard-and-fast rule can be laid down on the subject'. Most

men, according to the auntie, objected to powder but 'Still
I cannot imagine your lover would break the engagement
for such a trifling thing'. This same auntie was, however,
less permissive to a young girl who'd been experimenting
with home-made face cream. 'Your duty is at home
helping your over-worked mother and not gadding off to
girlfriends' cream-making to improve your complexion,'
she was firmly told.

Edwardian problem pages devoted a certain amount of
space to the specialized beauty requirements of emigrants
to distant parts of the Empire. 'LB' in the 13 December
1902 issue of *The Family Herald* was advised to content
herself with her present wardrobe but to sell her linen and
take the resulting money. *The Queen*, read by a more
elevated clientele, gave hints to girls being shipped over to
India in the so-called 'fishing-fleet'. Under the heading
'Dress and Toilette' on 4 July 1903, the expert revealed:

> *October to March is the gay time so you should take out to Calcutta*
> *plenty of evening dresses not of a rich material, but of thin silk, chiffon*
> *or net. Tulle spoils a good deal … Vests should be much the same as*
> *worn in Europe, but young people do not wear them more than*
> *can be helped … People are smart and dressy in Calcutta …*

The Great War brought sudden changes. On the eve of the
conflict *The Ladies' Field*, a county alternative to *Queen*, had
some exotic advice for 'Freda':

> *A new concept which has decided charm is to use a perfume to*
> *harmonise with the colour of your dress. For instance, when one is*
> *gowned in a delicate sweet-pea pink one must have the mouchoir*
> *perfumed with sweet-pea blossom …*
>
> (The Ladies' Field, *20 June 1914*)

By October the tone of the page had been transformed. In
the first weeks of heady patriotism the buying of any
luxuries was regarded as self-indulgent, unless intended
for an invalid. This retrenchment in the spending of the
middle classes soon, however, led to large-scale
unemployment, particularly in the cotton trade. It would
be months before the War Office could redeploy the men

and women involved into a volunteer army and an embryonic munitions industry. In a state of mild panic, the government encouraged the women's columnists to advocate a less determined campaign of penny-pinching. *The Ladies' Field* told their readers where they could buy shirts for soldiers, and discouraged the indiscriminate donation of hunters to the army for cavalry horses.

When gently nurtured middle-class girls rolled up their once-frilly sleeves and poured out tea for soldiers on Victoria Station, or nursed wounded men in emergency hospitals, they sloughed off their elaborate skins permanently. The *Woman's Magazine*, in 1927, provided a retrospective account of the revolution in women's clothing which began during the war, and continued in a more exaggerated way in the 1920s:

> *What do you think of the modern woman's scanty clothing? Isn't she a product of a very decadent age?*

> Not exactly. When war broke out, the dress-making world had to wrestle with two big problems that were also confronting other businesses – shortage of materials and shortage of labour. But those in command among the dress designers found an easier way out of their difficulties than the rest of us did. For one bright brain evolved the idea of cutting the material down to about half the amount originally used in a garment, and reducing the work of making it to still less than half. With the result that we became a nation of shapeless females, with a clothing as 'fitless' and unadorning as it could possibly be, and as short as public opinion would tolerate – then! It has tolerated a much greater amount of shrinkage since! ...
> It is easy to try to condone this on the grounds that to the pure all things are pure. This is true. And it is equally true that to the impure scanty skirts and a lavish display of bare flesh suggest anything but purity!

Shingling provided the great beauty debate of the 1920s. In *Pam's Paper* for 9 January 1926, for example, 'Marguerite (Buxton)' read:

> *Do not worry what your friends say. If you do not wish to have your*

hair shingled and think it would not suit you, then keep it long ... after
all it is you who have to wear it.

Such new fashions, and the new manners of the young,
gave offence not only to parents but also, and more
worryingly, to the servants. In January 1934 *Woman's
Magazine* received a letter from 'Isabella' who needed
guidance over 'What to do about some of these very
modern ideas like sun-bathing in the garden in bathing
costumes, which may be all very well but shocks her old
servants, the village and many of her old friends.' She was
advised to put a stop to it, politely.

The Victorian problem of corsets and stays had
disappeared, only to be replaced by queries about that
new-fangled invention, the bra:

> *I often go to dances and my girl friends assure me that I should wear a*
> *bust bodice as my bust shakes about and is very conspicuous, but I do not*
> *like to do so as I feel very uncomfortable and my evening dresses are*
> *backless.*

> I think few things look worse than a loose, wobbling bust
> and I strongly advise you to wear a bust bodice from now
> on. I can assure you that it is very bad for your health and
> your figure to let a heavy bust hang without support.
>
> (*Peg's Paper*, 17 April 1937)

Even the Second World War did not sweep such feminine
concerns from the minds of women, serving though they
might be in the Forces or on the land. Behind the up-lifting
Churchillian rhetoric and the battle-news lay more
niggling problems. With Hitler poised across the Channel,
girls could still fret about their hair. 'Mrs Marryat', the
auntie on *Woman's Weekly*, answered a letter on 20 March
1943 from a correspondent whose chief worry about
joining-up was that she would no longer be able to get to
her hair-dresser regularly:

> *Wrens serving at stations where it is impossible to go to ordinary hair-*
> *dressers, are now able to have their hair trimmed, shampooed and set*
> *by their own hair-dressers. Every Wren is allowed one free trim or one*
> *free shampoo every fortnight. Setting costs 6d ...*

By 1945 the agony columns were filled with letters from women whose husbands had been away for the duration of the war. What would the response be of men who had left a young slip of a girl and returned to find a solid matron, marked by the passage of five or six years? Such women were encouraged to give advance notice of the changes time had wrought. One reader, for instance, was told to joke in her letters about her newly-grey hair, so that her husband would not be shocked when they were reunited. Others had to be reminded that men returning from Japanese or German POW camps would not initially resemble the well-rounded, physically-alert boys who had set out years before.

The consumer boom of the 1950s brought a new set of problems. With more than a decade of ration books behind them, shoppers ran amuck. The women's magazines were flooded with advertisements for nylons, skin-care products, cosmetics and clothes. Bombarded on all sides by the media's idea of ideal beauty, women looked in the mirror and found themselves wanting. Would their men still love their stretch-marked, flabby bodies after gazing at Jayne Mansfield's lissom, well-endowed form? Denise Robins was once again a realist and less than reassuring in her replies to women worrying about their attractiveness. Not for her any comforting words suggesting husbands loved the inner soul and not the crumbling outer-casing:

> *I'm stout and not very smart. My husband is a judge of pretty girls. I am frantically jealous and afraid of losing him. Don't you think it is cruel of a man to stop loving a wife who has been faithful for 20 years?*

> Yes, but look at it from the other point of view. No doubt you were pretty and smart when he married you. If you want to keep your man you must do something about controlling that figure and dressing attractively. The most faithful wife in the world can't afford to let herself go to pieces.

> (*She*, March 1955)

The inimitable Marje Proops was equally forthright when

approaching the dilemma of hard-working mothers trying desperately not to become frumpish:

> *I'm in trouble because I wear curlers in bed. My husband says they look awful and often gives a yell in the night when he suddenly turns over and catches an unlucky one on the chin. However, he is so tight with his money that he would not pay for me to visit the hairdresser. What CAN a woman do? – Patty.*

Dear Patty, Tell him straight. Either he continues to put up with a permanent eye-sore or he pays up. It would be worth his while to give generously in any case. There's always a chance your steel structure will miss his chin one night and give him a black eye. So if he wants some changes made, he'd better fork out. You could call it danger money.

(*Woman's Mirror*, 25 February 1961)

By the 1960s the consumer generation had grown more youthful, with beauty tips, fashion and luxury goods all being aimed at a newly-rich teen-age market. Simultaneously the young had become more rebellious. 'Kelly' in *Weekend* was one of the first aunties to deal with a problem later to become widespread. Sandra's Mum had written to Kelly, hoping she would concur that Sandra, at thirteen was too young to wear make-up. 'Sorry, I don't agree,' replied Kelly, on 14 September 1960. 'If you ban make-up Sandra will almost certainly wear it behind your back, so teach her instead to use it with discretion.'

The demand for beauty hints in women's magazines has often been misunderstood. Most readers do not aspire to radiant beauty. They wish simply to conform. A fear of inferiority or malformation, rather than an empty-headed frivolity, usually lurks behind requests for new creams, nose jobs or crash diets. But whereas the Victorian miss fretted about her facial spots or, just possibly, the depth of her cleavage, her modern counterpart can be concerned about the normalcy of more intimate parts of her anatomy. Claire Rayner of *The Sun* has been much quoted on this topic:

> *For Heaven's sake, everyone's face is different, what makes you think*

that the rest of the body should be the same? The saddest thing is that
people won't risk any sort of relationship because of this. They write
and say, 'I couldn't possibly go out with a boy because we might get to
have some sex, and he would find out I'm not normal.'

Ironically the page three offerings of her own newspaper
have done little to reassure her female readership, who
now have ample proof of their own short-comings.
Indeed, the more explicit such photographs become, the
greater the grounds for womanly worry. The continuing
practice of touching-up photographs is particularly to
blame, since certain attributes, such as protruding vaginal
lips, are invariably censored by porn-publishers. Anna
Raeburn, like Claire Rayner, devotes inches of her column
to persuading women that to be different is not to be a
freak. 'There are no figures available on the number of
women having what you regard as a deformity, and as far
as I know, nobody's ever gone round measuring,' she
wrote in reply to a correspondent worrying about the
protruding vaginal lip in *Woman* on 19 June 1976. 'The size
of the vaginal lip varies as much as the size of feet, noses,
hands or ears, and I wouldn't describe a big nose as a
deformity.' Such replies could be called many things.
Frivolous, however, they are not.

6

Genteel experiences
ETIQUETTE IN THE PROBLEM PAGE

Etiquette, unlike manners, has tended to be the exclusive preserve of the upper classes. As the other great distinguishing mark, wealth, began to be more widespread, etiquette became the crucial test which separated the true nobs from the mere snobs. The founding of the problem page coincided with the final collapse of the rigid Mediaeval social order. As the new code of polite behaviour slowly took shape, the aunties found themselves deeply involved in its development.

Echoing the generally relaxed attitude of a well-entrenched class not yet under pressure from below, the earliest problem pages devoted little space to the matter. John Dunton was not expected to pronounce upon the desirability of the fish-knife, or to arbitrate between the rival claims of an elderly maiden aunt and a recently married cousin to a place at the right hand of the host at a dinner party. The particular dearth of etiquette problems in Dunton's publications may, however, also owe something to the feeling that a publisher who knew more about the tap room than the boudoir (despite his two marriages) was an uncertain guide to refined behaviour. On at least one occasion he was himself happy to oblige a lady on a matter pertaining not merely to the boudoir but to the marriage bed. In *The British Apollo*, in 1708, a female correspondent was told 'since it is the custom and the fashion to go into the bridal bed with gloves on, we think it not genteel to go to bed without'. Whether the removal of the gloves symbolised the loss of virginity (as Laurence Stone suggests in his book *The Family, Sex and Marriage*), or whether their presence simply protected a husband from his new wife's nails is not made clear.

But if Dunton was not widely considered an expert on etiquette, he believed himself well qualified to expound on manners. When asked whether fondness after marriage was more pardonable in a man or a woman he replied:

> It is silly enough in both – and besides cruel, to set other people's mouths awatering, as if you were cutting a melon. Further, 'tis indecent, to be always flabbering like a couple of horses nabbing one another. Again, it oftentimes shows that all things are not well behind the curtain, when there's such a deal of love before folks. And last of all, there's danger lest their love should not last too long, if they squander it away too fast at their first setting up. But to compare this fondness of both sexes, we think it seems worst in a man, because there 'tis most unnatural, and looks like a woman with a beard so very monstrous that all the street points at him whenever he appears, as they may easily do, for the world is not much inclin'd to that vice.
>
> (The Athenian Oracle, *1691*)

Addison shared this distaste and published a letter from a reader complaining of 'the unsociable fondness of some husbands, the ill-timed tenderness of some wives'.

In an era which still conducted its affairs through the arranged marriage, the artificial marriage-mart of the London season had yet to flourish. But visits to the metropolis could still present problems of behaviour. Girls accompanying their fathers on the three-monthly visit to attend Parliament found the soldiers based in Hyde Park an agreeable distraction from the young men favoured by their parents. Army officers discovered, to their cost, that a fashionable posting to guard the Serpentine could lead to considerable expenditure on well brought up girls, who rarely gave more in return than a little flirtation. One middle-aged soldier, 'Captain Bluff', wrote to *The Visiter* on 25 June 1723, to complain that even he, despite his advanced years, was always met by a bevy of young ladies eager to be seen with a red-coat. The editor, in reply, promised to print the names of the offenders if they

continued to plague the colonel and to drink his
champagne.

Polite accomplishments became an important topic very
early in the eighteenth century. A correspondent of *The
Censor*, in 1717, who signed herself 'Miranda Love-Wit' and
explained that 'fate and my birth plac'd me in a middle
station of life; the thrift and good fortune of a husband
have raised me above that quality', was worried about the
education of her children. She believed that good manners
alone were not enough and begged the editor to let her
husband know that 'there are other improvements, beside
teaching them to behave well in company and training
them up to the knowledge of genteel experiences.' *The
Censor* agreed with her, and its stress on 'acquisition of
knowledge' was echoed a year later in a poetic answer in
The British Apollo:

Can you to noble blood just title claim,
And education that becomes the same?
The want of riches no distraction bears
For worth in rags, as well as robes, appears.
But virtue best illustrious birth does trace,
And generous acts proclaim a generous race.

Even in those less artificial times, however, one sure sign of
an imperfect gentleman was an inability to talk rationally
to a lady. 'There is,' according to one fair correspondent of
The Spectator, 'a language particular for talking to women
in, and none but those of the very first breeding – who are
very few and who seldom come my way – can speak to us
without regard to our sex ...' She continued, with perhaps
a hint of self-satisfaction, 'I am so handsome that I murder
all who approach me; so wise that I want no new notices,
and so well bred that I am treated by all who know me like
a fool, for no one will answer as if I were their friend or
companion.'

Conversation with unknown gentlemen continued to
involve difficulties, as a letter which appeared in *The Ladies'
Magazine* in 1817 makes clear. While spending the evening
at a provincial public assembly, the correspondent had
turned down a dance with the younger son of a lord,

preferring the addresses of another gallant whose dress made him the beau of the ball. During the galop she discovered that the young man's conversation was not altogether genteel. But worse was to follow. On handing her into her carriage at the end of the evening, her partner pressed a note into her hand which the lady fondly imagined to be a billet-doux. Suspense reigned while she was driven home in an unlit carriage. On reaching home she opened the note and discovered a trade advertisement. She had spent the evening in the company of a tallow merchant, the lowest of the low in the tradesman's pecking order, who was soliciting her custom rather than her person.

'The Matron' shared her disgust and regretted that the nature of public assemblies made it difficult to exclude such highly ineligible men. Society's arteries were hardening – a hundred years before, an influential adviser like Defoe had himself been the son of a tallow merchant.

The gulf between trade and the genteel or professional classes was particularly pronounced. A correspondent of *The Ladies' Magazine*, in November 1791, asked the editor's opinion of a merchant who 'was on a friendly footing with all his neighbouring gentry, amongst whom he both frequently pays and receives visits, in a style somewhat transcending the hospitality of tradesmen'. The ostensible cause for complaint was that his sons must be neglecting their business by making afternoon calls. Its real thrust, however, was clearly that a tradesman had no right to mix with social superiors as an equal.

The Ladies' Magazine considered itself the arbiter of polite behaviour from 1770 to 1832. Mrs Martha Grey's subject matter reflected a growing obsession with rank, formal manners and those little nuances of behaviour that separated the born lady from the manufactured copy. The tone, however, remained moralistic and any clergyman would have been proud to possess 'The Matron's' gift for preaching.

In the second decade of the nineteenth century *The Ladies' Magazine* revived 'The Matron'. The column was now supposedly written by the original Mrs Grey's granddaughter, Sophie, and dealt almost exclusively with problems of etiquette and polite behaviour. By this date the code was clearly becoming stricter. In the 1770s Mrs Grey had countenanced the idea of a girl's being brutal to discourage a thick-skinned suitor. The new 'Matron', in June 1817, allowed no such latitude:

> ... *nothing is so easy as keeping men at a proper distance, and that without prudery or affectation, and if her own actions are such as are not calculated to invite freedom, one may depend on it, they will never be offered, except by the ultra-impertinents, and even they are to be managed with a little address.*

Mild flirtation as a device with which to punish a neglectful loved one was similarly forbidden:

> *I'm afraid the young lady who complains of the fastidiousness of her lover condemns herself – innocent freedoms no man of sense will object to; and beyond these no woman of virtue will go – how far coquetting with the smartest in the room to punish a prude comes within the description remains to be determined. I would advise her in future to consider her love always the smartest man in the room, and as by her own information he seems to have been the most sensible, I think she had better take care, lest by punishing prudes, she should eventually punish herself.*
>
> (The Ladies' Magazine, June 1817)

Gentlemen had received scant attention from magazine moralists in the late eighteenth century. A true gentleman was expected to know how to behave, and the moral code he followed was understood to be different from that governing his wife. Boswell spoke for his age when, in a famous passage of the *Life of Dr Johnson*, he argued that although a woman must be faithful she should not object if her husband 'from mere wantonness of appetite ... steals privately to her chambermaid'.

By the mid-nineteenth century men began to face a moral code which, officially at least, was the same as that imposed on their women-folk. In practice considerable differences continued to exist. Men could enjoy a degree of sexual freedom as long as they were discreet. The maintenance of such a covert double standard required a complex code of etiquette. Society evolved elaborate rules for the turning of blind eyes. A girl was not at fault, for example, if she cut a young man of her acquaintance (even her brother) when she met him with what the problem pages euphemistically called 'flower-girls', 'milliners' or 'girls of a lower social order'. Indeed she was grossly at fault if she greeted him or sought an introduction to his companion. Mothers, too, were expected to pass their sons without acknowledgement in this painful situation.

Respectable women, etiquette decreed, had the right to determine the degree of acquaintanceship. A man was not expected to remove his hat, or to approach a lady, unless she had civilly bowed to him first. This, as *Cassell's* pointed out, was a useful defence against men to whom one had been polite in the artificial circumstances of a ballroom:

> *A lady who is introduced to a gentleman at an evening party is not bound to recognise him the next day, even though she had danced with him and conversed on a familiar footing the previous evening. This is one of the laws of politeness wisely framed to protect ladies from those overpowering coxcombs who infest our drawing rooms.*
>
> (Cassell's, *17 January 1857*)

Both *Cassell's* and *The London Journal* strenuously warned their readers against associating with strangers in the street. 'Julia', for instance, was told by *The London Journal* that she would seriously compromise her dignity if she allowed herself to be drawn into a clandestine conversation:

> *Love, as we know it, is very bold; but vice is bolder, and always prefers secrecy – it cannot exist in the sunshine of honour and candid explanations to those to whom explanation is peremptorily due.*

'Clandestine conversations' did nonetheless occur, and once a young man knew where a girl lived, short of locking her up or moving, the parents could find it difficult to prevent them meeting:

> *A Mother – It would be useless for a family to remove their residence*

because a gentleman in the neighbourhood, who is objectionable to the parents, persists in paying attention to one of the daughters to whom he is not objectionable. They would contrive to meet even then. The only way is to persuade the young lady to do right; nothing else is of any avail.

(The Home Magazine, *No. 421, Volume 17*)

Another piece of advice, in the same volume of *The Home Magazine*, suggests that it was not necessarily men whose attentions were unwanted:

Tom Jones – You would only degrade yourself by having words in the public street with a woman capable of behaving in the manner you describe. So long as she keeps her hands off you should pass on without taking the slightest notice of her, and if she resorts to violence, you should give her in charge.

(The Home Magazine, *No. 426, Volume 17*)

This letter describes an outrageous hussy who was clearly not a lady. But, whatever the provocation, our correspondent was evidently expected to follow the example of his sisters and, with head held high, ignore the incident. In other words, whatever her status, he at least was expected to behave like a gentleman.

What, however, were the qualities of that elusive being? *Cassell's* obliged with a definition:

Expectant wishes to be a gentleman and requires a recipe for that article ... If we were asked to speak positively, we should say a gentleman in the best sense of the word is but an embodiment of the abstract idea of manhood ... The difference between the true and false gentleman is that the one is an actor, the other is not; in this case, as in every other, the most finished piece of acting can never rival the beautiful 'Simplicity of nature'. A good heart shines forth in fine manners and plain manhood, seek it where you will and comprehends something higher and nobler than that which fine gentlemen call honour. We define a gentleman to be he who amidst the pressures of worldly business, can yet find time to hold his soul his own, manfully to oppose the wrong, give shelter to the weak and work his way towards Heaven.

(Cassell's, *April, 1856*)

The description is highly uplifting but was hardly, one suspects, the formula required by the correspondent. *Cassell's* and *The London Journal* were read by the lower middle classes, whose income outstripped their education and knowledge of polite society. They needed something closer to a step-by-step guide to correct behaviour – what to do and when to do it. Even more urgently, perhaps they wanted to know what should not be done.

The giving and receiving of presents was a particularly complicated area of etiquette for unmarried girls. It was, according to *The London Journal*, within the bounds of propriety to give a departing curate a pair of embroidered braces, although he might prefer that you should have expended the same amount of labour in some article to have been sold for the poor. But to give a young man a photograph as 'Tulip', a correspondent of *The Ladies' Treasury*, had done was rash since 'a young girl's fair name is so easily "smirched" by the ribald nonsense of grown up boys, that she cannot be too careful not to give colour to any liberty of any kind'.

One worried mother counselled her daughter 'Jessie' to send a money order to a gentleman friend of her brother's who had sent her a pair of gloves. This was a wrong move, obviously, but *The London Journal* felt:

> *Apologising would only make matters worse, and Jessie could not make one without compromising her mother, under whose dictation she acted. The affair must be looked upon as one of those mistakes which cannot be avoided, even by the most precise people.*
>
> (The London Journal, *14 June 1862*)

Mothers could be hindrances in other ways as well:

> *... Marian complains that her parents talk about nothing but chairs and tables, and carpets and engravings ... housemaids, housemen and house business in general. There is a lack of sympathy and kindness for herself and her sisters, which she most keenly feels. No one comes to see them, and she thinks it must be because her parents are such vulgar and disagreeable people. They offend all who know them, and never keep a friend for more than a few months, and so Marian continues for several pages, and in that delicate tracery on the 'cream laid' which is*

> *so charming to the sight of an editor wearied with proofs. We really*
> *don't know what to say to Marian. She cannot send her father and*
> *mother to school to learn manners so much is certain. She can, however,*
> *do this – it has just struck us, she can be kind and civil and well-bred,*
> *even if her parents are uncouth, uncivil and vulgar. Thus there will be*
> *an angel in the house that may do some good to the more mundane.*
> (The Englishwoman's Domestic Magazine, *June 1862*)

This reply may well have been composed by Mrs Beeton who knew something about appearing a lady under adverse circumstances. Though she was given a good education (including a spell at a Heidelberg finishing school), much of her childhood was spent with her sixteen brothers and sisters in the grandstand of Epsom Racecourse, where her step-father was Clerk of the Course. This mixed background may have given her a certain sympathy for 'Marian', unlike most aunties who believed that nothing could justify want of respect towards parents. The adviser in *The Family Friend* in 1852, for example, insisted that:

> *It is due to yourself to treat the relation with respect and the more*
> *perfectly proper your manners are, the greater will be your influence ...*
> *So much of safety and happiness is gained by being open and*
> *confidential with the natural guardians of your youth that it is*
> *worthwhile to make some sacrifices to it of momentary repugnance and*
> *fastidiousness of taste.*

Such fastidiousness of taste was, however, supposed to operate in the presence of strangers, even when invigorating sea breezes blew every carefully learnt rule of etiquette from a young girl's mind. It was bad enough if a pure young girl allowed herself to be lured into conversation in Broadstairs or Brighton, but if the setting was Boulogne then the worst was feared:

> *'Rosa R' says she met at Boulogne sur Mer at a public Ball with a*
> *French gentleman of captivating appearance and manners, who*
> *taking advantage of the custom of the country, asked for a dance*
> *without an introduction; and in defiance of French and English*
> *etiquette, joined her in her walk the next day when she was out with*
> *her little brothers and sisters and their nurse. 'Rosa R' adds that her*

partner made a declaration of love, and that though she did not know whether she liked him or not, she agreed to his meeting her again next day, that for several days he continued to do so and at last forced on her a locket containing a piece of hair, at the same time imploring one of her locks. 'Rosa' says she was weak enough to comply and went to a celebrated worker in hair to get him to set a curl of her hair when, to her dismay, the artist en cheveux, after examining her locket and its contents, assured her that the case was ormolu and the lock, according to an unerring test of his, cut from a wig! We advise our weak and imprudent correspondent, of whose whole plan of conduct we disapprove, to have nothing more to say to a man whose heart is probably as false as his hair, and his conduct as brazen as his locket.

(The Ladies' Treasury, *October 1859*)

This hair-raising episode would prove, it was hoped, a valuable lesson to the flighty Rosa. Back home, another girl was facing difficulties over conduct in the ballroom, though her head rather than her heart seemed this time to be the cause of the trouble:

THS complains that in waltzing she turns dizzy after a dozen rounds or so and is then obliged to sit down. She has consulted a doctor on the subject and he tells her as soon as she feels the dizziness coming on to turn round in the opposite way; but THS very naturally observes, few partners would like me to do so. We think not indeed ... The expedient recommended by him would soon, we apprehend, bring our lady friend and her partner to the floor. Would it be any great deprivation to our correspondent to abstain from waltzing altogether?

(Cassell's, *5 January 1856*)

Entertainments at home were unlikely to include energetic dancing or the possibility of meeting an ineligible stranger, but a chaperone was still essential to ensure that no one overstepped the bounds of good taste. Party games sometimes strayed towards the boisterous and the aunties insisted that young girls should only play forfeits, with the penalty of giving or receiving a kiss, in the company of relatives. As *The Ladies' Treasury* remarked, in April 1866, 'it must be pleasanter for any pure-minded young girl to feel that her lips have been kept intact from rude embraces, although they might only have been given in play'.

Match-making mamas following the rules of etiquette

faced a dilemma. One set of rules rested on the assumption that men were potential ravaging beasts, ready to pounce on any defenceless girl. Another convention declared that a man should be given the chance to be alone with a girl so that he might propose. A certain manipulation of circumstances was therefore necessary if it looked as if a suitor was coming up to scratch. Sometimes, however, the best laid plans misfired:

> *N puts the following question – Suppose a Gentleman is spending the evening at the house of friends, among whom are several young ladies and as the time for his departure draws near, he finds that all the ladies have left the room save the one with whom he is conversing, and on accidentally looking at an aperture in the ceiling he discovers one of the ladies who had recently left the room watching him – to what should he attribute such conduct?*
>
> (Home Magazine, *No.* 270, *Vol. XI*)

Perhaps, replied the auntie, it would not be rash to attribute it to curiosity.

Operating in an essentially virtuous clime, in fact, the problem pages could afford to be jocular about those who broke the rules. One such was 'Despairing lover' in *The London Journal* of 1 June 1850. He had fallen in love with a 'charming young member of the company who administers to the gratification of large audiences at the Theatre Royal, Manchester', and wished to meet her. *The London Journal* drily suggested that he should applaud violently and be so fulsome in his tributes that he would, doubtless, be ejected from the theatre. Of course he would resist and 'then, "all bleeding and torn" he would be carried behind the scenes to receive medical assistance, and there behold the peerless and perhaps scantily attired beauty for whom he had perilled garment and limbs, and excited doubts as to his mental condition'.

In a similarly satirical mood, *Punch* gave some unhelpful advice to those who needed a guide to the complexities of calling:

> *Votary of Fashion – 1. In paying afternoon calls, be careful to leave as many cards as there are persons in the family. Thus, if there are 13 in*

all, leave 13 cards. This is always done in the highest circles. 2. If you wish to 'make kind enquiries' write PPC in one corner. It is a formula well understood. 3. Do not take up the gravy in your plate with a spoon. It is contrary to good etiquette – you can get as much as you want on the blade of your knife, but be sure not to cut yourself in so doing. 4. Buy Etiquette for the Million or How to Behave like a Gentleman on Nothing a Year, *published at this office.*

(Punch, *1 January 1887*)

Now that most men worked at some distance from their home, calls were made during the afternoon almost exclusively by their womenfolk. It was customary for a married woman to leave one card in her own name and two in her husband's. This gave credence to the polite fiction that the husband, whose work prevented him from accompanying his wife, had made the call in spirit. Daughters, unless they had passed that uncertain 'certain' age, were included on their Mama's card, by the expedient of turning down a corner. If a family was about to leave the district, go on holiday, or leave London at the end of July when the season ended, then PPC (Pour Prendre Congé) was added to the card. Cards had always to be left after attending any ball, reception or dinner party, preferably the following day and certainly within a week. To fail to acknowledge a card by a call meant, in effect, that the recipient did not wish to further the acquaintance.

It would be wrong to dismiss this social habit as merely a device to fill the hours of unemployed middle-class women. For many these formal afternoon visits constituted hard work, which was only undertaken in the knowledge that it would help their husband's livelihood. As late as 1908 *Myra's Journal*, the magazine founded by Matilda Browne, former editoress of *The Young Englishwoman*, had this to say to a doctor's wife:

Topsy ... I'm afriad that you will find yourself forced to call and receive visits. It is one of the real aids which his wife can give a medical man. The wife of a famous physician can do as she likes. Your chief object should be, without extravagant outlay in dinners etc., to enlarge your circle of acquaintances and (probable) patients for your husband.

(Myra's Journal, *1 April 1908*)

Calling, in other words, could be the middle-class equivalent of the tradesman's soliciting for custom. The only difference was that the tradesman used the back entrance and stated his wares on his card.

The educative function of the problem page was reinforced towards the end of the nineteenth century by the publication of etiquette books, written by such experts as Mrs Humphreys (who as 'Madge' had run a society column in *Truth*) and Flora Klickmann, later the editor of *Girl's Own Paper* and *Woman's Magazine*. This left the aunties with more space for the straightforward denouncing of social blunders. Any attempt at unfeminine, or boyish behaviour was censured or ridiculed:

> *Eustacie wishes to know 'up to what age a girl may climb a tree?' If a pack of wolves were after you, we should advise you to climb a tree up to 90 or 100. Otherwise why make yourself look like one of Mr Darwin's monkey-progenitors? Were there apples in the tree we should excuse your so doing; but otherwise it is not so delightful to be up a tree, nor a suitable position for a girl.*
>
> (Girl's Own Paper, *18 September 1880*)

Three girls, on 20 November the following year, were reminded how to conduct themselves in the street. They must never look at a strange man, never speak or laugh and, if accosted, the auntie held 'It is generally a girl's own fault if she be spoken to and as such is a disgrace to her, of which she should be ashamed to speak'. Another correspondent was encouraged, on 17 March 1894, to deal with an attempted pick-up by saying 'I am obliged to you, but I go nowhere without my mother's knowledge and sanction'.

It would appear that the *Girl's Own Paper*'s colonial readers were particularly in need of the magazine's hints on etiquette, and it saw no reason why the tribal customs of the English middle classes should not apply to the far-flung empire, however strange they might seem in Alice Springs or Alberta:

> *Dollie and Nettie (Australia) enquire whether it be 'the correct thing for a gentleman to embrace a lady when he is first introduced to her?'*

Certainly not. Possibly, after 50 years acquaintance, and on some special occasion, such as the Christmas Festival or a wedding, the rule might be relaxed.

(Girl's Own Paper, 7 October 1893)

At home the importance of the introduction was constantly stressed and those who dispensed with it clearly paid for their rashness. *Woman's Life* in 1899 could not resist pointing out that 'AP', a reader who had fallen for the lion-tamer in a visiting circus, had not been formally introduced to him and that, although isolated cases of happiness resulting from the meeting of two unintroduced strangers did occur, they were very rare. The auntie comforted her with the reflection that 'Time heals all wounds of the heart ... and depend upon it, the right man will yet come along, and AP will settle down in a happy and comfortable life.'

By the turn of the century many magazines had specialist etiquette columns in addition to their general problem page. Here the niceties of the subject were discussed – how to set a table tastefully, how to peel an orange with a knife or compose a letter of condolence. But, while up-market magazines dealt with such esoteric matters, the publications of Newnes and Harmesworth continued to face the really basic question:

... I have decided to become engaged to the girl of my heart. I believe in doing the right thing if I can. So tell me, do I ask her father's consent, her mother's, or anybody's? What do I say? What questions ought I to have asked me? ... 'Answers to the Front'

'Answers to the Front' seems fairly sure his sweetheart will accept him. But he had better ask her first and not make too certain. Put it plain and plumb. It's easy enough to find the words once you've got started. Asking Papa is the next step. That is harder. 'What's your income?' is the first question you'll have fired at you. Also your prospective father-in-law has every right to ask a great many questions as to your character, antecedents, family and prospects ...

(*Answers to Correspondents*, 1 January 1900)

Getting married may have been a complicated business,

but so too was dying. Queen Victoria's own fascination
with the subject (she wore her widow's weeds for forty
years) may bear some responsibility for the highly
ritualised nature of mourning during her reign. Crepe, the
material most commonly used, was highly impractical and
spotted badly on contact with water. One tip from an
adviser was to restore its pristine blackness with ink.
Ingenious as this solution was, it tended to make matters
even worse on the next rainy occasion.

Black was the colour donned immediately after the
death of a close relative. After a certain period it could be
relieved by flashes of white, grey or mauve. But mourning
was not standardised, and almost every reply in the agony
columns of the late Victorian period recommends a
different period of full and half-mourning for the various
degrees of relationship. *The Queen*, that upper-class oracle,
suggested the following system in the early twentieth
century:

> *Orchids – The strict period is 12 months; ten months black and two
> and half months half mourning, but this is modified in young girls and
> for children and also as regards young married women. The latter
> frequently lighten the black period with touches of white after six
> months and mauve and grey after 9 months. Young girls often wear
> white shirts and blouses with their black coats and skirts after three
> months and continue to lighten the black with white the following three
> months and wear half mourning after 9 months. Very young children
> wear white trimmed with black when they are very young, middle-
> aged daughters often wear black for six months unrelieved by white,
> while others commence wearing touches of white after three months.
> Crepe is not worn at all by the many, and only as a trimming by others.
> Gold bracelets, bangles, etc. may be worn after six months and
> diamonds after four months.*

> (The Queen, *10 October 1903*)

A remark made in *The Queen* some twenty-three years
earlier may explain the frequent variations. Ultimately,
The Queen felt, 'This must be a matter of individual feeling;
we only indicate the conventional periods required by
custom and everyone naturally is at liberty to lengthen
them at pleasure'. There was no suggestion, however, that
they could be shortened at pleasure. The *Girls' Own Paper*

was shocked by queries from daughters who wished to know whether they could attend dances within a year of their mother's death, and another question, enquiring 'How long a young widow need wear mourning for a husband she did not like', was felt to show 'an utter lack of good feeling'.

The First World War drove the first nail into the coffin of elaborate mourning. The shortage of material, the emphasis on economy and, above all, the extent of the carnage prevented mourners from assuming a distinctive status. Had the periods of mourning remained those specified by *The Queen*, there would by November 1918 scarcely have been a single colourfully dressed woman. As early as 1916 a girl writing to the aptly named *Forget-Me-Not* was told:

> The usual period of mourning would be a month. Only a very little quiet visiting is done amongst intimate friends during that time. Jewellery, except for a brooch or watch, is not worn with deep mourning. But nowadays mourning is greatly shortened and even, in some cases, not worn at all.
>
> (Forget-Me-Not, *12 February 1916*)

This letter marked a significant change in etiquette. Seven months earlier a girl had written to the same column, upset that her decision not to wear mourning had been misunderstood by her friends and her late lover's relatives:

> I have lost my dear, brave soldier boy and all my friends and also his family are angry with me because I do not wear black. But neither he nor I approved of mourning; he always begged me never to put it on for him, and so I do not. He loved me best in white, and when I can I wear it, and think of him and long for him to be with me again. But it is so hard to be looked upon as heartless that I have nearly given way more than once. Do you think I ought to do so?

No, my dear, I do not. You are showing as much respect to his memory by doing as he preferred and as you promised, as by wearing the deepest symbols of woe. Time will accustom people to your opinions, and you will have the satisfaction of knowing that you kept your word and did as he would have wished. My very true and deep sympathy in

your loss. May you receive comfort to go on with life and its
duties as bravely as did your hero boy.

(*Forget-Me-Not,* 17 July 1915)

War brought in its train sweeping social changes. One
immediate change was the slackening of chaperonage so
that sweethearts could enjoy each other's company during
the few days of leave. Indeed, by February 1916, parents
who selfishly demanded long descriptions of events at the
front from their daughters' sweethearts home on leave
were described by *Betty's Weekly* as showing 'a want of
thought' and the girl and her lover suffering this situation
were told to confront the parents and not to 'make
martyrs of yourselves as you are doing'.

Nice social distinctions were relaxed during the war
when patriotism over-rode almost everything. One girl,
for instance, writing to *Betty's Weekly* to complain that
soldiers let their girls walk on the gutter side of the
pavement, was told that 'It isn't the first time I've walked
on the outside of a pavement myself, and proud to do it,
too, when the man in khaki kept alongside.' This magazine
was aimed at working girls and reflected the dramatic
change in their readers' lives after the exodus of men to
war. A girl working in an armament factory could earn
considerably more than a Tommy in the ranks, and this
revolutionised the traditional manners of courting
couples:

> Do help me, and tell me if I'm in the right. I'm making a good screw,
> 30 shillings a week, and my boy, who is in the Welsh Fusiliers hasn't
> much more than that in pennies. So being the one who has the most
> money, I, in the meanwhile, want to pay for our seats when we go to
> the pictures, but he won't let me ... 'Gwen'

My dear little girl, I'm so glad you wrote to me about this,
and I back you up from the bottom of my heart in your
desire to pay a little towards your mutual enjoyment. Tell
your boy to swallow his pride and let you do your tiny bit. If
I could whisper in his ear I'd tell him he ought to be proud
of his girlie. I think you have hit on one of the ideas that
should be fostered wherever Tommy and Jack and their
sweethearts meet. The boys are making so little money at

the present so why shouldn't every one of their sweethearts
do the entertaining for a bit, just like 'Gwen'. Let the lads
pay the piper in peace-time, girls, but wartime's your time.
Be sure you see to it.

(Betty's Weekly, 12 February 1916)

The vote, shorter skirts and financial independence meant
that the post-war girl no longer presented herself as a
delicate hot-house flower – and was no longer treated as
such. This worried some girls:

> *Is it only the fact that your sweetheart does not give up his seat to a lady
> that annoys you with him? If so, I do not think that you have any cause
> to complain. Times have changed, as you must know, and in these
> days, when women claim equality with men, it is only right that they
> should be taken at their own valuation. You say he gives up his seat to
> an elderly person or to a woman with a baby. Then, surely, that is all
> that matters. Don't worry about trifles, my dear. Good manners are
> only kindness of heart and consideration for others, and a hefty, golf-
> playing, hard-dancing young woman is quite as able to stand as any
> young man. It's all a matter of opinion, of course, but that's my view.
> At the same time I call it simply piggish for a woman to keep her seat
> when a lame man or an old man or another woman who is older or
> heavily laden is standing. What you tell me shows that your boy simply
> discriminates and shows very good sense.*

(Polly's Paper, 7 June 1920)

A more relaxed approach to manners did not, however,
mean that the whole paraphernalia of middle-class
visiting, formal dances and calling cards disappeared
overnight. Indeed a query about who calls first and how to
make a call was printed in the January 1932 edition of
Modern Marriage and it was by no means the last of its kind.
But problem pages increasingly provided tips on how to
serve a meal in front of the mother-in-law, rather than
how to eat grapes while wearing gloves. This adjustment
to changed circumstances has continued. The difficulty
today is likely to be how to give a speech of thanks at the
W.I. flower arranging class or, to take an example from
Woman's Weekly of 1 April 1978, how to write a retirement
letter. Was it 'done', this correspondent enquired, to say
that one had enjoyed the work?

In the 1940 edition of Emily Post's *Etiquette*, that doyenne of advisers defended herself against the accusation that she dealt with an unimportant area of life:

> *One is apt to think of etiquette as being of no more real service to the average citizen than a top hat – something that is of importance to none but brides of diplomats or the newly rich or persons lately elected to political office. As a matter of fact, there is not a single thing that we do, or say, or choose, or use, or even think, that does not follow (or break) one of the exactions of taste, or tact, or ethics, or good manners, or etiquette – call it what you will.*

Though one might be tempted to ask what a bride was doing with a top hat, Mrs Post's general point is valid. To modern readers the manners of polite society in the 1850s or 1890s seem foolish, time-consuming and repressive. And no one writes to 'Mary Marryat' to ask how to behave at a pop concert. But modern readers do still frequently seek advice on matters of behaviour which appear reasonable to us because they refer to current customs.

However horrific the formalities of calling, card-leaving and tea with the vicar may now seem, they at least helped people to meet their peers. Strangers moving into a new district would have an accepted means of contacting local society. Not until the Second World War, when the age of formal etiquette was largely over, do we find a letter from a desperately lonely woman, recently moved to a large, impersonal housing estate, whose nearest approach to company was the photograph of the adviser in her weekly magazine.

Today aunties are more likely to be experts on psychology than on precedence, and few write guides to etiquette in their spare time. Their columns reflect the change of emphasis. As the printed page was gradually liberated from a publisher's morality which banned the intimately personal (be it homosexuality, incest, sexual difficulties or the mechanics of birth control), less room was given to form and more to content. Problem page advisers who previously had been content to repaint the face of society now had the opportunity to do some major surgery. As a result etiquette problems have been elbowed to one side. The subject has not, however, been dismissed. Aunties know perfectly well that most of their readers are quite as worried about having their husband's boss to dinner as they are about having an orgasm.

7

Absolute quietude on a bed
MEDICAL PROBLEMS

Not all doctors are illiterate, despite their difficulties with calligraphy. John Keats, Richard Gordon and Somerset Maugham were all medical students who preferred the pen to the scalpel. But, conversely, few journalists are skilled in medicine. Bernard Mandeville, doctor of both medicine and philosophy, and Queen Anne's physician John Arbuthnot (who may have provided *The British Apollo* with some of its more expert answers) were rare early exceptions to the rule that problem page counsellors rely principally upon bluff when diagnosing the illnesses of their readers.

Ignorance, however, was no deterrent for their fellow advisers. Readers used to the patter of quacks were eager for second opinions. In response to this demand, Grub Street published medical queries in profusion. *The Athenian Oracle* and *The British Apollo* carried answers to such questions as 'Did Adam have a navel?' and 'Was abortion always a crime?' Not every answer was definitive. 'When may it properly be said a virgin hath lost her virginity?' Dunton was asked. 'When she hath it no longer,' he replied, avoiding both the technical and the potentially offensive thereby.

Some of the early questions were obscure in the extreme. 'Why,' Dunton was asked in *The Athenian Oracle*, 'are eunuchs never afflicted with gout?' Such teasers only put him on his mettle:

There is not one eunuch in a million men, and if one eunuch of a thousand be gouty (as 'tis reasonably supposed such an instance be found amongst those luxurious ones in Turkey) 'tis near proportional and perhaps as much as falls their share.

Dunton had a genuine tolerance for the passions and frailties of human nature, a quality perhaps surprising in a man whose friends and relatives were mostly dissenters of a notably puritan cast of mind. Stern towards readers flirting with serious dissipation, he remained sympathetic to those who had indulged and were beginning to show the after-effects. To escape censure in the case of unwanted pregnancy, for example, he recommended a discreet vacation:

Gentlemen, I am a young gentlewoman in the prime of my youth, and if my glass flatters me not, tolerably handsome, likewise co-heiress of a very fair estate; there being but two sisters of us to enjoy what my aged father hath. He hath ever shown himself lovingly tender, yet he hath ever had so great an awe over us that we shall never durst give him the least suspicion of any ill conduct of our behaviour, he often assuring us that nothing should so soon quench the flame of his paternal love, as our deviation from the strict rules of pure charity and its handmaid, modesty. Now to my utter ruin and eternal shame (if anything unknowingly committed may be termed shameful) I am now with child; how, when and by whom to my greatest grief I know not; but this also I know too well, that the hour wherein my father hears of it, I am disinherited of his estate, banished his love etc. Gentlemen I earnestly implore you to give me some relief by solving these two queries:

1. Whether it be possible for a Woman to so carnally to know a man in her sleep as to conceive for I am sure this, and no way other was I got with child?

2. Whether it may be lawful to use means to put a stop to this growing mischief and kill it in the embryo; this being the only way to avert the thunderclap of my father's indignation?

To the first question, Madam, we are very positive that you are mistaken, for the thing is absolutely impossible if you know nothing of it; indeed, we had an account of a widow that made such a pretence, and she might have better credit than a maid, who can have no plea but dead drunk or in some kind of swooning fit, and our physician will hardly allow the possibility even then. So you may set your heart at rest, and think no more of the matter, except for your diversion.

As for your second query, such practices are murder and those that are so unhappy as to come under such circumstances, if they use the fore-mentioned means will certainly find the remedy worse than the disease. There are wiser methods to be taken in such cases, as a small journey and a confidant. And afterwards such a pious and good life as may redress such a heavy misfortune.

(*The Athenian Oracle*)

Such quasi-medical replies, printed with an eye to the more voyeuristic end of the market, led fellow Grub Street journalists to satirize Dunton's outpourings. The short-lived *Lacedaemonian Mercury* published one letter purporting to be from a sailor married to a tripe woman's daughter. He'd been taken by the press gang, and after an absence of fifteen months returned to find his wife giving birth. When he taxed her with the parenthood of the child she insisted it was his. 'She told me it was customary in Wapping for a woman to go fourteen months with child and sometimes seventeen and sometimes twenty as it happened.' Her reason was that the proximity of the water prevented children from 'ripening in their bellies as soon as it would in other places'. The sailor wanted to be convinced, and his informant in *The Lacedaemonian Mercury* of 21 March 1692, tried his best:

> We can tell you then, for a certain truth, that though vulgarly receiv'd opinion has fixed it at nine months, yet every day's observation shews that time to be as uncertain as the Jewish Trial of Maiden-heads or the sinking of old women to be witches. Several women, and those of no mean quality, at the other end of town, have been delivered at five or six months after matrimony; nay, we have heard of some, who to be sure were of a sanguine complexion, that had occasion for a midwife after two.

'Friend Tar' was encouraged, 'since the bone of your side fairly assures you that it is the custom in Wapping', to accept the overlong gestation period and 'we'd even advise you not to heed what Aristotle or Culpepper say, but believe her ...'

Dunton's record with the fanciful is uneven. He rejects the idea that the blackness of negroes was the result of Noah's curse upon Ham and his posterity since 'We rather think that their going naked in a climate where the sun is extremely hot did contribute a little to it'. On the other hand he evidently shared the popular belief that a child's appearance was formed by the imagination. He was asked 'Why are children oftener like the father than the mother?' His answer ascribed it jointly to the 'good women who are present at the gossiping' and the thoughts of the mother, 'she having the idea of the father's face, not her own, in her mind, that of the child may be form'd accordingly like him, not her'. He gave a similar reply to another reader:

Q. What is the reason when a Woman cuckolds her husband, the child is commonly like the father?

A. Pray – whom shou'd a child resemble sooner than his father? But perhaps the querist, somewhat in haste to be fingering his wager, has mistook the right stating of his question – If he would know why a child begotten in adultery is commonly like the husband of the adultress; 'tis our opinion that this seldom happens to any but women of a very timorous nature – who being touch'd in the action, with a deep sense of the enormity of the crime they are committing, have their thoughts attentively on the person of their absent husbands, so that a likeness is stamp'd on the child then begotten by the active force of a powerful imagination.

(*The British Apollo*)

Dunton's purported postbag sometimes owed more to his own spite than to his readers' curiosity. He was particularly merciless to Sir William Read, a former tailor turned quack oculist, who was knighted by Queen Anne in 1705:

Q. I am by trade a weaver and was forced to make a break of it by reason of great losses I had, and you must know that I have a great many recipes to cure a festered wound … Now I will be advised by you gentlemen whether I shall turn doctor or set to weaving again?

A. Turn doctor by all means, man, since you talk so learnedly of the matter, and never fear of offending the physicians, for you are likely to take a great deal of work from them.'

(The British Apollo)

Nice 'Mr Bickerstaff' on *The Tatler* never used so blunt a hacksaw. The lightest flick of irony was sufficient weapon for him:

Mr Bickerstaff, I am very much afflicted with the gravel, which makes me sick and peevish. I desire to know of you, is it reasonable that any of my acquaintances should take advantage over me at this time, and afflict me with long visits, because they are idle and I am confin'd. Pray, Sir, reform the town in this matter …

It is with some so hard a thing to employ their time, that it is a great good fortune when they have a friend indispos'd that they may be punctual in perplexing him, when he is recover'd enough to be in that state which cannot be call'd sickness or health, when he is too well to deny company, and too ill to receive 'em. It is no uncommon case, if a man is of any figure or power in the world, to be congratulated into a relapse.

Mr Johnson in *The Censor*, in 1717, found himself dealing with the fashionable disease of 'melancholy'. He was solicitous for the health of a young lady, come to town on an annual visit 'for new cloaths and a turn in Hide-park'. But, instead of being cheered by such gay dissipation, she wondered 'whether I shall be able to wear those I have bought with any tolerable satisfaction. The continual tolling of the bells at night has thrown such a gloom on my temper and disturb'd me with such melancholy that I cannot rest for the apprehension of death laid in a cold grave.' 'Emilia' was diagnosed to be suffering from 'a poverty of the Animal Spirits' and the remedy proposed was to 'guard against solitude and contemplation … and whenever she must think of death, let her consider it as the end of nature and her best privilege.'

For over a century medical queries became, first unfashionable, and then unmentionable, in magazines adhering to Bowdlerised standards. But when the general problem page re-emerged in the 1840s it carried a proportion of medical letters, with a new emphasis on psychosomatic illness. The reasons for this are not clear-cut. The doctors themselves may have been responsible. At an average fee of a guinea a visit, a little hypochondria could help a struggling practice, and strained only the bedside manner, not the competence, of the attending physician.

But the explanation may lie in the increasing isolation of the middle-class Victorian woman. She lived in a suburban house, separated by a rail journey from her husband during the day, with only the company of her children and a teenage servant. Those edging their way up the social ladder were particularly prone to loneliness and hence depression. It has been estimated that the average middle-class couple in nineteenth century Britain moved house three times in their lives, each move involving an improvement in their status and a consequent need to establish a new circle of friends. This was a daunting prospect for many women, with little time to spare for making formal social contacts, despite their desperate need for helpful neighbours. In some respects they were little different from the librium-popping suburban housewives of today. But though laudanum may sometimes have served as a substitute for contemporary drugs there was nothing equivalent to the modern companionship of radio or television.

Children, idolised in the problem pages as a cure for depression, were frequently its cause. Yearly confinements brought annual post-natal depressions, and almost as soon as many Victorian women emerged from the mental desolation of child-birth they were faced with morning sickness and another nine months of pregnancy. For some women it was not a cheering prospect, and the following advice might have struck them as somewhat inept:

> *An unhappy woman – You ask us for a few suggestions to relieve you from your constant state of depression ... The safest and best of all occupations for such sufferers as are fit for it, is intercourse with young children. Next to this comes honest genuine acquaintanceship among the poor; not the parade of mere charity visiting grounded on soup tickets and blankets, but an intercourse between the parties.*
>
> (The London Journal, 27 September 1845)

This letter is only one example of the many from married women who found their lives dull, empty and without point.

Daughters living at home were also often affected by an atmosphere of despondency. Those who did not devote their energies to escape through marriage often turned their health into a hobby, imagining that they had new and horrible diseases daily. Though *Cassell's Illustrated Family Magazine* always referred its readers to a doctor, it recognised that many queries did not come from the gravely ill. It wrote to seventeen year old 'Sarah M' on 15 March 1856, for example, 'The very circumstances of your health being good, and your countenance rosy would, independent of youth, be quite sufficient in themselves to satisfy us you are not suffering from cancer.' Specifically, however, Sarah had been worried that she had cancer of the breast and, unlike the modern problem page which provides detailed instructions on how to hunt for unusual lumps around the nipples, *Cassell's* did not give any self-diagnostic hints.

Were Sarah to take *Cassell's* advice and seek medical help, she could not be examined by the doctor unchaperoned. A wise precaution, perhaps, if many doctors felt like one who corresponded with *The London Journal*:

> *GAF (Dublin). Unless you can control your passions, the sooner you quit the medical profession the better. Temptation, we know, is very powerful; even the good St Anthony could not resist the witchery of a pair of laughing black eyes, but a man of rectitude is capable of resisting the longings of an impure heart and can so train himself, however impetuous his temperament may be, as to be able to walk through life as becomes a man and a Christian. When in the throes of your distemper, think, upon all occasions attempt to impart vigour to the tone of your*

mind, and depend upon it, you will gradually become more cool and collected in your deportment.

(The London Journal, *8 December 1849*)

The memory of this letter lingered on. And in the last decade of Victoria's reign, girls such as 'Flighty Seventeen' (*Girls' Own Paper,* 2 June 1894) were still firmly admonished 'You should never go to the doctor or the dentist unaccompanied by an older woman.'

As the nineteenth century progressed, the social status of the medical profession improved. Even surgeons, formerly on a par with butchers, were allowed to use the front entrance and leave their hats in the hall. At the same time the midwife lost ground, except in working-class areas. Woman patients now had no choice – even for the most intimate of complaints they must face an examination by a male doctor. Modesty however, on the part of both doctor and patient, was often so strong that essential examinations were omitted and women sometimes found it difficult even to talk to these busy, professional men. Despite an expansion in the number of doctors by 53 per cent between 1861 and 1891, women became more rather than less reliant on problem pages and health manuals. Many magazines responded by adding a medical note-book to their page.

Others had a separate medical problem page, run either by a doctor, or by a journalist who spent the major part of his time compiling home medical manuals (big business in the Victorian era) and providing the medical snippets for general compendia such as the best selling *Enquire Within.* By the 1880s there were several popular monthly magazines, such as *The Family Doctor,* devoted solely to medical matters and home nursing. These would discuss the detailed treatment of particular diseases, while the more general family magazines concentrated upon illness on a grander scale.

In the 1840s the causes of most infectious diseases had been a mystery. Although cholera was known to strike hardest in the slum areas of large towns (though not, by any means, exclusively, as the death of Prince Albert was to prove), its connection with tainted water was still only one of many theories. *The London Journal* in 1846 plumped for a decidedly eccentric explanation:

> *AF – The volcanic origin of cholera is a theory that has attracted some attention because of its feasibility. In the fiery centre and fermenting bowels of the earth there are constantly being generated millions and millions of cubic feet of the most deleterious gases, highly inimical to animal and vegetable life, which ordinarily are safely emitted from the vast belching mouths or craters of more than 4,000 permanently active volcanoes, or volcan chimneys – some 10,000 feet above the level of the sea ... whence the noxious vapours are partially decomposed by the air, and safely ascend to the upper strata of the atmosphere. The cholera and many other epidemic poisons most probably arise from the well-known temporary inaction or blocked condition of some one or more of these volcanic tunnels.*
>
> (The London Journal, *14 April 1846*)

Another entry had cholera 'stalking from East to West', claiming victims in its wake. By 1862, however, Chadwick's energetic campaigning had led to a general acceptance of the connection between cholera and water-carried germs. The mid-nineteenth century accordingly saw an enormous expansion in public health legislation and the creation of effective sewerage systems in towns.

But in some respects Chadwick and his fellow reformers did their work too well. Already in middle-class households dirt had become associated with the indigent, gin-swilling lower classes. But now that it was also actively associated with disease, the middle-class matron became convinced that cleanliness was not only morally next to Godliness. It might also prevent a premature departure for His realm. As a result she both risked working herself to death to keep her house spotless, and endangered her family's health by connecting fresh air (you never knew where it had been) with germs. Draughts were consequently banned, as far as possible, with rooms deprived of all ventilation but the chimney, where a smouldering coal fire filled the air with dust. It was because doctors were well aware that fresh air was being excluded from many households that they so often suggested a holiday by the seaside. This killed several health hazards at once. It provided fresh air and exercise. But it also provided the chance of a rest for Mum.

Sea-bathing for reasons of health, however, was a complicated business and not to be embarked upon lightly. *The Family Friend* gave details of how to derive the maximum benefit from a quick dip in the sea:

> *Seabathing M – To have the greatest benefit from sea bathing, it is proper to remain but a very short time in the water – not exceeding two or three minutes. If longer, the body should be kept immersed under the surface the whole time, and in constant motion, in order to promote the circulation of the blood, from the centre to the extremities. It is much better to remain completely immersed in deep, than to take repeated plunges in shallow water. On coming out, the body should be wiped dry with a rough cloth and the ordinary dress resumed as quickly as possible. It is more necessary to replace the usual vestments quickly than to be extremely anxious that the surface of the skin is completely dry, as any wetness from salt water is not likely to be prejudicial. After bathing use moderate exercise to promote the return of the heat of the body; taking care that it neither be violent nor too long continued. If chilliness occasionally ensues, breakfast in the forenoon, some warm soup or broth may be taken, and remember that if immersion, instead of being succeeded by a glow on the surface of the skin, is followed by dullness, langour or headache, bathing in the sea should not be persisted in.*
>
> (The Family Friend, *1852*)

Walking was made to sound an equally complicated business by *Twice a Week*. On 25 June 1862, 'Mouth Open' was told to shut it. 'The nasal passages are clearly the medium through which respiration was, by our Creator, designed to be carried on,' the doctor wrote. 'The difference in the exhaustion of strength by a long walk with the mouth firmly closed, and respiration carried on through the nostrils cannot be conceived as possible by those who have never tried the experiment.'

Bicycling, in the view of some aunties a somewhat 'fast' sport, was encouraged by others on the grounds of health. *The Family Doctor* on 2 July 1883, declared: 'We believe bicycle riding to be free from any injurious effects, if indulged in moderately. Many medical men, however, maintain that it is harmful, no matter how practised.' The

usually censorious *Girls' Own Paper* also found bicycling a
suitable and healthy sport, but only after Queen Victoria
had given one of her young grand-children a machine.

At the start of the Victorian era most homes operated as
their own hospital, with one room almost permanently in
use as a sick-room. Every middle-class girl, long before
Florence Nightingale had made nursing outside the home
socially acceptable, was taught the basic skills of the nurse.
Mothers bore their huge families in the bedroom and their
infants died there; elderly parents were nursed through
final illnesses upstairs while consumptive sisters wasted
away in the drawing room. Many diseases which clear up
on the swallowing of a couple of pills were then treated by
enforced rest, and those which now hardly warrant taking
time off work were often severely disabling:

> *Diarrhoea – The first, the most important and the most indispensable
> item for the arrest and cure of the looseness of the bowels, is absolute
> quietude on a bed. Nature herself always prompts this by disinclining us
> to locomotion. The next thing to do is to eat nothing but common rice,
> parched like coffee, and then boiled, and taken with a little salt and
> butter. Drink little or no liquid of any kind. Bits of ice may be eaten and
> swallowed at will. Every step taken in diarrhoea, every spoonful of
> liquid only aggravates the disease. If locomotion is compulsory, the
> misfortune of the necessity may be lessened by having a stout piece of
> woollen flannel bound tightly round the abdomen, so as to be doubled in
> and kept well in place. In the practices of many years we have never
> failed to notice a gratifying result to follow these observations.*
>
> (Twice a Week, *11 May 1862*)

Common sense, rather than medical expertise, was the
Girls' Own Paper's forte. Rejection of the Bloomer costume
did not lead them to countenance tight lacing and other
excesses of the fashionable.

> *Ruby – So many of our girls complain of indigestion that we have taken
> the matter into serious consideration, and we recommend them to stiffen
> their dress bodices with whalebone and leave off wearing stays. Let the
> ribs expand well, and the process of digestion will not then be interfered
> with. This is likewise our prescription for the red nose trouble, of which
> many of our readers complain. An extra woven vest would be an
> excellent substitute for stays because it would be elastic. You would all*

then approximate a little nearer to the classic forms of a Venus, instead
of a wooden figure.

(Girls' Own Paper, 11 November 1893)

Delicate health in a man, or more particularly a boy, was regarded as highly suspect. If the word consumption trembled on the pens of the *Girls' Own Paper*'s aunties, masturbation was what leaped into the minds of their male counterparts on the *Boys' Own Paper* as the most common 'disease' likely to attack the adolescent. Dire warnings abounded for self-admitted practioners of the solitary pastime. The columns of the *Boys' Own Paper* in the 1890s covered little else. Run by a Dr Gordon Stables, who wrote in 1902 'I cannot recall that I have ever given my boy readers a single sentence of bad advice,' they specialised in predicting feeble-mindedness, blindness and premature senility for readers spurning the right path. 'Bad habits', for instance, was told 'Coffins are cheap and boys like you are not of much use to the world.' 'Pimples' received more reassurance, 'Nothing to do with the bad habits you have given up, and thus saved your life or reason.' Dr Stables frequently suggested that readers indulging in the awful vice should seek medical help:

> *School vice – Have you not a family doctor you can trust? Glad indeed you have seen the terrible error. Yes, there is an operation for the evil after-effects; but I don't think it is necessary in your case. The cold bath every morning and take plenty of good, non-stimulating food. Why should they make withered, shaky old men of themselves before their time, or be just like an old thistle after it has shed its down?*

(Boys' Own Paper, 28 February 1899)

Dr Stables may have added to his readers' neuroses, but he probably saved some of them money by inveighing against quacks selling cures, stretching from rubber bands to electric belts. More than usually dangerous was a device widely advertised in boys' magazines. This consisted of a spiked ring, which fitted relatively comfortably over a limp penis, with no harm coming to the wearer so long as an erection was avoided. Dr Stables, however, preferred his boys to rely on such British virtues as self-control and courage:

> ... *I credit you, however, with honest bulldog pluck and staying power, and I feel sure that having made a fixed and determined resolve to get rid of any bad habits, smoking or anything worse and more fatal, though you may stumble, and fall at times, you will never quit hold. Having laid hold of the plough, you will not look behind you till you stand victor at the head of the furrow.*
>
> (Boys' Own Paper, *August 1902*)

Following years of stern remonstrances to individuals, Dr Stables finally doled out 'some advice to struggling lads' wholesale. At no point did he directly refer to masturbation:

> *1. Do not lie awake in bed of a morning. Never give way to any thought while in bed.*
> *2. Be up and doing when you are awake, no matter how long the morning may seem. But it can hardly feel long if you have books to read, or studies to engage your attention, pets to see or walks to take.*
> *3. Get into the cold tub as you turn out. Verily, it is life to the nerveless.*
> *4. Take exercise at the same time every day. Join a gymnasium, but see to it that you make no bad or careless companions thereat.*
> *5. Eat slowly and well of strengthening, non-fattening food. If you eat more oatmeal and less pudding, you could grow up as healthy as a pipe-major.*
> *6. Pray to Heaven to assist you. Prayer gives comfort, encouragement and strength. You cannot do wrong, then, to make your life a prayer. Yet do not forget that there are means within your power to retain health, and we have ample instinct to guide us to these. Heaven helps those who help themselves.*
>
> (Boys' Own Paper, *1901*)

Masturbation was long regarded as an exclusively male vice. There is no mention of it in the *Boys' Own Paper*'s stable-mate, the *Girls' Own Paper*, although it is possible that the aunties did, in private replies, foster the prevalent Victorian myth that protruding vaginal lips were a permanent disfigurement resulting from masturbation by girls. It was not until the 1930s that *Peg's Paper* and *Woman* finally recognised that girls did masturbate, and then their advice tended to be very much in line with Dr Stables. A typical answer appeared in *Glamour* during the Second World War, 'A cure for this "trouble" depends on your friend – she must control herself, or she will get into an unhealthy nervous state.' Female masturbation is still today regarded, if not as a sin, then as a poor substitute for the real thing and a sad admission of a failure to have a well regulated sex life. The revelation, for instance, by Ms Hite in 1977 that most American women not only masturbated, but found it more satisfactory than the climaxes achieved through intercourse, was regarded as slightly shocking, even by the trendy 'Look' page in *The Sunday Times*.

Often what did not appear in Victorian problem pages was as significant as what did. Venereal disease was one topic which was taboo, in fact though not in implication. Though it appeared explicitly only in the highly specialised correspondence column of *The Lancet*, it lurked behind much moralistic advice elsewhere. Indeed, the implication was often that any loose behaviour was bound to lead, in the girl's case, to pregnancy, and in the man's to VD.

It was not until the 1920s, in fact, that discussion of VD became possible, although it was still not entirely explicit, as is shown by the following letter:

> *Paddy (Salford). I certainly think you did the right thing in giving up the first boy, my dear. As you are probably aware, the dread disease from which this boy suffers, is extremely infectious and marriage with him would have been the natural result of keeping up this friendship and would of course have been little short of disastrous. So really, you have been very wise in acting as you have done.*
>
> (Pam's Paper, *6 November 1926*)

Only with the explicit advertisements put out by the Ministry of Health during the Second World War did VD become a mentionable word. The official message 'better safe than sorry' was loyally backed up by the more personal approach of the problem page. Widespread ignorance as to how the disease was transmitted, however, continued:

I am in terrible distress. I have been engaged to a boy for nearly three years and now find that whilst he has been away he has caught VD. What worries me is – can VD be caught by kissing, as I kissed him a lot since he's been home? Worried 29.

No, you can dismiss your worry. Venereal Disease, or VD as it is called, is spread through intercourse with an infected person. So long as you avoid loose behaviour, and are chaste and modest, you need not fear you will get this terrible disease.

(*Glamour*, 11 November 1945)

When Dr Schoenfeld, the 'Dr Hippocrates' of *The International Times*, was asked, over thirty years later, whether it was possible to catch VD from using the bathrooms of bars in the rougher parts of town he replied more sharply. 'Certainly it is possible to get a venereal disease in the bathroom. But bathroom floors are usually very cold and hard ...'

The open discussion of VD on problem pages, at the time of the Second World War, was roughly contemporaneous with the thawing in printed attitudes towards birth control. Prior to the 1930s, contraceptive methods were not openly discussed on problem pages although newspapers had, long before this date, carried advertisements for leaflets explaining the right way to a planned family. This omission reflected the curious double standard which had led to the trial and conviction of Charles Bradlaugh and Mrs Annie Besant in 1877, and the odium surrounding Marie Stopes. Their crime lay not in espousing the cause of contraception but in publicising birth control methods to the working classes, as Richard Carlisle and Francis Place had done before them.

Books on contraception with a limited, middle-class readership, priced at five shillings or half a crown, could be sold freely, as Annie Besant pointed out at her trial. The woman with only sixpence to spare, however, was not allowed to purchase a cheap pamphlet on the same topic. Women's magazines with mass circulations prudently decided to play safe and ignore the topic entirely. For this reason, problem pages throw no light on the debate as to why middle-class family size, which peaked in 1877, declined thereafter. Was it that the publicity following the Bradlaugh/Besant trial served to further the case of contraception amongst the middle classes more effectively than any pamphlet? Or was it, as the Banks suggest in *Prosperity and Parenthood*, that the middle-classes coincidentally decided at this date, for compelling economic reasons, to limit the size of their families? No easy answer is available. Even in the mid-1930s, the only methods of birth control discussed openly were withdrawal and the rhythm method. And still today, *Woman* publishes two editions of its problem page if contraception is mentioned – one for Great Britain and another for Roman Catholic Ireland.

'Nurse Janet', the medical expert on *Peg's Paper* in the 1930s, confronted an increasing number of sexual and gynaecological problems. Resolutely optimistic in the face of missed periods, she doled out anaemia charts like sweeties even when 'we have the knowledge you have been acting foolishly, so there is always a risk'. 'Nurse Janet' would hint at the rhythm method or withdrawal, encouraging her readers to write to her privately but warning them that these methods cause 'a good deal of nervous strain' and are 'far from trustworthy'. On the printed page, however, she preferred to advise 'live a natural and complete life' – so long as the correspondent was married, of course.

That marriage should be synonymous with procreation was Nurse Janet's view and she dealt firmly with one correspondent who, though married, did not feel ready yet to 'sink into motherhood'. She wrote reprovingly that motherhood 'should be a most uplifting experience, and I do not feel that you are too young to have your first baby when you are 19'. A mother with one child, who wished to know how to avoid having more, was reluctantly told of the existence of birth control clinics (though no address was given on the printed page) but was warned that 'The world would be in a very bad way if every mother who had difficulty rearing one child should immediately decide she did not want any more'.

Some aunties were both more sympathetic and more informative than 'Nurse Janet'. The counsellor on *Mab's Weekly* was less convinced that marriage must immediately bring children in its wake:

> *My fiancé is earning enough for us to set up home – providing we do not think of having a family yet. We shall have to be economical even then, but we feel it would be worth it, particularly as at present he lives away from his home in uncomfortable 'digs'. But my mother, whom we have told, is utterly shocked, and says that marriage is primarily for having a family, and it is not right deliberately to avoid it. I want to consider her opinion, but I simply do not see it that way. Shall we marry on the understanding that we put off having a family yet, or ought we really to wait? – Wendy.*

Frankly 'Wendy', I think you should get married. Don't you remember that in the service it also says marriage is for the 'mutual society, help and comfort of married folk'? Try not to upset your mother who is only sharing an opinion held by many of her generation, but just go ahead. Don't however, put off the family longer than you must, for everyone who knows anything about little children realises that parents just have to sacrifice a lot of their freedom for them ...

(Mab's Weekly, 17 November 1934)

In the mid-1930s, contraceptive methods were still largely the same as those available to the Victorians – the condom, the diaphram, and pessaries. But, by the 1930s, the average middle-class family had one or two children, where 75 years earlier six children had been common. So although the aunties preserved their public silence over the mechanics of contraception, it was probably to protect the sensibilities of their 'maiden aunt' readers and the more adventurous of the unmarried young, rather than to prevent their married readers from taking precautions.

Most aunties, however, preferred in the 1930s to discuss matters above, rather than below, the belt. 'Nerves', a disease first discovered in the Victorian problem page, reappeared in the 1930s. Deprived of any chance of marriage by the death toll of the First World War, working at dull, repetitive jobs, many girls found they were becoming snappy, depressed and desperate. One girl, writing to *Woman's Magazine*, wondered whether 'I'm very wicked and do you think I ought to go away and live by myself?'. No, the auntie didn't think she was wicked, what she needed was care and affection rather than censure:

> *I'm sure what is really wrong with you is physical trouble, no doubt you are tired and strained to such a degree that your weariness is poisoning your mind ... No, I don't think you should live alone; that will but lead to introspection and further depressions.*

The auntie recommended going to bed early, fresh air and good, wholesome meals, with lots of milk. But above all, 'When you are rested, your mind will be more balanced and you will begin to realise that God is lovingly protecting you and that this world is not such a terrible place after all.'

The preoccupation with 'nerves' disappeared in the events of 1939, with the aunties dealing with the more fundamental problems of war and its victims. And there is one very notable difference between letters on medical subjects during the Great War and the Second World War. The former dealt exclusively with physical injury. The latter gave more and more attention to mental and psychological damage. During neither war did aunties allow their columns to be filled with depressing tales of maimed and broken men returning from the battle fields. But in the Second World War it was clear, from a couple of letters slipping through the aunties' self-censorship net, that for some the tragedy was not that the war had removed their heroes for ever, but that it had returned them fundamentally altered:

> *... My husband was employed in the building trade which took him a lot from home, but we were always very happy. Then he had his call up and went into the Navy, as both his brothers were serving there. In less than a year he was invalided out, and he has some kind of heart trouble, although I don't think it can be very serious. But since he has come home he has acted very strange, and has always wanted a separate bedroom, which he never did before. He is very quiet and not like he used to be. Do you think he loves another woman?*

No, indeed I do not. Although you appear to think the heart trouble is not very serious, what is the truth about this? ... I think you should be more sympathetic for a man wouldn't have been excused duty in the navy unless it was more than a trifling ailment of the heart ... It is quite enough for a man to be invalided out and know that he is not sound and fit to make him relapse into quiet ways. Do your best to cheer him up instead of letting nasty suspicions enter your mind, for which, as far as I can see, you have not the slightest foundation.

                                        (*Glamour*, 10 April 1945)

An auntie with a suspicious mind might today probe further. Had her husband in the heady atmosphere of an all male ship discovered he was a homosexual? Was the diagnosis by naval doctors of a heart attack a euphemism for a mental breakdown? Was he feeling emasculated and uninterested in sex because he felt that, since he was not fit to fight, he was not fit for anything? None of these possibilities was discussed in *Glamour*. But her reply to the nagging wife was probably sound, whatever lay behind her reader's current marital difficulties.

Prisoners of war, rather than fighting men, led to some of the most severe problems when couples were reunited. Many POWs returned emaciated and mentally scarred, and their wives found it difficult to cope with their nightmares and violent changes of mood:

My boy was taken prisoner in Libya and sent to one of the enemy's worst camps. He should have been dead except for the Red Cross parcels and he nearly died through brutality. He has just got home a wreck of what he was and he seems so moody at times I am half afraid. Do you advise me to put off the marriage for a time or should I give in to him and get married?

... no wonder he gets moody at times. Wouldn't you be after all the privations and horrors he has endured? Nazi brutality has much to answer for, and I can well understand how this dreadful treatment will have changed him ...

                                        (*Glamour*, 17 July 1945)

Injuries sustained during the Second World War led, as in
the previous conflict, to a crop of letters from readers who
found their lovers returned to them disfigured or
incomplete. Some of these letters displayed a fundamental
ignorance of physiology:

> *I am engaged to a young airman who has lost three fingers of his left
> hand and also lost the sight of an eye. This happened on his 39th trip so
> you can see he has been through a lot. Now he is grounded, but he says
> he hopes to fly again. What is worrying me is that I have been told if I
> marry him, my children might be blind or cripples, and as we both love
> children and had planned to get married at Easter I should like to know
> if this is true. I cannot give him up whatever happens.*

No, it is not true. Put that fear out of your mind. When an
accident causes some disablement, this kind of disability is
not hereditary and transferable to the children.

(Glamour, 13 January 1945)

It would be premature of us to mock the ignorance of
women a mere thirty years ago, and to presume that the
readers of women's magazines today are better informed.
Similar confusions are still common. In October 1977,
Lesley Garner, a columnist on *The Sunday Times* 'Look'
page, was astonished to read a letter in *Woman*, written by
a white girl who had, some years previously, given birth to
an illegitimate, racially-mixed baby. She was now about to
marry a Caucasian, but feared that the negro blood 'still
inside her' would produce more black children. Lesley
Garner might have been shocked and surprised, but the
problem page aunties were not. They assured her that
such ignorance, and incidentally such guilt, are
commonplace and that ignorance about bodily functions
and appearance are one of the staple components of the
modern problem page.

The 1960s and 1970s have seen the arrival of a new range
of moral problems, created by the development of medical
techniques. Children who would once have died now live
to be burdens to their parents, many of whom feel guilty if
they sentence them to perpetual institutional life. Other
children are never born.

Abortion, once dismissed on the grounds that 'such practices are murder', is an area of medicine which remains highly controversial. Claire Rayner was one of the first aunties to tackle the subject after the Abortion Act had made National Health abortions more widely (though, contrary to a wide-spread misconception, not universally) available. Writing in *Petticoat* on 18 October 1969, she explained the procedure for those who wished, or were forced, to by-pass their G.P. and the N.H.S. Conscious that doctors are willing only exceptionally to consider an abortion later than sixteen weeks, and that most prefer a dead-line of twelve weeks, aunties always give letters dealing with abortion priority. It is, however, a subject rarely discussed in their columns. Most counsellors believe the 110-word published answer is insufficient space to devote to the implications of abortion.

But even more emotive is the contemporary recognition that certain kinds of anti-social behaviour have their roots in mental disturbance. Alcohol is one social malaise now recognised as a disease; gambling is another. Neither of these, however, even approaches the shock effect of child-molesting:

> We have been married for six years; we have no children but have always been very happy together. Last year, however, I had a horrible shock when my husband was arrested for molesting a young girl. I could not believe he had done such a thing; I kept thinking I would wake up from this nightmare.
>
> My husband was given a suspended sentence and ordered to have psychiatric treatment, which he has been having. Nothing like this has happened before, and he has promised it will never happen again. I hate living here now as we are shunned by most of our neighbours, but my husband does not want to move because he says the psychiatrist is helping him. But I think that if we move we could put the past behind us and make a fresh start in a new area.

Miserable as it may be for you to feel that you are being ostracized by your neighbours, I am afraid that if you did move without your husband finishing his treatment, you could be taking your problem with you and your nightmare might start all over again. Ask you husband if he could arrange for you to talk to his psychiatrist so that you can be helped to understand what led your husband to commit this offence. It really is more important for him to have the treatment he needs than to move house; otherwise another young girl could be harmed and your husband might then be sent to prison.

(*Woman's Realm*, September 1976)

This letter would probably not have appeared on the printed page even a decade ago. Many of Claire Shepherd's readers may well have considered that she was too 'soft' in her attitude towards the offender. The view that the modern criminal should see the doctor, when his predecessor would have faced the warder or the hangman, is not universally popular.

Though counsellors today are unwilling to invade the doctor's province, and are particularly wary of being used as an anti-doctor device, they will often admit to an anger at the physician's insensitivity to the problems of his female patients. One publication for doctors, *The General Practitioner*, has discovered that eighty per cent of its readers do not bother even to skim its articles on women's diseases. It is not altogether surprising that some women's magazines now run a doctor's column, such as 'Dr Meredith' in *Woman's Own*, in tandem with their agony column. Increasingly the conventional problem page tries to refer medical difficulties back to the reader's general practitioner. But many letters are a hotch-potch of medical problems, depression, financial difficulties and emotional strain. Not every G.P. has the time, skill or inclination to unravel the strands and help a patient cope. In a world compartmentalised by specialists, the problem page remains one of the few places where the bewildered can get comfort and, possibly, help.

8

Benefit of clergy
RELIGION IN THE PROBLEM PAGE

Given His omniscience, it is not surprising that God has always figured largely in the problem pages. The word of God, suitably interpreted, has been used to reinforce morality buckling under temptation, to chivvy the indecisive, and to threaten the wicked. His character may have changed somewhat, from the vengeful figure of the seventeenth century to the more helpful presence of recent years. Essentially, however, His role as the ultimate arbiter of morals has not altered.

In the formative stages of the problem page, the years between 1690 and 1720, the ethics of the Ten Commandments were binding and took precedence over all man-made standards. God was the judge, the jury and the hangman, with a more occasional function as comforter. By the middle of the nineteenth century religion was beginning to be used rather differently. Increasingly it was invoked to reinforce standards which society had independently decreed to be correct or desirable. God was awarded the role of an elevated school-prefect, with eyes in the back of His head. But He was not now presented by the aunties as the source of immediate retribution. That function was more and more left to the moral judgement and social pressure of one's neighbours. By the mid-twentieth century God was used by the agony column as a friendly witness, a sympathetic ally in the difficult fight to establish and obey moral standards. His job, no longer punitive, was to strengthen good resolves, and to reassure the lost and the puzzled.

Throughout this long process of adjustment problem pages have very rarely been used for simple religious propaganda. Many of the earliest writers, the hacks of Grub Street, were clergymen manqués whose wild behaviour, or failure to obtain a living, had obliged them to turn to the only other employment for which their learning qualified them. Most of them could, when required turn out a pugnacious sectarian pamphlet. But as aunties they were of necessity confined, like their successors, to the practical bearing of their creed, the humdrum questions of everyday morality. As clergymen they would have been free to choose their own text from the Bible. As advisers their starting point came from their readers, and the confines of the medium left little room for doctrinal self-indulgence.

John Dunton, the father of the problem page, was never himself a clergyman, though he did have strong ecclesiastical connections. For three generations his family had been country clergy. His wife was a minister's daughter and at least one of his sisters-in-law married into the cloth. What is more, he was intimately acquainted with religious disagreement. His in-laws were evenly divided between those whose conscience allowed them to remain Anglicans, and those who chose instead the thornier path of dissent.

Such division and debate were a central part of the life of his age. As a loyal subject, however, Dunton carefully avoided any unorthodox or rash pronouncement on religious matters. Despite his claim to have a bevy of eminent churchmen on his team of advisers, he confined himself to such inoffensive topics as whether or not angels conversed, and if so in what language.

Above all he was concerned with the practical application of Christian morality, and with dissuading his readers from sins with which he seems himself to have been all too well acquainted. One correspondent admitted to a 'vicious course of living' which involved drinking and, while under the influence, contracting 'too great a familiarity with a Woman who being sensible how much I despise her in my more sober and sedate thoughts, endeavours chiefly to seduce me in my extravagance'. She usually succeeded, though the writer recognised that 'while I embrace her, I embrace my ruin'. Dunton was more concerned with actions than intentions:

> *That fornication is damnable without repentance is own'd by all but Papists and Atheists – and 'tis plain that there's no repentance without amendment and we doubt an amendment while you are near her, which if there not be, you ought to flee the fair destroyer, tho' twas to the ends of the earth. We have given you our advice as brief and close as possible, and pray God give you the grace to follow it.*
>
> (The Athenian Oracle)

Another of Dunton's readers wished to know whether he could pray to God asking for the death of his wife. He had been separated from her for some years but, of course, was not free to re-marry until death did them part. *The Athenian Oracle* felt that 'If she's fit for Heaven, she's fit for you' and suggested that 'twould yet be handsomer to submit to God's will and wait with patience'. Alternatively he might pray instead that God would convert her into a more lovable human being.

Just occasionally Dunton allowed good works to atone for past misdeeds. *The British Apollo* advised a former pirate, whose conscience was troubled by his bloody deeds, to hand over his invaluable charts of the East Indies to the British authorities. Dunton did not commit himself as to the forgiveness of God, but was sanguine that her Majesty, the head of His church, might in these circumstances grant him a royal pardon.

A similar brand of enlightened pragmatism was displayed when a clergyman wrote to *The Post-Angel* about a wicked wretch in the next parish who was living with his niece and had several children by her. He asked 'whether it does not concern every good Christian (and minister especially) to take cognizance of such villainy, and to do as much as in them lies, all they can to suppress this complicated sin of adultery and incest'. Dunton thought so, but warned the vicar to avoid taking punitive action which would leave these children fatherless and dependent on the Parish for support.

One genuinely ecclesiastical member of Dunton's small team of regular answerers on *The Athenian Oracle* was Samuel Wesley, father of the founders of Methodism. His moral attitudes were harsher than those of his editor, and he was eventually to break with Dunton after accusing him, justly enough, of licentious living. Failure to keep one's word was, in his eyes, a particularly heinous offence:

> *Q. ... I am a single woman and there is a certain marry'd man that has made all the vows and protestations that can be, that if his wife should die, he would never marry any woman but me, I making the same to him, and wishing if he did marry any other, God might strike him dead, the same minute: However, his wife is still in good health and he has disobliged me so highly that out of revenge I would now marry: Pray your judgement, Whether I may do so without committing a sin?*

> A. ... Your mutual resolution and promise was highly imprudent, tho' we cannot say 'twas simply considered absolutely unlawful, therefore we think it obliged; nor are such imprecations as these to be played with, or made to be broken on any caprice or pique that may happen, much less out of revenge, as you yourself acknowledge which would be adding a new sin to perjury, and perhaps others that we know nothing of.
>
> *(The Athenian Oracle)*

A slightly more sympathetic reply was given to a young man faced with a faithless woman. While courting her he rashly wished 'a most dreadful mischance might befall me, if I ever married any other' but the lady concerned had proved 'a base woman'. Did this free him from the curse? *The British Apollo* thought so, but advised in future that their correspondent should 'avoid all manner of imprecations and not rashly venture to entangle yourself in such ensnaring as well as unwarrantable circumstances'.

This strict view of the sanctity of a promise was obviously not universally held, for it gave rise to a number of parodies. *The Spectator*, for instance, published a query from 'Clara', a widow, if 'she be obliged to continue single according to a vow made to her husband at the time of his presenting her with a diamond necklace, she being informed by a very pretty young fellow of good conscience, that such vows are in their nature, sinful'. Tom Browne, another Grub Street journalist, took his parody one stage further. His correspondent had made a solemn vow 'to touch no flesh this Lent, and his wife being lately come out of the country to town, he is in earnest to know whether she be comprehended in the vow'.

Daniel Defoe did, from time to time, find himself plunged into the obscurities of theological controversy. The Gentlemen of the Scandal Club, in *The Review* of 1 December 1704, were asked whether it was 'possible to prove, demonstratively, the Immateriality of the Soul?' Defoe chose to duck. The Scandal Club's members, he declared, 'have received a great many letters on this head, which they think too weighty for the authors of this to decide'.

Most churchmen seem to have been preoccupied with more practical questions. In an age when a curate earned scarcely more than a lady's maid, the struggle for advancement to a living could be a desperate one. Steele found himself dealing with a particularly material manifestation of this problem in *The Tatler* of 21 September 1710:

Q. ... *I have been for some time in Holy Orders and Fellow of a certain College in one of the Universities, but weary of that unactive life, I resolved to be doing good in my generation. A worthy gentleman has lately offer'd me a fat Rectory, but means, I perceive, his kinswoman should have the benefit of the clergy. I am a nonce in the world and confess it startles me how the body of Mrs Abigail can be annexed to the cure of souls.*

A. ... I do not see why our clergy, who are very frequently men of good families, should be reproached if any of them have the chance to espouse a Hand-Maid with a rectory ... since the best of our Peers have often joined themselves to the daughters of very ordinary tradesmen upon the same valuable consideration.

Such underhand influence upon the appointment of vicars did not lead to an immediate slackening of the church's grasp on congregations. Competition from alternative sources of entertainment was limited on a Sunday, and became more so as the various societies for the suppression of vice gained ground. And, quite apart from the joys of the sermon, the church provided a useful meeting place, with the chance of a little sly dalliance. Glances could be exchanged during the sermon, notes passed from prayer book to prayer book during the hymns and, if the family pews were conveniently positioned, hands could brush each other as the collecting plate circulated. Such practices were frowned on by the more upright members of society, and by those Grub Street journalists who donned that disguise for the purposes of running a problem page:

> *Gentlemen, I have long admired a young lady that sits over against me in Church, to whom I have sent several letters, none of which are ever answered, otherwise than to forbid me ever to look at her. Now, I believe that they are read and answered by some other person since I never see her, but she seems to love me as much as I love her, our eyes being seldom off each other; and if I endeavour to obey her (supposed) letter, which is not to look at her, she sits seemingly displeased with me, till my eyes are on her again. Now, gentlemen, what shall I do in this case, since I cannot possibly come to speak with her?*

Repent that you spent your time so ill at church, and then, if your designs are just and honourable, you may have better hopes that Heaven will prosper them.

(The British Apollo)

Flirting in church was evidently a national past-time, with endless variations, as we can see from another of Dunton's discouraging replies. In this case the young lady had been described to the correspondent as extremely witty, with a 'wisdom inferior to none'; she was beautiful and she spent her time in church ogling him, 'which fixes a fancy in my mind that she loves me well'. Dunton believed him to be mistaken, either in her ogling or in his friend's report that she was wise. For if the latter, 'she would be cautioned

thereby (had she really conceived a passion for you) to
conceal it till addrest and not prostitute it by glances'.
Perhaps, suggested Dunton, she was trying to feed his
pretensions and so amuse herself and her associates.

The stern tone of these answers masks the fact that in
the early eighteenth century Sunday was still quite a jolly
affair. Officially no one was supposed to gamble, to
procreate (except with a married partner), or to drink to
excess on the sabbath, and various Societies for the
Reformation of Manners acted as unpaid informers. A
significant victory was won by such pressure groups in
1757, when nonconformists prevented Parliament from
passing a bill to allow Sunday drilling by the militia,
despite Britain's involvement in the Seven Years' War. But
the need for constant vigilance on the part of these self-
appointed guardians suggests that most people kept one
eye on the pulpit and the other on some more attractive
sight, such as a buxom blonde or a frothy head of beer.
Problem pages reflected something of the battle. *The Court
Miscellany* in 1765 answered a young reader's query as to
why routs were so called by stating that godliness, good
sense and good manners were put to rout at these
occasions, which frequently took place on a Sunday.

Late eighteenth century problem pages, and their
audience, were notably less rumbustious than those of
Dunton's era. Finer feelings and more delicate moral
discriminations were the new order of the day. Typical of
the columns of this period was that run by 'The Matron' in
The Ladies' Magazine. In 1781 she dealt with a lengthy letter
from an aggrieved 'Miss D' who wished to know whether
Christian charity obliged her to support a spend-thrift
friend. The friend in question, when rich, had shown up
the others of her set with smart dresses and reckless
indulgence in whist. Now her small competence was
frittered away and she was penniless:

> *I am not ashamed to own, Madam, that I am myself one of her frugal
> friends, and can, therefore, afford to do something for her, though not so
> much as many others in more roomy circumstances; yet, I am often in
> doubt, whether money, when it is so bestowed, is not misapplied.*

Mrs Grey appealed to the spirit, as well as the letter, of Christian principle in her attempt to make the pursed-lipped 'Miss D' open her purse strings:

> *I am sorry to enforce that which ought to come freely from the liberal mind. Her friend's conduct is indefensible, granted; yet when she considers how severely that friend is at this moment punished by recollections for past misdemeanours (for her failings cannot, with any propriety, be strained into crimes) she will not, I hope, want any spur from the Matron's pen (ever ready to promote acts of benevolence) to quicken her feelings in favour of one of her own sex.*

Moral action is here becoming as much a matter of sensibility as it is of divine decree.

When problem pages returned, after their thirty year exile, in the 1840s, they were initially dominated by factual enquiries of a secular nature. Most early Victorian advisers did not feel qualified to deal with queries which Dunton had taken in his stride, and actually discouraged too minute an enquiry into religious affairs:

> *Bits and Scraps – We would not advise our correspondents to pry too curiously into the mysteries of creation, or the operations by which the Deity executed the conceptions of His will. The phenomena of nature are freely given to our investigation – the visible miracles respond for the invisible. It is useless as well as presumptive to draw aside the veil which shadows the Holy of Holies. There is a gulf which man, while in the flesh, is not permitted to pass.*
>
> (The London Journal, *1 June 1850*)

A nervousness about the scientific challenge to faith was perhaps natural. But the Oxford Movement, Anglo-Catholicism and the bitter intellectual disputes over the sacraments of the church were similarly ignored. Decorum among the parishioners, rather than theological debate, was the province of the correspondence columns, and the fabric of the church was more in view than its spiritual content. One thing that hadn't changed was flirting during services. Young lady readers of *Cassell's Illustrated Family Magazine* seemed to be particularly liable to such weakness:

Anxious ... We must inveigh against the practice of falling in love in church, which appears to be very common. How young gentlemen can continue to keep one eye on their book and the other directed towards a bonnet in the gallery is more than we know. How ladies manage to observe gentlemen seated four pews behind them, we are equally unable to say. But such things are done and the worst of it is, that the perpetrators appear altogether unconscious that there is the least harm in what they are doing. We beg to remind our young friends that they go to church for far other purposes and if they find their attentions distracted from the service by any particular person, it would be better for them to go to some other Church, or even to stay away altogether, rather than to profane the sacred edifice by making it a place of assignation.

(Cassell's, *10 May 1856*)

Our modern view of Victorian life as one devoted to regular church attendance is not borne out, either by the 1851 Census (admittedly statistically suspect), or by the problem pages. Mothers with infants were told, by *The Home Magazine*, to stay at home rather than 'disturb a whole congregation that you may attend service'. And children, according to the same source, should not be forced to attend long services 'of which they cannot comprehend a word and tend to give them a disgust of that which, at a later period, would be pleasant to them'. As these children grew to years of indiscretion, of course, church attendance could cease to be a penance:

Jemima – That any respectable girl of nearly 17 should spend her visits to church in giving and receiving passionate glances from a stranger, accepting notes slipped into umbrellas, subsequently obeying requests for a private meeting at dusk and then earnestly listen to, and afterwards ask our opinion upon, a proposal of elopement, appears to us so outrageous that we can only look on the letter as a hoax. Such things as Jemima describes may happen under the fiery skies of Italy and Spain, but long may it be before our fair, pure English maidens, the best of their country, and the pride of our hearts, imitate such shamelessness, and forfeit that modesty and delicacy of thought and deed which is their birthright.

(Cassell's, *14 March 1857*)

But not every girl in the congregation spent her time

sneaking glances at the talent in the rows behind her. Some concentrated intently on the imposing figure of their vicar. From listening to the sermon, however, their minds could wander to more romantic scenes. 'Lizzie', for instance, writing to *Cassell's* on 6 October 1860, was warned against such dangerous day-dreams:

> *Your friends are much to blame in encouraging you in hopes that can only end in disappointment. We do not doubt you are very pretty and that you make a good match, but you are likely to die a spinster if, in spite of your being an uneducated member of the working classes, you can be satisfied with nothing less than a clergyman.*

The status of a clergyman might be high, but his pay was not. The adviser on *Every Week's* correspondence page showed little sympathy for the ten thousand ministers whose income was less than £100 a year. On 17 January 1863 he declared, 'If men seek to live by their religious persuasions, they must make up their minds to take the market price of their services', adding the dour advice, 'If their object is simply to benefit their fellow creatures – well, there is a way; the apostle found it: tent making is not a dignified profession, but it satisfied him.' Clearly the indigent poor were not to be found only outside the vicarage gates, and a debt-ridden clergyman raised a particular social problem. How could he, or his wife, be dunned politely, as befitted his cloth? *The Young Ladies' Journal* of 1 November 1869 felt 'a Bankruptcy Court was not the place for a clergyman' and advised one of their readers, a milliner, to come to some arrangement for the long-term repayment of a sum owed to her by a clergyman's wife.

Unreasonable expectations by parishioners could take other forms. Gimlet-eyed, long-memoried Mrs Grundies often gave new curates a hard time. One woman, for instance, wrote to Samuel Beeton complaining that her vicar had given the same sermon three times in a year. Beeton felt that this was not unreasonable in a parish where the congregation rarely numbered more than twenty. Another dissatisfied communicant found she was sent to sleep by the local preaching:

Mrs Morfey – Doubtless it is difficult to keep your eyes open in the dog days, whilst your minister is preaching on the vulgar, everyday subjects of practical morality and home virtues, preferring as you do, discussions of predestination and essays on free will. You have not heard, perhaps, of the parish of Lunan where there existed a habit of sleeping in church, much to the disgust of the minister who, one unlucky afternoon, endeavoured to stir up his hearers by an earnest objuration, concluding with the pointed fact: 'You see even Jamie Fraser, the idiot (who was in the front gallery, wide awake) does not fall asleep as many of you are doing.' Jamie, not liking the publicity or the designation, replied: 'An I had na been an edjet, I would ha' been sleeping too.'
(The Englishwoman's Domestic Magazine, *August 1860*)

Increasingly the church was to lose its exclusive right to Sunday activities. And while the popular literature of the period remained overtly devout, indeed grew more so, the nation as a whole became steadily less willing to devote its day off to religion. The quasi-religious magazines of the 1870s and 1880s must be seen against this background. Their message had to be conveyed very much more aggressively than that of their Georgian predecessors. Eighteenth century readers had sometimes to be nudged into correct behaviour by a reminder of God's awful power, but the vast majority of them had an unquestioning faith. In 1700 none of the fundamentals of the Christian faith needed reiteration. By the 1880s they did. This new missionary role is one reason why a modern reader finds Victorian magazines so strenuously religious.

Just occasionally the true state of affairs is glimpsed in the problem pages of the 1880s. Before that date the majority of mixed marriages referred to had been between Christians and Jews, with magazines such as *The London Journal* of June, 1849 advising the suitably named, but actually Gentile, 'Rachel', to ignore prejudice and 'Consult your family, and above all, your own heart – not forgetting the gentleman's.' But increasingly the problem became one of girls marrying the simply irreligious. The advisers were not pleased:

Forget-Me-Not – Had you asked our advice before your engagement, we should have endeavoured to dissuade you from marrying one to

whom religion appears very distasteful. But now your marriage is
about to take place, what can we advise? You should let him know,
now at once, how far above all earthly affection is the love of Jesus, the
Redeemer, and that it will be a sure trial to you, if you do not have him
accompany you to church on Sunday.

(Girls' Own Paper, *8 January 1881*)

Three years later, however, the same magazine found itself
warning a reader not to make too much of such
differences. Reputation, they hinted, might be more
important than doctrinal fastidiousness:

Mary C – Certainly it would be very wrong for a believer in Christ to
marry an Infidel. Can two waltz together except that they be agreed?
And we are plainly forbidden to be 'yoked together' with a denier of
Christ. But it seems to us that you have strained this point beyond its
due limits, and perhaps unintentionally, have raised yourself on a sort
of elevation above others, which superiority you have no right to
assume. Of course, if you knew him to be really a denier of the faith of
Christ, you have no right to encourage his addresses, and if you do not
accept him now you have much compromised your character as one
who makes a very high profession of religion.

(Girls' Own Paper, *4 October 1884*)

Religion could get mixed up with courtship in other ways
as well. Aunties repeatedly found themselves discouraging
the use of God as a superior matrimonial agency. On 19
May 1888 the *Girls' Own Paper* told 'Agatha' that 'You
should not pray for a husband. How do you know it would
be for your happiness or your advantage, and not a
hindrance to your usefulness and your spiritual life?' The
Girls' Own Paper gave similar treatment to the slightly more
shocking case of 'Pearl' on 19 April 1890:

Under the circumstances you name, the question is no subject for prayer.
We mean you are not promised the granting of a prayer for a man to
love you, with whom you are not acquainted and who does not want
an introduction. Your state of mind is an unhealthy one.

What was made in heaven, according to the aunties, was
less marriage than consolation for the broken romance.
'Columbus' was advised to 'humble yourself on your

knees and never be in the man's society alone again'.
'Katie' was warned: 'Leave your future in the Lord's
hands and He will order your life as He thinks best for you.
Matrimony is not the end and aim of a woman's existence,
nor the certain road to either health or happiness.'

Next to God, problem page writers liked to call upon
the help of the local clergyman. His brief was wide. He was
asked to rescue young girls maltreated by their guardians,
to recommend a good lawyer to a suffering woman, to
protect those persecuted by unwanted suitors and to warn
of the likely consequences of hoydenish behaviour. The
vicar and, to a lesser extent, the local magistrate were in
pre-Welfare State days the fount of most help, the source
of most knowledge.

The clergy's pastoral role was particularly significant in
the late nineteenth century, when the traditional forms of
caring within a close-knit community had largely broken
down without yet being replaced by the modern bevy of
probation officers and social workers. This hiatus came,
unfortunately, at the very time when modern life, with its
income-tax forms and government regulations, was
becoming more complex.

The rich, of course, had their specialist advisers. The
rest, without access to accountants, solicitors or bank-
managers, muddled along as best they could, with
frequent calls on the vicar's help. Given their
responsibilities, it is perhaps fortunate that most Victorian
clergymen were solid, upright men. So great was the
clergyman's aura of respectability at this date that he could
even be visited by a young lady without her chaperone.
Just occasionally, however, the local curate turned out to
be a wolf in clerical clothing:

Litro — ... *There is no acquaintance more demoralising than anyone
who makes very high public professions and follows a very low course of
private practice. When a man of that kind is in the church, exposure
one day is inevitable. But since the young lady you speak of does not
admire him, and has determined to see him no more, there seems little
harm done as far as she is concerned. It is men such as you describe who
bring noble things into contempt with the unreflecting, who forget that*

hypocrisy is only the tribute of vice to virtue, and that right itself stands like a rock amid the missiles of the unworthy.

(The Young Woman, *November 1894*)

In many Victorian parishes the clergyman had the glamour of a modern pop star. Part of his job was to prepare young girls for confirmation and this left him constantly open to adolescent crushes. But marriage to a clergyman was not always bliss. Just as the Victorian God could be stern, unbending and joyless, so too were some of His ministers. One of the saddest letters to appear in the *Girls' Own Paper* was written by a clergyman's wife who had found to her cost that Christian charity did not necessarily begin at home:

Lonely Girl Wife – ... *You had better write a letter, having asked divine direction and a blessing on your so doing. Represent your utter loneliness from the 7 o'clock breakfast to 10.30 pm. Say that if your husband desires you to give up your old work in the school and the parish, he, as a vicar, has a right to do so, and you submit, but that, by Divine ordinance, the wife's duty is to 'guide the house' and that you could not be set aside by the old housekeeper's declaration that your husband detested strangers 'meddling' nor by being told that 'children must be seen and not heard'. That you desire to do your duty as a wife and mistress of the house, to please him as far as you may, and to show him you are worthy of his confidence, respect and love. May the Lord help, direct and comfort you.*

(Girls' Own Paper, *23 June 1894*)

Clergymen's wives were frequent correspondents of the problem pages. So common was the pseudonym 'minister's wife' in the Methodist magazine *The British Weekly*, that one such was begged on 5 March 1891 to use a more distinctive title 'else Minister's Wife B writing this week to inquire about a hair wash may next week take to herself the advice intended for Minister's Wife A. "Apply Jackson's Varnish Stain; if the surface looks thin try a second or third coat", which might lead to awkward complications.'

By the end of the nineteenth century, not only had God's forbidding aspect changed to a more loving concern with the condition of mankind, but the omnipotent God allowed a greater latitude to those who had taken His name in vain. *The Athenian Oracle* had held that a vow over the permanence of a relationship could not be broken without breaking faith with God. *Woman's Life* thought differently:

> *MG tells me she is a governess and has been in the same family for the past four years. The house is presided over by a widower and MG has charge of the three children. Recently she has noticed that her employer has shown signs that he has an affection for her ... Seven years ago she was engaged to another man. He broke off the engagement and married another woman. At the time of his breaking his engagement she turned to him and said, 'I shall never love anyone but you.' She has kept this promise faithfully, and now she has evident signs that someone else is fond of her, she is wondering whether she ought to be true to her promise and simply refuse to think of any other man who may come her way. How should she act?*

> *... I would be the last person in the world to suggest to anyone not keeping a promise, but a promise such as MG made was, so to speak, a promise of degree; and seeing that her old lover left her for someone else, there is absolutely no reason why MG should not think again and ... forget what was for the moment, the outburst of her heart ...*
>
> (*Woman's Life,* 1 July 1899)

Though the problem pages of such Victorian stalwarts as *Girls' Own Paper* may seem cloying, they are actually outdone by the 'Chat that Cheers' column of the Edwardian *Home Companion*. Here it seems that God is lurking on the subs desk, next to the auntie, ever-ready to jump helpfully in. He is an understanding deity 'who can do all things, no matter how impossible they seem to our weak, human eyes'. A widow tired from 'climbing life's rocky hill for fifteen long years', for example, is urged optimistically onwards. 'Take courage with you as your companion, and ever keep your eyes fixed on the bright reunion which one day will be yours.' Count your blessings was the general philosophy of the page. One childless wife, who felt depressed by her barrenness, was comforted in true *Home Companion* style on 5 June 1909:

Take up your cross, dear sister, and bear it bravely, and the weight of it will disappear. If we wish for what God thinks fit and wise not to send us, we forfeit the true enjoyment of the blessings He gives. Try to remember that you deserve no more than others, and your life in many respects is free from care, and you are surrounded by that great crown to womanhood − a good man's love. Let the love of those around you − those sad and weary ones that you can help − fill your aching heart. Don't turn from the little ones − God's blossoms − because none are in your garden. Just gather the drooping ones and crumbs of comfort will shower upon you.

Christianity, however, was not the only version of the supernatural peddled by the women's magazines. Graphology was a popular craze in the 1890s, with one correspondent writing to *Mothers and Daughters* to inform their expert that she had married the man whose handwriting has passed her test and now, a year later, was not regretting it. *Woman's Life* boasted a graphologist who rarely liked what she saw. One girl was told in 1899:

A disagreeable handwriting, this, indicating a peevish and discontented nature. She would probably affirm that she is highly sensitive − and so she is, but sensitive only in regard to her own feelings … The temper is irritable and quickly called into action. She is unforgiving and fickle in her affections …

One suspects that the correspondent took care to type any future letters to problem pages.

The fashion for the occult boomed during the First World War. Conventional religions were unwilling to offer specific predictions about the safety of loved ones. Crystal ball gazers and astrologers had no such inhibitions. *Leech's Lady's Companion* made constant use of 'Amethyst', an astrology expert. Her reading of the stars produced such information as 'Your son will go to the Front during the Spring. He appears to return safely to you again.' Another worried woman − this time a fiancée − was encouraged not to lose hope, despite having received no letters recently. 'Do not give up hope; you will hear from your fiancé soon, but he has not been able to write as he has been dangerously ill. He will recover, and appears to get leave in about a month's time.' Whether such magazines lost readers when it transpired that the loved one had been dead for some weeks, is not clear. But certainly, as the war progressed, most seers began to cover their options.

Peg's Paper, a post-war creation, had a 'Madame Sunya', specialising in dream interpretation. In May 1919, 'Helen of Leeds' dreamt that she had lost a brooch which was returned to her by a 'foppishly-dressed stranger'. The mysteriously-oriental 'Madame Sunya' interpreted this to mean 'You are shortly to fall in love with a very plain but steady man who will make an excellent husband'. Madame Sunya evidently worked on the principle that dreams always meant the opposite of what they seemed. On 26 June 1919, 'Elizabeth of Kingston-on-Thames' learnt that 'To dream of going to church to be married signified that the dreamer, for the greater part of her life at any rate, will remain single'. *Peg's Paper* readers must have spent some troubled nights.

The aftermath of war left some Christians finding it hard to reconcile their faith with the horror of war, or the disappointments of life without a man. In 1925 the re-titled *Girls' Own Paper and Woman's Magazine* reassured a depressed 'Muriel' that she was not alone in her feelings of alienation from Christ. These feelings 'were apt to occur with tormenting force during the late war; but they were vanquished wherever there was true Christian experience in the background'. Fresh air, plenty of exercise and sufficient rest were prescribed for this particular religious crisis.

The problem pages of the 1920s mark a quiet revolution in society's attitude to religion. Formerly religious convictions were worn openly, and were enforced by those with social and legal authority. By the 1920s religion had become a matter of private conscience, and would-be moralists were firmly discouraged from imposing their standards on others:

I am in the midst of very worldly, pleasure-loving people. Ought I to speak out and tell them plainly that I think their mode of living is wrong?

No! Our instructions are to strive to reflect the Lord Jesus in our life; not to criticize or judge others. There is a wide difference between letting our own life shine and accusing other people of living in darkness ... A preacher or teacher or a person in authority is expected to give a lead. But an ordinary citizen of the rank and file is not justified in offering gratuitous and unsolicited criticisms on the conduct of his or her fellow citizens, unless there is distinct wrong-doing which threatens injury to others.

(*Woman's Magazine*, 1927)

For most people religion was becoming strictly a part-time affair. Though the Church Rambling Club and the Sunday School still attracted supporters, the church was losing its social side to such purely temporal attractions as the cinema. Good works had been, in the view of the Victorian problem page, far more likely to lead to an eligible *parti* than an evening spent dancing. By the 1930's columnists had lost their faith in good works as a medium for match-making. 'MC', a girl brought up on 'rather restrictive religious lines', had a pleasant job, devoted two nights a week to religious work, lived at home with Mum, and wrote to *Woman's Magazine* asking whether she should try to cure her feelings of loneliness and depression by playing the piano for a slum-district settlement. The auntie recommended 'a more balanced life'. This meant less good works and more good fun. 'MC' was encouraged to join a debating club or amateur dramatic troupe, 'so that the girl can return to her religious work refreshed and zestful'. The auntie concluded 'I am not advocating a butterfly, whirl-of-pleasure existence, but I am suggesting that you, "MC", and many other women in your position, owe it to yourself to have some social life of culture and to enlarge your circle of friends of both sexes.'

The recommendation of broader interests did not, however, mean that the reader should forget God, or fail to count her blessings. One self-pitying reader was put right in no uncertain terms:

You say you have never got anything you have prayed for. My dear, isn't that a rather sweeping statement, for on your own assertion, you have a good situation with a kind Christian mistress, and this includes food, shelter and freedom from financial worries. Don't you think all that is a good answer to your prayer: 'Give us this day our daily bread'? I wish I could take you down to the East End houses of London to some of the sad homes from which my cheerful Girl Guides come, and then you would see how far more blessed is your lot than many others ...

God as provider grew in importance during the depression. Servants might be confident of their future, but employers were less so. One middle-class reader wrote to *Woman's Magazine* with a considerable moral dilemma. Should she sack her old family servant now, since she knew she would not be able to pay her an allowance in her old age? The auntie was reassuring:

Do your duty and be kind to her now; that is all God expects of you. Be sure you try to follow His word and put your trust in Him. If He wants you to give Janet a pension He will provide the where-withal when the time comes.

The arrival of the Welfare State in post-war Britain must have seemed an answer to this employer's prayers.

Some problems of the period are still more ticklish, and suggest how much more private and personal religion was becoming:

Should husbands and wives pray together or each alone in secret as directed in the New Testament? My father told me that he found he prayed for what he thought his wife would like at first and then they prayed separately — Retired Commander RN.

I think the idea of a husband and wife praying together a beautiful one. I suppose that where there is perfect unity of spirit and love between a husband and wife, such prayer would be as natural as mutual converse with a close friend. But the average British couple are very shy about anything as personal and delicate as their devotions, and unless such prayers of either were completely simple and straight from the heart, it would perhaps be wiser to pray separately.

(*Woman's Magazine,* 1937)

The astrological problem page continues in such

magazines as *Peg's Paper* throughout the 1930s. It disappeared with the coming of war, partly because of a suspicion that the German propaganda machine might use these columns to spread alarm and despondency. Women, therefore, no longer received the spurious re-assurance of fortune-tellers that their men would return safely. Prayers to God, however, remained both socially acceptable and safe from German interference:

> *My fiancé has recently won his wings and will be going on flying operations over enemy territory. So now I am one of the thousands of women to whom the fateful announcement that some of our planes failed to return has become a personal anguish of fear and depression. Do you sincerely believe it will help if I pray for his safety? Do you yourself believe that there is an Almighty God who has the power to bring my man through all the dangers and hazards which lie ahead of him?*

I do believe most strongly in the power of prayer. We must add, though, faith in prayer. By this I mean it is no use invoking Divine Help unless we are prepared to believe in Divine Judgement. For instance, it doesn't necessarily mean your question hasn't been answered if the answer doesn't come in the way you expected it. Often I myself have found that, what at the time appears to be one of life's disasters, turns out in the passing of time to be a great blessing. But yes, pray for your man, and cheer yourself that many more of our planes return to their base than fail to make home.

(*Glamour,* 13 March 1945)

In retrospect, the death of six million Jews in the gas chambers of Nazi Germany has given the Second World War overtones it only partially possessed when Britain went to war. German treatment of Jews in the 1930s was recognised as shameful. The Nazis, however, did not have exclusive rights to anti-Semitism. *Woman's Fair*, a film mag with an auntie called Olive Wadsley, published a reply in July 1938 to an Irish girl whose wish to marry a Jew was meeting fierce parental opposition:

> *The Jewish faith is as great a faith as any other, and this I say with no*

Jewish blood in my veins. This man seems to be a true man, 'kind and gentle' as you say yourself. Every living person has the right to follow what creed he or she chooses ... If you truly love this man, then marry him. What does your family offer you by way of compensation for giving up a home, love and the hope of children?

Even after six years of war and the discovery of the death camps, letters still appeared from couples whose parents couldn't stomach such a mixed marriage:

I am deeply in love with a Jew, and he with me, but my family are horrified at the idea of marrying a man of that race and religion. His father and mother strongly object, too, unless I take his faith, and my boy is anxious for me to do that. Do you advise me to go against my parents' wishes? As you will have gathered, they are violently anti-Semitic.

Yours is a problem which certainly requires very careful consideration ... I think personally, one should not change one's religion for any reason except a conviction that the new one is likely to give more spiritual help and comfort. Therefore if I were you, I should put it very strongly to your boy, that you will each follow your own method of worship. I know, however, that the Orthodox Jew, as his parents appear to be, take a very grave view of 'mixed' marriages, and you will probably face an estrangement from his family as well as your own. Your parents are exaggerating, I think, when they warn you you will be shunned on marrying a Jew, but it is plain you must make very sure you love this boy sufficiently for it to be worth the sacrifices and difficulties you will encounter when you do marry him. Don't be in a hurry to make up your mind, and remember to think well over the problem of your children, which undoubtedly he will wish to have brought up in his own faith.

(*Glamour,* 22 May 1945)

Mixed marriages still figure in modern problem pages, as do the questions of divorce and contraception for Roman Catholic readers. Religious convictions are evidently a great comfort and strength for some readers of *Woman's Weekly* and the *People's Friend*. But they can also lead to couples trapped in loveless marriages and to the birth of

unwanted children. Anna Raeburn underlined this point
on 8 May 1976:

> *My problem is that my husband, who is a Roman Catholic, doesn't*
> *believe in any form of contraception. He's so much against it, he won't*
> *even talk about it. We have three children and I'm pregnant with my*
> *fourth. My husband demands sex every night and sometimes he even*
> *comes home in the middle of the day for more. We can barely manage*
> *on his money now, so I don't know what we're going to do if we have*
> *any more children.*

Religious beliefs are a very private matter, but it seems
from your letter that, even if contraception is out of line
with your husband's beliefs, you don't share them. If you
visited your doctor, I'm sure he could recommend some
form of family planning which would be acceptable to you.
   I was disturbed to read about your husband's insistence
on intercourse. He sounds like a selfish man, and the next
time he sounds off about his religious principles, you might
remind him that coercing you isn't very Christian of him.

(*Woman,* 8 May 1976)

Marriage Guidance Counsellors, Citizens Advice Bureaux
and social workers are today mentioned more frequently
than the parish priest. But spiritual advisers still have their
place – even in the trendier versions of the problem page.
'Dr Hippocrates', for example, who ran an advice column
for a Californian magazine in the late 1960s,
recommended the services of a priest to a reader who
found that doing chin-ups gave him an orgasm. Would
this, the athlete wondered, be considered by the catholic
church to be masturbation 'and therefore a sin?' One can
only hope that the priest he consulted was a believer in
muscular Christianity.
   In some respects, when religion lost its exclusive
authority, the aunties lost an ally. But in many ways the
decline in church attendance, and the diminished status of
the local vicar, have enhanced the advisers' job. Their
pages have, to some extent at least, replaced the power of
the pulpit. But whereas the emphasis in church has
traditionally been on what one should not do, most
aunties find that they spend most of their time giving their

readers permission to do innocuous things which have, for one reason or another, come to be regarded as wicked.

Some aunties are clearly Christian. Peggy Makins, the 'Evelyn Home' of *Woman* for thirty years, is a converted Quaker whose religious beliefs were central to her advice, although she did not seek to impose them on her readers. The implication was that 'where there's love, there's God'. Her column, she maintains, was a mixture of the Ten Commandments, the Sermon on the Mount and common sense.

'Evelyn Home' was perhaps the last of the traditional aunties. Most modern advisers run a strictly secular column in which a rule of thumb utilitarianism seems to be the guiding philosophy – do what makes you happy unless it hurts someone else more. Absolute standards of morality are becoming rarer. If the problem pages no longer appear perceptibly Christian, one reason may well be that three of the most influential aunties – Claire Rayner of *The Sun*, Marje Proops of *The Daily Mirror*, and Irma Kurtz of *Cosmopolitan* – were born into the Jewish faith.

That religion can be positively harmful is a view of several of them. Their mail bags include letters from readers whose lives have been blighted by a sense of guilt induced by early religious training. Other letters attest to the destruction caused by religious bigotry, and to the callousness of some pillars of religious society whose hands seem to itch to pick up the first stone. Angela Willans, an agnostic who writes as 'Mary Grant' in *Woman's Own*, maintained, in a television discussion with Peggy Makins in 1978, that religion could wreck lives and prevent people from fulfilling themselves. Enlarging on this point, she claimed that religion could reduce self-confidence, and could be used by parents and spouses as an unhealthy means of control. Her denial of God, however, only strengthened her belief in a caring attitude towards human beings. 'I think it is important to watch over each other, because I don't believe anyone is watching over us.' The remark sums up the direction in which the modern problem page seems to be moving.

9

Happy families?

Problem pages have always concentrated on the snappy, rather than the happy, family. A successful domestic circle resolves its own internal conflicts, an embattled one resorts to the auntie or to the rod. Though the high divorce and delinquency rates of the mid-twentieth century have often been taken as an indication of the breakdown of the family, they do not in fact reflect a less convivial fireside. The evidence of the agony column is that families are no more, and probably less, miserable now than they were a hundred or two hundred years ago. The only real change is that today the alternatives to the family are more inviting.

Victorian and twentieth century publications devote considerable space to practical child care. By contrast, the early advisers steered clear of such mundane matters, preferring a discussion of metaphysics to the niceties of nappy-changing. That most of the earliest aunties were men without legitimate heirs, and with a positive disregard for the claims of home, may well have been responsible for such neglect. But it was also the consequence of a less soft-hearted approach to the family and to children.

Though sentiment had begun to creep into marriage by the end of the seventeenth century, love still came a poor third to portions and position. Maternity too was a more detached experience. Investing too much feeling in a baby was rash when there was a fifty per cent chance of its death before the age of five. The following letter, which appeared in the first decade of the eighteenth century, illustrates the no-nonsense approach to one's progeny.

> Q... *It hath pleased God that hitherto we have had no Children, nor probably may; on which my husband for sometime hath grown a little melancholy. I entreat you would be so kind as to send him what comforts you can under such circumstances.*
>
> A ... Providence is so indulgent to mankind as to afford comforts in all conditions of life, how (seemingly) unhappy so ever they might be, if man takes pain to search them out, and submits to the conviction of them. As to the case before us, most sure it is, that their insensibility of our kindness to them renders us little gratitude of our returns. As they increase in years, we but more and more part with them to schools, then to university, Inns of Court, trades etc. during which the distance prudence commands us to keep, prevents all pleasures of conversation. And when they come to years of discretion, too often the return of all our cares, pains and expenses on their education etc., is, Pray, Father be pleased to die ...
>
> (*The British Apollo*, 1708)

In this, somewhat cynical, portrayal of the joys of parenthood Dunton may be remembering how unsatisfactory his own father, a sober clergyman, had found a son who wasted his schooling by a refusal to study, and then spent his years of apprenticeship as a book-seller chasing unwary young females.

The seventeenth century child, such as Dunton, did not enjoy the moral idealization which Rousseau was to make so fashionable. Children were born, according to Calvin, with natures designed as 'the seedbed of sin' and they were treated accordingly, even by non-Calvinists. A child born in pre-industrial Britain was also likely both to have a far shorter childhood, and to see less of his parents during it than a child of today. Put out to wet-nurse almost immediately after birth, the children of the literate classes of the eighteenth century would probably leave home between the ages of twelve and fourteen, either to be educated or as apprentices. These factors do not mean that children of the period were unloved. They simply had to obey different rules, and it is noteworthy that while the problem pages of this period do produce instances of a neglected wife complaining of boredom, no child ever writes of being so afflicted.

Where the Victorian child was expected to love his parents, the eighteenth century child had the more limited task of implicit obedience. Dunton was at one point called upon to perform a complex moral judgement upon the relative wickedness of disobedience and prostitution. As always he was equal to the occasion:

Q ... *Which is the greatest sin, to be a Night-Walker, or to rebel against one's parents?*

A ... Either of 'em big enough for Damnation; nor doth the greater at all excuse the lesser, as 'tis often designed in such Comparisons; but to return a direct answer, we refer you to the order of their setting down in the Ten Commandments, where duty to parents is pressed before adultery is forbid.

(*The Athenian Mercury*, 1691)

Despite their unanimous sense of the importance of filial obedience, however, most eighteenth century advisers did their best to avoid family disputes, especially those involving the younger members. One auntie, for instance, when asked by a youthful correspondent of *The Ladies' Magazine* 'At what age could she go to a masquerade?' answered Sphinx-like 'When you have reached the age of discretion.'

As the eighteenth century progressed, the young seemed increasingly less inclined to dissipate their youth in the pursuit of knowledge. Where *The Spectator*, *The Tatler* and *The Censor* were able to offer a straight-forward concentration on educational matters, their mid-century successors were obliged to conduct repeated campaigns against the distractions of pleasure. Mrs Haywood, the auntie of *The Female Spectator*, received a letter from one 'Sarah Oldfashioned' whose daughter chose to spend her time at Ranelagh Gardens instead of practising the spinnet, sewing or conversing with her French mistress.

Her mother remembers how she spent her own childhood paying her 'devotions to heaven' and studying 'dancing, music, writing and those other accomplishments of my sex', and reveals that her daughter's alternative programme is a morning in the pleasure gardens and an afternoon's discussion of her wardrobe with her fourteen year old friends. Mrs Haywood shares the maternal shock:

> *Could children be sensible of the endless cares, watchings, the anxieties which attend parental tenderness, and how impossible it is for them to return in kind those obligations, they would certainly avoid doing anything that might render fruitless the pains and labours employed for their interest – gratitude as well as self-love would make them use their utmost efforts to improve the education bestowed on them; but how hard it is to bring young people to a just way of thinking …*

Hard it might be, but the distressed 'Sarah Oldfashioned' was not entirely at a loss. Young 'Biddy' would be sent to stay with a Cornish relative, whose nearest neighbour lived twelve miles away.

One-parent families were even more common in the eighteenth century than they are now, with the difference that death rather than divorce was the invariable cause. Re-marriage was also common, and although full-parents were generally given the benefit of the doubt by problem pages when dealing with accusations of cruelty or neglect, step-parents often seem to have stepped straight out of *Cinderella*. One correspondent of *The Female Spectator* observed:

> *How many young ladies, merely to avoid the severity and arrogance of their step-mothers, have thrown themselves into the arms of men whose addresses they would otherwise have despised, and afterwards, finding they had but exchanged one slavery for another, either broke through the chain by unwarrantable means, or pined themselves almost to death under the weight of it!*

The journal itself, in a sceptical vein unworthy of Mrs Haywood and her 'three admirable helpers', gave its own account of what might be hoped for from a step-mother:

> *She will have all the fondness as well as the care of a mother for them*

and do that by inclination which she is bound to do by piety ... Such
instances are, however, very rarely met with, and both Husband and
Children ought to be content, when a step-mother acts in everything like
a mother, and not to scrupulously enquire into her heart for the
sentiment of one.

(The Female Spectator, *Book XVI, 1744–46*)

This letter suggests that historians and sociologists are
wrong to maintain that the pre-industrial family had little
shared affection. Clearly the love of a mother was already
recognised to be of a different timbre from that of a nurse
or a step-mother by the readership of the mid-eighteenth
century problem page.

Recent social historians may well, however, be correct in
their rejection of the traditional belief that the Industrial
Revolution brought about a decisive change from the
extended to the nuclear family (two parents and their
immediate children). Cousins, uncles and grandparents are
occasionally mentioned in the eighteenth century,
normally when as guardians they have some role to play in
a wedding. But problem pages do not record the sort of
family rows which would inevitably have arisen in
extended households had they been the norm. Quarrels
were then, as today, between husband and wife, or parents
and children living together on a day-to-day basis. The
disputes with relatives usually concerned money, a
commodity which can start long-distance rows with ease.

One development certainly did occur in the Industrial
Age. This was the growth of an ostentatious familial
fondness. The problem pages give us repeated glimpses of
this phenomenon. A reader of *The Ladies' Treasury* in 1859,
for example, had a family which unfailingly gave her a
birthday party, and had the tactlessness to continue doing
so when she reached the critical age of twenty-five. When
'Tryphena' admitted that she, 'On beholding them
interested in the preparations and looking so merry and
joyful, cannot help feeling quite provoked', suspecting
that 'they are glad that she has continued year after year, a
neglected spinster at home', she was sternly told:

... if they are glad, share their joy; do not mar it by your discontent. If

no gentleman has yet elected you to be his bride, be sure it is for your own good that you have remained single.

When Marx claimed in *The Communist Manifesto* that the bourgeoisie had 'torn away from the family its sentimental veil, and reduced the family relation to a mere money-relation', in fact, he was certainly not referring to the bourgeoisie's own, immediate domestic circle. It is true that servants, apprentices and other non-related members of the household largely lost their semi-familial status. But Marx's accusation that the bourgeoisie put an end to 'all feudal, patriarchal idyllic relations' ignores the imposition of just these things (the last one only in theory, of course) on the family at home. The less cosy, depersonalised world outside brought into being a well-insulated, claustrophobic and inward-looking family at home. Safety extended only as far as the garden gate – and then only if the female members of the household were cautious. As *The London Journal* pointed out to an early Victorian reader who had contracted a clandestine engagement, 'The serpent found his way into Eden, and why not into the park adjoining your father's house?'

For those dutiful daughters who did not seek illicit excitement in some quiet corner of the paternal estate, virtue had to be its own reward. Only Samuel Beeton in *The Englishwoman's Domestic Magazine* made an attempt, albeit an ironic one, to understand the destructive boredom suffered by the unmarried middle-class girl:

> *Poor Puss – Your case is a sad one. To have nothing to wear is bad enough. 'Nothing to eat' is worse, but to have 'nothing to do' is indeed lamentable. Shall we send you Florence Nightingale's address or Mrs George Dawson's, or Lady Shaftesbury's or perhaps Miss Burdett Coutts would accept off-hand the services of one who 'yearns for some congenial employment for mind and hand'.*

(The Englishwoman's Domestic Magazine, *November 1861*)

Florence Nightingale would probably have welcomed any letter from 'Poor Puss', since she had only to turn to her diary to re-discover her own feelings of despair and boredom at the age of twenty-five.

The cult of the perfect family made it difficult for nineteenth century aunties to sympathise with children who complained about the behaviour of their parents. If parents were wise and godly – as all Victorian parents were depicted – then ructions must logically be the fault of ungrateful children. Only very occasionally did the weight of evidence force the aunties to depart from this polite fiction. One answer which appeared in *The London Journal* dealt with a complaint from 'Emma and Louisa' about their mother's shocking bad temper. Some mothers, the adviser recognised:

> ... nag at their children, especially the marriageable daughter, all day and finish off with a grand Babel chorus of wrongs and mistakes with their husbands at night. Such conduct is not merely censurable – it is inexcuseable.

Both parents, according to *The London Journal*, were to blame, for the father should be head of his own house, and ought to insist on its being properly managed, 'instead of tamely submitting to the ungovernable whims of a virago'. A nagging wife was such an unnatural phenomenon, they felt, that 'we cannot repel the intrusion of the suspicion that she drinks on the sly'.

Certain irregularities could free a child from his duty to honour and obey. 'Kit Carling', for instance, was told by *Cassell's* on 3 January 1857 that 'the man living with your mother has no legal control over you and if he beats you, or turns you out of the house, he could, if brought before the magistrate, be punished'. But another correspondent of *Cassell's*, on 18 April 1857, was advised to conciliate his step-father by every proper means:

> ... avoiding most scrupulously all allusion mentioned in the latter part of his letter to us. For if the marriage could be invalidated, which from what he says we do not believe possible, what good could arise to our correspondent sufficient to compensate for bringing shame and dishonour upon his mother?

Another *Cassell's* reader, who signed herself (with considerable allusive skill) 'Cordelia', was told on 5

February 1859 that although her case was a painful one she had no recourse in law. 'As your father maintains you at home, how harsh so ever he may be (no personal assaults being proved) there is nothing in which the law may assist you.'

The proper limits of child punishment became a central topic of problem pages in the second half of the nineteenth century. In the mid-1850s, for example, a concerned father asked *The London Journal* whether a school mistress was justified in birching a fifteen year old, female pupil. 'Certainly not' was the reply:

> No misconduct would justify such a disgusting act; and a woman who would inflict such a degrading punishment on one of her own sex, should be at once removed from her post, or her school broken up.

But not everyone agreed. Some readers, as the correspondence in *The Englishwoman's Domestic Magazine* shows, warmly supported the idea of birching girls. Over a two year period, the 'Conversazione' column of this journal acted as a forum where readers (and occasionally the editor) could exchange views on the desirability of corporal punishment.

This correspondence, coupled with an equally lively one on corset wearing and the charms of be-spurred lady equestrians, has led subsequent generations to think of this as an overtly sadistic age. C. W. Cunningham, for instance, in his book *Feminine Attitudes in the Nineteenth Century*, claimed that these letters reveal an 'orgy of sadism in the upper middle class during the late '60s and '70s', and ascribes this to females who have 'missed the more normal forms of sexual gratification'. Some letters certainly seem to support his first accusation:

> The mother of 2 boys and 6 girls (the youngest now 25) writes: It seems to me all your correspondents omit the first principle of the usefulness of punishment by whipping – namely, that you cannot begin too early. Permit me to state my method, as it fully answered. As babies in arms, my children were never allowed what they screamed for, and at the age of one year I began to chastise them, that is to say, at first to give perhaps two or three strokes with a small birch twig, increasing the

punishment between one and three ... At the beginning, before the child can reason, the slightest fault should never pass uncorrected – certainty of punishment is even more important than severity, though I think a severe whipping is more useful than 3 light ones. A bad fit of obstinacy is one of the most trying naughtinesses, such as suddenly refusing to say a letter or word perfectly known. As the fit must be subdued, I used to inflict a whipping every ten minutes until the word was said. Sometimes the fit would last an hour or even longer. For lying, the most deadly of all childish sins, the most severe punishment was reserved. Whatever the time of day, the culprit was sent upstairs to prepare for bed, and when ready was brought in to me. I had in the meantime told their father of the occurrence and on the child's appearance led it to the study door, leaving it to enter it alone. After pointing out to the child the fearful nature of its fault, and praying with it that it might never again fall into such a sin, my husband saying 'All liars shall have their portion in the lake that burneth with fire and brimstone' inflicted an invariably extremely severe whipping proportionate to the age of the delinquent who was then sent to bed. One unanswerable argument in favour of my system is that my dear children, who are all married, have adopted it in every detail with their own little ones. Depend upon it, children chastised systematically from a year old will seldom require the rod after 10.

(The Englishwoman's Domestic Magazine, *March 1870*)

Other letters in support of corporal punishment for girls indicate that, in some homes at least, the birch, the slipper or the taws was never far from the parental hand. One correspondent, for instance, who signed herself 'Another Lover of Obedience' recommended the leather taws, which she regularly used on her two children aged seven and fourteen, giving them between fifteen and fifty strokes. 'After this, I can assure you, they are perfectly docile for some time to come.' Another correspondent warned that 'salutary care should be taken to purchase rods with good buds, the handles being about the thickness of the wrist'.

Some recommended beating the children across the back, others preferred laying them across a bed and giving them a sound whipping in 'the old-fashioned style'. How much clothing should be removed was evidently a vexing question. Some boarding schools had a special garment – much like a modern hospital nightie – which fastened at

the neck and then fell open down the back. But most
parents had a straight choice between leaving a protective
layer of clothing on their daughters, which would make
the punishment smart less, or reducing them to
nakedness. A perplexed mother in November, 1868 asked
whether a thin garment could be retained so that the
punishment would be less shameful. 'Or is it good to have
it shameful,' she enquired, 'and should the pain be really
great to be effective?'

Most readers of *The Englishwoman's Domestic Magazine* felt
that shame was an intrinsic part of the punishment. They
recommended that daughters should be birched after
prayers when the family was assembled, or in front of
younger sisters, or laid across the counter of the local
grocery store (there being apparently no suitable whipping
horse at home) and whipped semi-publically. As one
mother, who signed herself 'Experience', wrote 'It is no
disgrace to a girl to be whipped by her mother – the
disgrace is – in deserving it ...'

What, then, were the heinous crimes which led to a
birching? Disobedience, whining, temper-tantrums, lying
and refusing to eat the food put before them were
frequent causes. But so, as we have seen from the mother
of two boys and six girls, was a slowness to master lessons.
Another mother, when her fifteen year old daughter was
'turned' by her governess, birched the girl and claimed
that the effect had been wonderful: 'No girl could be more
dutiful and affectionate than she is now and she has
progressed rapidly in her studies.'

Such attitudes from mothers might have shocked John
Dunton. Writing in an age which is commonly regarded as
more brutal, he advised his readers to educate their
children at home, on the grounds that mothers lack that
'magisterial sourness which sticks so close to most
pedagogues, and frightens more learning out of children
than ever they can whip into them'. But they also shocked
Victorian contemporaries of such correspondents as
'Experience', 'Lover of Obedience' and 'Pro-Rod'.

The 'Conversazione' section of *The Englishwoman's
Domestic Magazine* in the late 1860s and early 1870s was

clearly a forum of deliberately controversial debate. Whipping was one of its longest-running topics. But the debate was by no means as one-sided as the carefully selected quotations of some historians suggest. It began with 'Home Discipline Pater' asking the advice of other readers whether he should, as suggested by an intimate friend, personally chastise his thirteen year old daughter who, apart from being obstinate and ill-tempered, did not hesitate occasionally 'to give her Mama a pert answer'. His other two daughters were also badly behaved, though his only son was more docile.

The initial response to his letter came entirely from readers opposed to corporal punishment. In April 1868, a month after 'Home Discipline Pater's' letter had appeared, he was advised 'On no account allow your children to be degraded by corporal punishment', by one reader while another suggested that he was responsible for the disharmony within his home by so evidently preferring his son to his daughters. 'Do not, for worlds, subject a girl of 13 to the ignominy of the lash, which is an insult to her reason, to her birth as a child of a rational being, and her destiny as the future companion of saints', this correspondent argued, recommending instead an appeal to the child's reason.

One month later the editor reported that one correspondent 'unyielding holds to a sound whipping', while another suggested 'imprisoning the child in handcuffs'. He commented, 'The lash and the handcuffs appear to us to be fit only for the vilest criminals and certainly not fitted for a comparatively innocent girl of 13.' Many readers agreed with him. 'A Scotch Mother', for instance, declared herself 'surprised and ashamed' at the opinions of some ladies on this subject and wished to know how the lovers of the rod would 'manage disobedient wives and second childhood?' And in January 1869 'Gentleness', a correspondent with the best of motives though a somewhat confused conception of what happened on cotton plantations, declared:

She should think those Mamas must have nigger blood in them, and

they are practising slaves' treatment on their children to their own
delight and love of beating. (It is the negro who is beaten not who beats
– Ed). How can the cowardly tyrants who use the whip on their
children dare to call themselves English? All her friends who are
mothers unite in saying that such a course of treatment brings the
children to being deceitful, ungrateful and hypocritical.

(The Englishwoman's Domestic Magazine, *January 1869*)

The English Vice does seem to have been closer to the
surface of public consciousness in the 1860s and 1870s than
at most other times. As well as appearing in the
correspondence columns of *The Englishwoman's Domestic
Magazine*, it was finding poetic expression in Swinburne's
early volumes, published at this time. But the taste for
physical pain was far from being universal.

Those Victorian children who did suffer under the lash,
moreover, were actually paying the price for the greater
interest now taken in their welfare by parents. The
deliberately detached attitude towards children of the
seventeenth century had gradually been replaced by a
fiercely active concern. In the 1880s parents, without
becoming less stern, turned increasingly to 'psychological'
punishments – hell-fire sermons, imprisonment in dark
closets and bread-and-water diets. The changing climate
of opinion can be sensed in a *Girls' Own Paper* reply of 29
January 1888 when seventeen year old 'Alice' wrote to
complain of her mother's treatment. 'If subjected to
personal violence, consult other grown up members of the
family about it, and be guided by them', she was advised.
The auntie even suggested that relatives might agree to
take her in. Alice was, however, firmly reminded that 'If
your mother is only cross and hard to please, you have no
right to leave her, for you owe to her the dutiful
submission of a minor.' In similar mood, the *Girls' Own
Paper* advised an eighty year old guardian, faced with
rebellious girls of thirteen and seventeen, to take the elder
one aside for a quiet talk:

After asking help from our Heavenly Father to speak with extreme love
and patience, lay before her the impropriety of her conduct, the bad
example to her sister, and the harm done to her own soul.

Moral suasion, if insufficient to force a girl to mend her ways, could of course be backed up by more convincing arguments. Most middle-class girls, in the absence of any form of respectable female employment, were financially dependent on their fathers. This was a point made frequently by aunties to girls dissatisfied with home life. *The Girls' Own Paper*, for example, told 'Rose' on 8 September 1894 that 'We are disgusted at letters enquiring "at what age is a girl free from her parents?" Why do you wish to be "free"?' Girls under the age of twenty-one, they decreed, might be more or less free if they were self-supporting but 'this is a great misfortune'. A correspondent who wrote to *The Young Woman* in December, 1894 about the openings for companions was reminded that a father could, legally, control his daughter until she was twenty-one in any way 'not detrimental to her physical and moral well-being'.

Most Victorian girls, of course, only obtained freedom from their parents when they promised, instead, to obey a husband and the ever longer wait for marriage in the late nineteenth century often led to internecine family warfare. Younger sisters wrote to the problem pages complaining of their elders' faultfinding. Brothers resented the obligation to squire sisters at evening dances, and to stand up with them if they failed to attract other partners. One correspondent, who complained that escorting his three, evidently unattractive, sisters left him with no opportunity to dance with other girls, was reminded sternly that this was a small return for all those tasks, such as the hemming of handkerchiefs, which his sisters performed for him. That he might prefer fewer handkerchiefs and more freedom to flirt is not considered.

Our conventional picture of the contented Victorian family, sternly bound together by their absolute dependency on the father's income, in fact bears little relation to the reality presented by problem pages, even if such obedient dependence is their consistent message. The paternal tyrant's subjects clearly rebelled, sulked, developed diplomatic migraines, took unchaperoned walks and corresponded during church services with

members of the opposite sex. The combination of moral
unctuousness and brutality in the late nineteenth century
was probably a response to an increasing loss of control. It
was this mixture which so disgusted Samuel Butler and led
him in *The Way of All Flesh*, to ask if there were 'any
decrepitude so awful as childhood in a happy, united, God-
fearing family?' And it is this which makes the Victorian
family still so unattractive to modern parents, however
much they may yearn for well-drilled children, who
chorus 'Yes, Papa' when ordered up to bed in the middle
of *Starsky and Hutch*.

Moral canting began to disappear in the Edwardian era.
The teenage correspondents of *The Cosy Corner*, for
example, were treated much like modern adolescents.
When forbidden to marry at the age of sixteen they sulked,
wrote endless screeds of poetry, and locked themselves into
their bedrooms with mementos of their loved ones (most
of whom, for some reason, seem to have gone to Manitoba
to seek their fortune). Their parents generally reacted
calmly, without recourse to whips, threats or talk of
eternal damnation. Similarly the problem page aunties
recommended that these sufferers should grow up and
learn housewifery, in preparation for the conjectural
return of their Canadian sweethearts. *The Cosy Corner's* no-
nonsense reply, on 30 June 1906, to a girl who'd been seen
by her brother 'kissing a man' was 'There is no harm
done, and I really don't see what you are worrying about.'

As the threat of an avenging God – or father – receded
so, too, did the fiction that a mother was invariably a girl's
best friend. In the fifteen years from 1880 to 1895 the *Girls'
Own Paper* only once, when faced with a clear case of
brutality, sided with a girl rather than her parents. By 1921
an auntie was openly admitting the fallibility of mothers:

*Miss EIR (Plumstead) – What a sweet letter, my dear. You are right in
saying that a girl should ask her mother and if she is a good mother all
will be well. Only, unfortunately, all mothers are not good; some are
very bad, and others are very foolish. That's one of the great reasons
why there is so much sorrow in the world.*

(Polly's Paper, *13 June 1921*)

Even the *Girls' Own Paper*, the bulwark of the Mother-knows-best school, finally admitted in 1918, in an article entitled 'Do they Misunderstand You at Home?' that there was no fundamental law which made girls like their parents. 'Most parents make a great mistake in taking it for granted that blood is always thicker than water, that members of the same family are peculiarly bound together with mind connection, heart connection and the bond of sympathy,' wrote Olson Swett Marden. 'Many a girl's heart has been broken because she was denounced for estranging herself from her family, when there was not a particle of affinity which bound her to any of the others.'

From recognising that some mothers were monsters, it was only a short step to admitting that papas could be pernicious too, and that the parental home was not invariably sweet. In 1901 a worried mother wrote to *Woman's Life* about her two daughters, aged nineteen and twenty-two, who wished to leave home, giving their father's drunkeness as the reason. But, claimed the loyal wife, 'he never abuses them in any way when he is intoxicated, but always goes quietly off to bed'. The auntie agreed with the mother that it was ungrateful of the daughters to wish to go, taking the view, 'It would certainly be more creditable on their part if they stayed at home and helped their mother in every way possible to cure their father of his bad habit ...' By 1929 even girls from working-class backgrounds, traditionally the most loyal to a family structure whether their own or their employer's, were asking the permission of aunties to leave home. 'Grey Eyes' and 'Sad Brown Eyes', for instance, were told by *Peg's Paper*, on 10 December 1929, 'If you think you would be happier in posts away from home, tell your parents so and try it for a time.'

The emphasis within the family has clearly changed. In centuries prior to our own, the corporate interests of the family were always seen to outweigh the inclinations of the individual. Whether a girl was happy at home was not deemed important. What mattered was whether she was needed at home, for whatever reason. One cause of this change was probably the rise of the limited liability company. The financial failure of a business could no longer bring in its train the stripping of a family's domestic assets, its house, furniture and clothing, a threat which had previously strengthened the sense of the family as an indivisible financial unit. Another cause of change was, more simply, the rise in women's wages during and after the First World War, and a consequent change in middle-class attitudes to work outside the home. Capitalism, as Marx had grudgingly foreseen, was 'building the new economic foundation for a higher form of the family and of the relations between the sexes'.

The new freedom was first enjoyed by the working girl, the reader of *Titbits*, *The Red Rose*, *Peg's Paper* or *Forget-me-Not*. The emancipation of the middle-class girl proved a lengthier process. Her education was more extended, and her subsequent chances of earning enough to support herself in the manner to which she was accustomed were appreciably less than those of her proletarian sister. But, whether explicitly or not, the aunties clearly recognised that the earning power of the new woman had given her an unprecedented independence. In cases where the girl was the provider they now adjudicated in her favour in family disputes. The following letter is an example of a girl who was clearly usurping the role traditionally held by the father – and receiving the support of the auntie:

> *Miriam's husband has quarrelled with the eldest daughter, who practically keeps the house going as she is in a very good position and pays the rent besides helping in many other ways. The two unmarried daughters live at home, and they have sided together against their father in a family quarrel about a small boy – a relative and an orphan – to whom the girls wish to give a home against their father's wishes. The younger daughter is out of work, but she is on her sister's side. Miriam tried to keep the peace but there is constant quarrelling and she is afraid that her daughter will bring the boy home some day, and that her husband will leave the house if she does, and he is not very strong. It seems a very complicated situation, and one's sympathy is naturally with the eldest girl for the little boy is very unhappy boarded out with strangers, and she is very fond of him. She would take a little cottage herself and adopt him if it were not for leaving the family in straits and deserting her mother. Miriam's husband is angry with her too, because he thinks she is taking the side of the girls.*

Well, Miriam, as your daughter practically keeps the house going, it seems to me that she ought to decide this matter. After all, she is a mature woman who has not married, you should take the daughter's part, and not in any secret way, but out in the open. If the three of you make a stand and have the boy, your husband would probably bend to the situation. I expect his threat to leave the house is made only to frighten you. It does make things more difficult for you that he is not strong, but it is no use allowing a peevish invalid to rule your lives ... the idea of a strange boy in the family must be upsetting to an elderly man, so do not let him think you are all against him; let him see he is considered, too, even if his daughter claims the right to adopt the boy if she wishes to do so.

(*Woman's Magazine*, December 1933)

By the mid 1930s aunties were lending their active support to girls who wished to leave home. Another reader of *Woman's Magazine* wrote in 1937 of how she and her mother constantly argued, after which her mother 'goes about like a martyr, and I have to keep pleading for forgiveness – in fact, I have to grovel before her to make peace again'. The correspondent had been offered a better job in another town, where she could live comfortably in lodgings. Was it her duty to stay with her fractious mother? The letter was unsigned since the girl was 'so ashamed at having to confess to not being able to get on with my own mother'. The auntie, though she pointed out that the mother might be at what she euphemistically termed 'a critical age', was nonetheless emphatic that the girl should leave her mother, and the scenes, behind her. Distance, she pointed out, would make 'you and your mother have a better perspective on each other and you will gradually understand each other, becoming more affectionate, forgetting past differences'.

Wartime gave a new twist to family relations. Traditionally parents had consulted the magazines about child-care and child-control, brothers and sisters had requested the adjudication of quarrels and, latterly, children had sought advice on how to find freedom. In the 1940s children began to usurp the responsible role of their,

sometimes absent, parents. Many staid married men saw
call-up, not merely as a licence to kill, but as a chance for
licence. And if their wives believed them when they
claimed to have been out late on Home Guard exercises,
their children often knew better!

> *I'm an only son of 15. My trouble is that Dad's carrying on with a
> WAAF in the town and Mother doesn't know about it. He's four miles
> out of town with the balloon barrage, and Mother and I live four miles
> this side. She doesn't go into town very often because she has a weak
> heart and the buses are very crowded, but I go in on my bike. Once I
> saw her coming out of the pictures laughing, this girl and Dad, and
> once I saw them looking in a jeweller's shop, hand in hand, as if they
> were sweethearts, and once I saw them through the confectioner's
> window having tea. She's awfully pretty and, of course, much younger
> and thinner than Mother. Mother keeps on saying how rotten it is they
> get so little leave from Dad's station, and when he does come home she
> can't make enough of him. Dad seems just like he always was – quite
> contented and listens and doesn't say much. He was talking 19 to the
> dozen when I spotted him with the WAAF and laughing. Ought I to
> tell Mother? Ought she to be sort of prepared? Could I make him
> promise never to see the WAAF again? Could I stop a divorce – if that
> is what Dad had in his mind after the war – by telling Mother now? –
> Only Son.*

You would be doing an incredibly stupid and short-sighted
thing if you breathed a word of this to your mother. This
war is, with many middle-aged men like your father, a
sudden return to youth and goes to their heads for a little
while and makes them feel young. You will not understand
until you are your father's age but you must take my word
for it. This is his playmate for the moment. He is playing he
is young and jolly, with no responsibilities. When you next
see him, tell him how much you miss him, and ask him if
you can cycle to the pictures with him. Tell him how lonely
your mother is. Make him feel that he belongs to you, and
that you are missing him, but don't let wild horses drag this
stupid story from you. He would not be the same as he
always has been at home, if it were important. He would be
restless, bad-tempered, uneasy, or he would not come at
all.

(*Glamour*, 3 February 1942)

Today children are less likely to be advised to make efforts
to accommodate their parents' life-style. Instead aunties
are recommending a deliberate detachment from
unsatisfactory parents. One nineteen year old young-
married wrote to Claire Shepherd's page in *Woman's Realm*
about how she should cope with her forty year old, fun-
loving mother who flitted between her husband and a
lover, and occasionally moved in with her daughter en
route. 'What with worrying about my mother and
listening to her troubles and trying to help my father, I feel
worn out at times, for their lives are in such a mess,' wrote
the nineteen year old. Claire Shepherd's reply was firm:

*Clearly there is no reason why you should not help your father if he
really needs it, but you do not have to entertain your mother's man
friend, nor need you have her to stay with you when she leaves her
home. Your mother sounds as if she is thoroughly enjoying the drama of
her life between this man and your father, and does not mind whom she
hurts in the process. So there is really no need to concern yourself too
much with her affairs.*

(Woman's Realm, *1 September 1969*)

'Mary Grant' in *Woman's Own* gave similar advice to a
seventeen year old whose mother was living with a man,
rowing constantly, and then demanding sympathy from
her son. 'Shift this load back to where it really belongs – on
your Mother's shoulders,' she sternly told him. 'You'll just
have to detach yourself as much as possible from the
goings-on at home.' Anna Raeburn also recommended
detachment to a young wife whose father-in-law was a
scrounger, a whiner, and looked like becoming a
permanent third in their small flat. 'I know blood's thicker
than water, but I think he's a problem you don't need,'
wrote Anna.

Filial obedience nowadays clearly does not involve the
sacrifices which were demanded even fifty years ago. The
welfare state has taken over many of the caring roles
which formerly were either performed by the family or
not at all. Another relatively recent development has been
the assumption by the young of the role of moral arbiter,
and youth can be surprisingly censorious towards the

lapses of its elders. Sex has acquired an exclusively youthful implication. To be old and to love is an offence against good taste. Some of the most agonised and indecisive letters in the modern auntie's postbag come from widows or, less frequently, widowers, who have fallen in love with a new partner and are facing fierce opposition from their children. One widow in her late sixties, for example, had given up her own home to help her crippled daughter. When she met a nice widower she knew that she could not leave her daughter in the lurch, however much she hankered after a new husband. Self-sacrificingly, she decided that she would embark on an affair. But her daughter and son-in-law threw up their hands in horror, refused to allow her to receive her lover-to-be in their house and acted the role of the repressive Victorian father to perfection.

Equally revealing, was the attitude taken by a son and daughter in a letter which appeared in Marjorie Proop's collection of representative letters, *Dear Marje*, in 1976. 'At the age of fifty-six,' wrote the sanctimonious daughter, 'my mother has suddenly changed from a sensible, dignified widow into a vulgar laughing stock.' The cause? She was having an affair with a younger man who, in the opinion of her children, could only be after her money. Marje Proops pointed out that their mother 'at fifty-six ... is still young enough to enjoy a man's company and love making. And at fifty-six she is old enough to know what she is doing.' Even if the man was after her money she might reckon she was getting her money's worth. Whatever was happening between their mother and her lover, Marje Proops insisted, it was none of the children's business.

Maybe I've been somewhat harsh with you, but I do get angry when grown-up children treat their parents like doddering fools who have no sense and no judgement. I'm sure you are concerned about your mother's future but don't get carried away by this image of dignified, sensible widowhood. If her lover provides her with company and consolation, be thankful that your mother has found some cheerful purpose in living.

Consideration towards parents is a central tenet of Marje Proops' counselling, and she has often favoured prevarication rather than full frontal attack when two different philosophies of life (and more particularly sex) reside under the same roof. Even in her early days as a counsellor on *Woman's Mirror*, she was too experienced a campaigner to be drawn into squabbles between mother and daughter over boyfriends:

> *Dear Marje, Whenever I go out on an evening date, my mother sees me off with 'Be good, dear. Enjoy yourself.' Why can't she make up her mind? Jezabel*

Dear Jez, Well, she has. Lots of Mums believe their daughters are angels and could not possibly enjoy themselves by being anything but good. Pity so many find out that the little darlings really want to be wanton. Knowing this, it's up to you to take care not to disillusion your mother.

> (*Woman's Mirror*, 18 February 1961)

But not all mothers are blissfully ignorant of their daughters' activities. A letter appeared in 1976 in *Woman's Own* from a mother whose thirteen year old daughter had been sleeping with her fifteen year old boyfriend, with her mother's knowledge and consent. This consent was withdrawn on the boy's sixteenth birthday since the mother erroneously believed that only now could he be prosecuted for having sexual intercourse with a minor. The irate mother's letter demanded a lowering of the age of consent, claiming that since the curtailment of her sex life her thirteen year old daughter had changed from a well-balanced, mature (some might say precocious) young adult to a sulky, unmanageable little girl.

Sulky little girls are themselves today frequent correspondents of the problem pages, allowing us to see family problems from the other end of the periscope. The new affluence of teenagers in the 1960s produced a whole crop of magazines, *Rave*, *Tina*, *Valentine* and *Pink* joining the long-running *Mirabelle* (formerly *Glamour*). This last magazine had its problem page of the early 1960s fronted

by Adam Faith and contained advice on such topics as how
to make parents like long-haired boyfriends, and how to
get a boy to kiss you:

> ... *Here's a trick a very pretty film star swears by. Look deep into your*
> *boy's eyes. Fine, now you have got his attention. Drop your eyes to take*
> *a lingering look at his lips and then raise your eyes to his again. It's*
> *practically irresistible.*

(Mirabelle, 18 November 1961)

This use of famous popstars to front columns has largely
ceased, possibly because editors have realised how
destructive the fantasy love of a thirteen year old can be. A
typical letter from a love-lorn fan appeared in *Pink* on 26
April 1975 and was answered by 'Sally', an auntie whose
photograph on the page suggests a seventeen year old. The
fan was obsessed by the Bay City Rollers, to the extent that
'I'm going off my food and I can't concentrate on my
school work. Also I lie in bed for about an hour, still
thinking of them.' Sally did not try to persuade her to
forget the Bay City Rollers. But she did advise, 'Oh, sure,
listen to your faves when you have a moment, but don't let
the thought of them stop you living your own life – which
could be just as stimulating and exciting as you choose it to
be.'

Interspersed with these fantasy loves are letters from
eleven year old girls who have fallen for the boy next door,
or in the next classroom. How to persuade the boy to drop
football and take up dating is one of the frequent
problems. Frets over school-work and a failure to live up
to parents' expectations (one girl from an academic
background revealed that she had been falsifying her
reports for five years to prevent her parents realising that
they had bred an unintellectual cuckoo) are other constant
themes.

Connie Alderson, in her book *Magazines Teenagers Read*,
undertook a systematic study of adolescent preoccupations
as expressed in letters to *Trend* in the mid-1960s. The six
main topics, in order of frequency, were getting a
boyfriend, worry about over-weight, spotty complexion,

wearing glasses or some other aspect of unsatisfactory appearance, difficulties about losing a boyfriend or complications arising when a romance was not working out, and conflicts with parents. The book was in fact highly critical of *Trend*'s team, consisting of a secretary, Sally, and an advisory panel of a psychologist, a fashion and beauty editress and a guest pop star. The latter very often proved to give the best advice.

Such teeny-bopper crises can easily, of course, seem trivial. But, though it is drawn on a smaller canvas, the torment of a twelve year old who is convinced that her parents no longer love her, after the birth of a sibling, is just as poignant and as deeply felt as the despair which seizes a mother four times her age when she discovers a much loved husband to be having an affair with his secretary. Most of the teeny-bopper magazines do have the courtesy to treat their readers' dilemmas seriously, if not always very grammatically.

In the past three years there has been a growing belief that the problems of the young, and even the major ills of society, can be laid at the door of the disintegrating family. In August 1976 the Archbishop of Canterbury argued in the House of Lords for a Ministry of the Family. Two years later, in August 1978, James Callaghan, with half an eye upon the hustings, announced that he intended to set up a Ministry of Marriage. Quite what these ministries would do was never made clear. But the idea behind them was obviously that the modern family should somehow be restored to the accepted model of stalwart security and in-built discipline. It was an experienced auntie, Anna Raeburn, who first, and most decisively, denounced the idea of a Ministry of Marriage. The function of a team of bureaucrats, in solving the problems she then dealt with every week, remains a mystery. And the problem page, if it does nothing else, reminds us at what cost those traditional family virtues have always been achieved.

10

In despair of a husband
WIDOWS, SPINSTERS AND RUINED MAIDS

The widow, the spinster and the ruined maid face such different problems that it may seem strange to discuss them together. In one crucial respect, however, they are alike. They all, in their different ways, lack a man. That deficiency and the troubles it brings have, over the years, filled more column inches of the problem page than almost any other topic.

Dunton's attitude to the plight of the single woman was brusque – a spinster's position could be ameliorated only by marriage. Accordingly, no holds were barred in the pursuit of that end, as an answer in *The British Apollo* in the first decade of the eighteenth century makes clear:

> *I have had the hard fate and misfortune to enter into the lists of Old Maids, and consequently to be slighted and despised by all. They say our very looks and qualities differ from the rest of mankind. Pray, Gentlemen, inform me what is the cause of this change, and whether marriage now that I have grown so stale, would have any effect upon me. But alas, I need not talk of that, for I am almost in despair of a husband. Therefore, good Mr Apollo, you that know all things, pray put me in the way of a husband for, in short, I would do anything to be rid of an old maid.*

It is no wonder if crosses, vexations and disappointments should alter the looks and qualities of a person. The only remedy we can propose to your forlorn condition is that you immediately take a lodging in Wapping and wait for the arrival of a West or East India fleet; and if there be any compassion left in human nature for the most obdurate of her sex, you are most likely to find it among the tars after their long Lent.

Dunton's reply has the frank brutality of Restoration Comedy. His attitudes are not necessarily, however, to be condemned as cruel or benighted. He had no sympathy with the automatic caricature of the old maid as narrow-minded and evil-tongued, and said as much, again in *The British Apollo*:

What is more unhappy than an ugly old maid?

It is possible for a handsome young maid to be more unhappy than an ugly old one. For happiness consists of our own ease and not in the opinions of others. Therefore, an ugly old maid, who thinks she looks neither old nor ugly (and there are such) is more happy than a handsome young maid who is not content with the beauty nature hath given her, and is continually trying to improve it by art (and there be such also). But if by happiness you mean what is most real and perfect (viz. a clear conscience void of offence towards God and man) an ugly old maid has much the advantage of a handsome young one, as being free from those temptations the other is always liable to.

Not everyone had spinsterhood thrust upon them. Some contemplated a voluntary choice of the single state. One group of girls wrote to 'Mrs Crackenthorpe' in *The Female Tatler* of 5 October 1709, requesting details of the original Vestal Virgins since they were 'almost resolved to establish such another order and become ourselves the first votaries'. With an eye on the recent battles of Tournai and Oudenaarde, the auntie replied:

Poor girls! I'm sorry to hear such lamentable complaints from such as you. If it be true what you say, you neither want fortunes, nor beauty to recommend you; but I'm afraid you may not be over-stocked with a more necessary qualification, I mean discretion. I hope your reflection on the last battles don't put you into this melancholy quandry, for fear a scarcity of men should ensue. Never fear, if you behave yourselves discretely, and have those other qualifications you'll not long want suitors.

In spite of her discouragements, 'Mrs Crackenthorpe' did take the trouble to supply them with the information they'd requested, though in the slightly indigestible form of a seventy-eight-line poem.

The dire fate of the ruined maid was discussed by both Dunton and Defoe. The latter, whose fictional heroines seem adept at following pre-marital sex with post-coital marriage, was rather more moralistic in his advice columns:

> *I am a young man and lately courted a young woman, and we had promised one another, but not being able to obtain her friends' consent to marry, I us'd my best endeavours to get her to bed without it; which I easily effected. I had no sooner done this but I began to talk of it (keeping a secret being none of my talent) and now her Father threatens to go to law with me. Therefore I pray your assistance in this affair.*

Though the Society thought the publication of this a sufficient caution to the Sex in general how they venture upon the honour of men; yet they could not but add some necessary remarks here, as
1. A woman that will take a man's word in this case, really ought to expect such usage.
2. He that lyes with such a woman on a promise of matrimony, is a knave if he does not perform his promise and a fool if he does ...

(The Review, 5 September 1704)

It was not, however, always the man whose approach to the altar was dilatory. One of Dunton's correspondents had loved 'a gentleman on whom Nature had lavished her stock, to render him an unresisted instrument of melting the breasts of the softer sex'. She had not resisted but, knowing him to be poor, she rejected him as a husband. This resolve was strengthened when her friends introduced 'a Gentleman of inviting estate to be my owner, whose person I could like, had I not first seen my handsome deceiver'. The usually mercenary Dunton would have none of this. 'First repent,' he wrote, 'then either remain unmarried or marry him that has been so well acquainted with you – for you can't justly be any

other – and besides the event may be tragical, since the
world is generally too lewd to be checked in matters of that
nature'.

The likely consequence of pre-marital sex at this date
was an illegitimate baby. Few such babies lived to be adult.
If their unmarried mothers lacked the nerve to dispose of
them, then the business could be left to the childminder,
whose methods led on average to a 60 per cent death rate
within the first year. Other expedients could be adopted by
less ruthless mothers. *The Post-Angel* of 1701 tells of one
enterprising girl who appeared in the Royal Exchange
carrying a covered basket with two turkey heads poking
out of the top. She was relieved of her burden by two
thieves, who subsequently discovered that they were
saddled with 'a lovely male-child and two necks of turkey
fastened at the corner'.

Until the 1834 amendment of the Poor Law,
maintenance provisions favoured the unmarried mother,
who was given the benefit of the doubt if a dispute arose
between her and the putative father. This did not reflect
an eighteenth century indulgence towards erring women.
Rather it safeguarded the parish rates from having to
support an indigent mother and child. In the draft of the
1834 bill, mothers were originally deemed solely
responsible for the upkeep of their illegitimate children.
An outcry in the Lords, however, restored the right to
bring a suit for paternity against the absconding man.

More draconian measures against the fathers of bastards
were favoured by *The Post-Angel*, in November 1701,
which recommended that such men should either pay the
woman a hefty sum or 'marry her (Prentice or not) or be
transported, if married and could not; or have a mark cut
on his nose, without a long process in law'.

A more humane attitude was taken by Frances Moore,
editress of *The Old Maid*, in an article about the much
criticised Foundling Hospital:

> It has been said by people who, though perhaps well-meaning, appear
> totally ignorant of human nature, that this provision is an
> encouragement of vice, but it is not, I think, to be supposed that any

person who gives way to animal passion thinks at all of the consequences of so destructive a folly; if they did, they would certainly avoid a conduct of which shame, remorse and sorrow are the unavoidable effects. I am inclined to believe that a parting with the child is a very severe punishment ...

(The Old Maid, *1756*)

The Old Maid was, of course, addressed to single women. It published numerous letters denying the view that spinsters were useless. They were, it was argued, essential for the smooth running of the home where frequent child-bearing eroded the time a mother could spend on child-rearing. In society the old maid proved her uses by acting as pianist for impromptu dances, or by making a fourth in a game of whist or speculation.

Such arguments cut little ice with parents whose attempts to secure husbands for their daughters sometimes smacked of desperation. A letter from twenty-three year old 'Biddy Willing' in *The Lady's Monthly Museum* in October 1798, related how 'My papa and mama have been trying for the last three years to match me, and have for that purpose carried me from our country seat to London, from London to Brighton, from Brighton to Bath, and from Bath to Cheltenham, where I now am.' The editor replied discouragingly:

I think the parents of my lively correspondent are much more to blame ... than she is for her ill-success. I allow it to be a natural and laudable wish to see a daughter matched to a man of probity and sense, who possesses an independent fortune, and who has abilities and diligence to acquire a decent competence at least, but this should not be too openly expressed ... nor should she be dragged from one scene of gaiety to another, till every fop knows her face, and the weakest understanding can penetrate the design. Jewels are not worn every day ...

(The Lady's Monthly Museum, *October 1798*)

The ruined maid was treated with growing sternness. But the increasingly moralistic tone of the nineteenth century problem page was occasionally softened by pleas for forgiveness:

Afflicted father — Your case is truly a terrible one, as unregenerated human nature goes; but a man who is willing to do by his own erring and ruined daughter as he would have his Heavenly Father do by him, would not have much difficulty in deciding upon his course under such circumstances as you are placed in. Think of your daughter's former goodness and innocence — of the great love you bore her and above all of her youth, her ignorance of the wiles of the world, her loving and trusting heart, and above all, of the downward course, and awful doom which inevitably await her unless she is shielded from such a fate under some protecting roof, and in some pure family circle. You should yield to your wife's entreaties and receive the erring one back into the asylum of the home. A mother's affections and instincts are as near divine as anything human can be, and should be allowed to govern in such cases.

(Home Magazine, *28 August 1858*)

Girls with forgiving fathers were the fortunate few. Many unmarried mums were servant girls living in their employers' attics, far from their parents' home. Taken at the age of thirteen from a close-knit village community and sent to an unfriendly urban environment, a pregnant servant girl could expect little sympathy from any quarter, least of all from her distant family. *The London Journal* wrote a reply to 'Katherine', on 14 July 1849, which discussed this very topic:

It is a very cruel custom to expose so young a girl to the perils of a situation as housemaid in a town so far removed from all her relatives and friends. We know not of any situation in life so full of danger as that of a servant girl in a large town with no friends to advise her against the snares and deceits of the world.

By the 1870s magazines were recommending an actively forgiving attitude towards the fallen servant girl. *The Englishwoman's Domestic Magazine* wrote to 'A Happy Wife' in June 1871:

You acted rightly as well as kindly. Servants as a class are exposed to much temptation. Should any mistress discover that the life of her intended servant has not been all it ought to be, and that a 'slip' has occurred; if she finds that this has been the one and only fault, expiated by sorrow and suffering; if the child is provided for, and if she has

> *reason to believe in the future decorum of the servant, it is the part of the Christian and good woman to help her fallen sister into the good path and, by sheltering her, watching her, caring for her and keeping her secret for her, to make the rest of her days a blessing instead of a curse ... the servant who is turned from the house has no refuge but the workhouse, no home but the grave, and no means of gaining a livelihood but by going from bad to worse ... In the case of this dreadful trouble happening in one's own house, it is the duty of every mistress to call in a doctor, and in his presence to obtain the name of the father of the child, and to use every effort to induce him to marry her at once. But it is illegal to send away any woman in or near actual labour. If her death ensues upon her confinement, the mistress or master is guilty of manslaughter.*

On occasion, of course, the name thus elicited in the presence of a doctor proved to be that of the son, or father of the house. *The London Journal* advised one young man, in love with the family servant he had seduced, to own up and marry her. An honourable course was, however, the exception. The brother of a flirtatious girl was told by the same publication in April 1862 that:

> *... her actions may lead to the destruction of her character and happiness. The gentlemen so much above her in station are only amusing themselves at her expense and, while paying her compliments, only think her a pretty simpleton.*

One troubled governess in a similar situation made apt use of Richardson's heroine Pamela, when she wrote to *The Ladies' Treasury* in the June of 1858:

> *Pamela — says she is a young governess, in a noble family and that one of the younger sons, a 'Honourable' (as the poor, simple girl proudly says), is in love with her. He has owned to her that, were he to marry her, he would be turned out into the world a beggar, but yet he threatens suicide if she refuses to allow him to address her clandestinely as a lover! 'Pamela', if she would deserve her name, must run the risk (no very great one) of her lover's destroying himself, else he will destroy her. She must leave her situation at once. It is evident that her own little citadel (her heart) is full of rebels, and traitors enlisted on his side. Her situation is one of great and immediate danger. If this clandestine attachment is discovered (and fire can never be hid long) she will lose,*

not only her situation, but her character. The man is not worth the risk since, for the sake of gratifying a passing fancy, he exposes the woman he loves to ruin and disgrace. Such 'Honourables' require the prefix of dis to their high-sounding names.

The social and financial troubles of the governess, the only obvious career for the middle-class spinster, were discussed in the agony columns with particular frequency. In the November of 1862 'A poor governess (Brighton)' was told by *Cassell's*:

We pity you; such people are not Christians; they are infidels, who profane the name of religion. Even the Russians – who we regard as benighted – set us an example in their way of treating governesses.

Girls desperate to obtain employment were tempted to blur the all-important distinction between governess and servant. This was discouraged in many magazines. The adviser on *The Young Woman*, in June 1895, wrote:

No governess should advertise her willingness to do light housework ... Everyone is entitled to a little time to herself; no one has a right to take anyone's whole life for themselves. I should advise you to leave the situation you describe; you could scarcely be in a worse one, and you might do better. There are reasonable employers, who recognise their duty to their subordinates as well as the duty of the subordinates towards them.

The real campaigning for the rights of the governesses, however, came not from the problem pages, and not from their own trade magazine *The Governess*. Instead it was *Punch* which took up the cudgels on their behalf, in the 1880s.

Apart from teaching, few occupations seemed possible for the unmarried middle-class girl. Several magazines, including *The Lady*, published articles on job opportunities and tried to give career guidance. Agencies such as The Society for Promoting the Employment of Women (which found girls jobs as book-keepers and typists) were given publicity in these columns and the advisers urged a realistic understanding of the skills required. The

magazines continued, however, to receive frantic letters
from untrained girls, whose meagre qualifications for paid
employment included on one occasion 'the ability to pour
tea'.

The precise watershed between girlhood and
spinsterhood remained something of a mystery.
According to *Every Week*, no man should consider
marriage before thirty, and no woman before twenty five.
Cassell's quoted Dr Harley's view that the life of an old maid
began at twenty eight. The editor did, however, add some
reassurance:

> ... *the sanitary measures of the present day seem to have extended a
> youthful appearance to a later period than in the times of our ancestors.
> Besides vaccination, in coping with that fell foe to beauty, the small-
> pox, has rendered beauty much more general and none can be called
> old who still look beautiful. Education has brightened the female
> intellect, intellect has reacted on the countenance, and as far as ladies
> are concerned, it has proved another agent in warding off old age, both
> in single and married people.*

The Beetons agreed that spinsterhood was a condition of
the mind, not the body. Women of fifty could escape the
dreaded categorisation as old maids 'if they can look kindly
on the world, talk cheerfully on all womanly topics and
eschew scandal and eccentricity'. But thirty was the
dangerous age 'if their hearts do not beat with the
sympathetic emotion at the joys of youth or the sorrows of
old age'.

Some Victorian women adopted, as a last resort, the
expedient of dressing mutton as lamb:

> *Ellen – The lady should take the advice of her brother. We fear she
> stands in need of advice, which may come too late. She cannot possess a
> large amount of common sense if she thinks that dress can make a
> woman of 55 pass for 30, and if she forms as false an estimate of the
> character and object of the man who appears to be courting her as she
> does of her own appearance, the result, if she is tempted to marry him,
> may not be conducive to her own comfort, nor to that of her relatives.*
> <div align="right">(The Young Ladies' Journal, <i>December 1869</i>)</div>

In other circumstances hopes were pinned on a fleeting interest shown some years previously by a still single man:

> *Florence – You write about a fourteen years' courtship, and complain that for a long time the dawdling swain has not replied to your letters. The sensible course for you to take would be to consider him dead, or married, or if neither, not worth your having. His heart, if alive, must be as cold and small as a cucumber grown on a barren and cold moor.*
> (The London Journal, *20 December 1862*)

The growth of female employment, towards the end of the nineteenth century, removed some of the desperation from the quest for matrimony. It also, however, opened up new areas of activity for the seducer. Many of the warnings against 'ruin' in late Victorian and Edwardian agony columns are concerned, for the first time, with the office and the factory:

> *I believe in your sincere penitence, but I am quite sure that at all costs to yourself and to others, you ought to leave your present situation. You pray 'Lead us not into temptation' yet you stay where you are daily exposed to it, and where you have yielded so often. There is no disgrace in flight. On the contrary it would show true courage. It would mean self-conquest as well as victory over a tempter … Amid other surroundings I believe you would again be happy and useful and be able to share in all Christian privileges with joy and thankfulness.*
> (Girl's Own Paper, *9 May 1903*)

Forget-Me-Not, a Harmesworth publication which appeared under the motto 'It will be as bright and pure as the flower from which it gets its name', published several letters from machine operatives whose piece-work wages had suffered after their rejection of the foreman's advances. Unlike the secretary, who merely had to dodge round the desk, the mill-girl who alienated a foreman might find her machines constantly breaking down, her materials disappearing and her reputation for efficiency destroyed. The aunties, despite the claim of the *Peg's Paper* editor in 1919 that 'Not so long ago I was a mill-girl, too', had few helpful hints for a girl in this position, other than to report the foreman to his boss.

The arrival of more jobs for women did not immediately lead the aunties to see such opportunities as an acceptable alternative to marriage. Widows were still encouraged to find a new male bread winner at all costs. Only in one extraordinary case did the advisers falter:

> *Yours is a very sad story 'Widowed one'. After six years of widowhood, to meet and love a man who also loves you but who would not consent to your crippled son sharing his home if you became his wife, is very hard indeed on you. Your duty is most definitely with your child …*
> (The Cosy Corner, *10 March 1906*)

Few letters from widows were published during the First World War. This conspicuous absence may have reflected a decision, taken for reasons of morale, that such letters should be answered privately. Death stalked the problem page only by implication. Information was given on how to claim a widow's pension and how to contact the War Office to find out why letters from the front had stopped coming. Women were also given hints on self-sufficiency and told how to manage their financial affairs. 'Beth' in *Woman's Weekly*, on 28 August 1915, for instance, was encouraged to put her money into the hands of the Public Trustee. She was worried that her brother might 'be called on to enlist, and if he was killed, I should – besides the grief of his loss – be in danger of being swindled out of all my money'. Quite which eventuality she feared the more is not at all clear.

The implications for women of the loss of a whole generation of men were sensed as early as January 1915, in a series of letters in *The Girl's Realm* dealing with their readers' future prospects:

> *We are all training for professions and mean to be happy and prosperous in our careers if possible, but we one and all realise that marriage is the vocation of healthy sensible girls and we are not going to pass by love for any high-flown notions about careers and fame …*

Once the war was over most aunties encouraged their readers to bury the past and flirt with the future. Just occasionally, however, an adviser would judge a girl to be insufficiently devoted to the memory of a lost man:

> *Sarah – You must please yourself, my dear girl. You know what your feelings are for the young man. As far as your sweetheart's people are concerned – well, if they think you have forgotten him, they will not be far wrong, will they? I should think that anyone would 'feel sad', when they visited the parents of someone who had given his life so nobly for his country; but if the feeling only lasts while you are there, and your thoughts are of the newcomer directly you leave, I should say you never loved the first boy at all.*
>
> (Polly's Paper, *29 December 1919*)

Four years of gloom, shortages and death led girls in 1919 to dream of gaiety, laughter and fun. The Twenties introduced a new species of spinster – one who charlestoned, smoked, shingled her hair and wore lipstick. Most of the changes, however, were only skin-deep. Girls were now faced with such competition from their sisters that an overtly aggressive approach was required when searching for a husband:

> *We have outlived the days when at the tender age of about 20 unless some obliging and, very probably, uninteresting young man took pity on a girl she was obliged to retire into the background with a piece of tatting for consolation and diversion and suffer the indignity of being styled an old maid ... Your modern maiden is not nonplussed if, at the ripe age of 35 or over, she finds herself husbandless. She is possessed of courage and a reckless independence which enables her to stand alone and fight her own battle, and she doesn't feel embittered if the right man dawdles instead of hastening to be on the step to realise her worth ...*
>
> (Pam's Paper, *17 July 1926*)

In 1934, the first year since the war in which the number of marriageable women roughly equalled the number of nubile men, *Woman's Magazine* at last broke with the established convention that every woman wished to marry. It recognised that 'there are many women who have no desire whatever to marry and who have a jolly and happy life as single folk'. *Woman's Fair*, a magazine aimed at film fans, was however unconvinced:

> *Any girl who declares she prefers to stay single is only fooling herself. No matter how full of life she may be, it isn't complete without marriage. Nothing else can satisfy this fundamental need. If you are clinging to single blessedness, the chances are that there is something wrong with your emotional make-up ... or that you are a victim of false ideas. Knowledge and guidance may help.*

A little bit of ill-digested Freud went a long way in many women's magazines of the 1930s.

But the assumption that most women would do anything to avoid sinking into spinsterhood was often based on a more sensible premise – the recognition that single women were still at a social disadvantage. A reply in *Woman's Magazine*, in February 1934, given to a spinster living with her brother and his new bride in a jointly inherited family house, illustrates how a married woman automatically took precedence when it came to domestic squabbles. The wife was the one who ought to run the house, according to the auntie, and the spinster should step back since 'that is the right and gracious thing to do'. Whatever the legal position, 'the opinion of all reliable people would be that your newly married brother, who may be having a family of his own, had more right to the family house than you, an unmarried sister ...'

Spinsters also lost out to their married siblings in that it was they who were invariably expected to care for their parents in old age:

> *I have recently lost my father and my mother is, of course, very much upset. She wants me to leave my job and come home to be with her. Both she and my brothers seem to take it for granted that I should do so, but to me it does not seem as simple as all that. You see, I am 34 and my job is a good one. Suppose that I gave it up. I should be dependent on my mother during my life-time as she has a pension, and later I should have to rely on my brothers because the older one gets, the more difficult it is to get a good job. Two of my brothers are engaged and the third is likely to be. It sounds horribly calculating, but I am really worried about it. What do you think I ought to do?*

I do not suppose for a moment that your mother – and still less your brothers – have realised just what they are asking of you. I think you should state the case quite bluntly to your brothers and point out that your mother's well-being is quite as much their care as yours. Daughters seem very often to be expected to shoulder an unfair burden in this way. You should point out to them that they do not propose to break their engagements and remake their lives for their mother's benefit, and have no right to expect it of you. I don't suppose that they have realised that a time might reasonably come when they might have to support you.

(*Mab's Weekly*, 26 May 1934)

Large Victorian families, with large Victorian houses had, in general, found caring for elderly parents less burdensome. The spinster of the 1930s was more likely to get landed with looking after her parents without help from either relatives or servants than her predecessors.

The widow of the 1930s also fared badly, becoming more socially isolated than ever before. The premature death of a spouse became rarer. Divorce was still not widespread. The single woman accordingly was surrounded by couples who wanted no truck with her. Married friends 'are afraid I am going to develop into a designing widow and make mischief with their husbands' wrote one widow disconsolately to *Mab's Weekly* when she found her social life had ended along with her husband's life.

But young girls, rather than designing widows, were the real danger, if the evidence of the problem page is to be trusted. They were the ones who had apparently dissociated sex and marriage. Morality was in a state of flux in the inter-war years with aunties, though never condoning pre-marital sex, nonetheless not being too shocked when guilty secrets were revealed – particularly if marriage was in the offing. But betrayed girls were variously advised. *Woman's Magazine* felt:

> It does not matter that no one knows but yourself, or that your future husband might never find out. The thing that matters is whether you are on the side of goodness, on God's side, or on the other. Do be on God's side.

'Evelyn Home', on the other hand, believed that girls with

lurid pasts (usually a reference to heavy petting) should not indulge in revelations. They might remember, she suggested, that their fiancés probably 'had quite as exciting pasts as them, but they have relegated it to its proper position – the hinterland of forgetfulness'.

'Evelyn Home' also departed from tradition when she advised a woman not to marry her child's father, a man 'who drinks and has a bad temper', purely so that the child would be legitimate. Most aunties in the 1930 thought a bad husband better than no father, the implication being that such a loveless marriage was the price of wrong-doing. 'Evelyn Home' also discouraged endless recrimination. She told one twenty seven year old, who as a teenager had let a man go too far and now wondered 'Could I ever presume to accept the love of a straight, honourable man?' that, yes, she could.

The punishment was not always self-inflicted. Life could still be tough for the ruined maid who, by the 1940s, was making more frequent appearances on the problem page. The rise in the number of girls in trouble partly reflected the gap between the date of the slackening in conventional morality and the time when birth control was readily available to unmarried women. But it was also indicative of a change in editorial policy towards what could be printed on the page. With the government launching explicit advertisements about VD, which were reproduced in the women's magazines, the aunties could afford to become more daring in the topics they covered.

Once men were whisked away into the military machine, it was not easy for a putative father to be shamed or shot-gunned into marriage. Some men, however, found that their love triumphed over their feelings of betrayal when they returned home on leave to find their girl cuddling someone else's baby. One serviceman who found his girl pregnant by another soldier wrote to *Modern Woman*, in December 1940, that:

> At first I thought this would finish everything between us, but now I know I want her as much as ever. I suppose it is all wrong. My mother would cut her dead if she knew.

The auntie advised swift action if he still wished to marry her and 'then trust her utterly and never tell anyone of the secret of the baby's parentage for "a secret confided to any one is no longer a secret".'

Girls wrote in about the same problem, often in less hopeful circumstances:

> *My friend and I are writing to you because we are in need of a friend. We were both engaged to two nice boys in the RAF. During their absence we have been keeping company with two soldiers who seemed genuine enough when they told us they loved us very much. They took us to a dance, and later escorted us home. They made love to us, and we lost our heads, and we are afraid there are serious consequences. Since then the soldiers have gone abroad and have not kept their promise to write. We have left our homes and now our own boys have left us ... We are both 19.*

My dears, I am indeed sorry for you. You have thrown away your happiness for the sake of an evening's excitement. I wish all girls would beware of men who 'lightly come and lightly go' such as the two men who betrayed you and left you to bring into the world two innocent children. The only thing for you to do now is to return to your homes, make full confession of what has happened, and ask for your parents to help you ...

(*Glamour*, 6 January 1942)

As in the previous war, death sometimes intervened to leave girls pregnant with no potential husband, and no potential maintenance order. The opening of the Second Front was the signal for a flood of desperate letters from girls whose defences had been stormed some weeks before:

> *This is not my trouble, but I am terribly worried as my mother has a weak heart and isn't strong in other ways. My young sister, who is not quite 17, was crying awfully the other night, and I thought this was because a young chap we both knew has been killed out in Normandy. But it turns out she is going to have a baby ... I simply dare not tell Mother and my father is dead. Will you tell me what to do to get her away before Mother finds out ...*

How I wish you had sent your name and address as then I

could have helped you straight away. Directly you see this, will you do so, and I will put you in touch immediately with someone who will help your sister in her trouble. I'm afraid your mother will have to know as it may be some little time before you see this reply ... if as you say, your sister is already three months pregnant, I am afraid changes in her figure will be noticed by your mother ...

(Glamour, 30 January 1945)

Aunties in the Second World War were generally much less keen on rapid, war-time marriage than their First World War counterparts. This was possibly because they had spent the 1930s dealing with the accumulated problems of the previous batch of hasty alliances. As 'Evelyn Home' put it in 1939, 'One marries for life and not for war'.

The Beveridge Plan of 1942 made more adequate financial provision for social misfits of all kinds. But the unmarried mum and the deserted wife could still be treated like pariahs by their neighbours:

> *I am beginning to think there are no decent kindly folk left in the world, because I have met with nothing but indifference since I've to fend for myself and my five year old daughter.*
>
> *I desperately need a job and a home for us both, but I cannot find one. I sank my pride and asked for temporary accommodation with some friends I once took into my house.*
>
> *They turned me away, and I've no relatives to help us and no job to provide for us.*

I am deeply sorry for your unhappy plight, but I think there are several possible (though only temporary) solutions for you to seek.

First to overcome your immediate difficulty, do go along to your local employment exchange and ask to see the assistance officer who will give you the financial help to tide you over.

Then enquire about the possibilities of a house-keeping job where you could have your little girl with you ...

(Woman, 4 July, 1953)

Those families who stand by a pregnant daughter still find

that the price can be high. A letter which appeared in a
teen-magazine in 1974 illustrates how unpleasant life can
be made for them. The correspondent was a school-girl
whose elder sister was an unmarried mum. Her family,
after initial ructions, had accepted the baby. Not so the
young sister's school chums who – probably parroting
their mums – taunted her with being the aunt of a bastard.
The problem page could do nothing but advise her to
ignore them.

Alongside the casualties of a permissive society which
does not accept the consequences of its tenets, are those
who think they must be odd, frigid or unacceptable
because they are not overcome by lust every time they
meet a boy. 'Were they abnormal?' asked the virgins.
They could be forgiven for thinking so:

> *Most girls who write to you seem to have trouble preventing themselves*
> *from sleeping with their boyfriends. I have a boyfriend, but find that I*
> *am not nearly so anxious to sleep with him as he is with me. Does this*
> *mean there is something wrong with me? – Ellen, Bristol.*

Not necessarily, but it could be you've got the wrong
boyfriend. Not every girl in the land is fighting down
uncontrollable sexual urges, though it might seem so
sometimes. Many girls have slow responses, but lead
happy, successful lives for all that.

(*Petticoat*, 19 July, 1969)

In the 1960s the aunties seemed determined to support
both those who decided, after due consideration and
proper precautions, to indulge in pre-marital sex, and
those who plumped for virginity until the honeymoon. It
was not the policy, however, of women's magazines to
encourage the latter to change camps and have an affair.
Without saying so in so many words, Anna Raeburn
finally broke this barrier in *Woman* on 19 August, 1978,
when she replied to the following letter:

> *In a few months time I'm getting married and like any other girl I*
> *want to be a virgin on my wedding night, but my boyfriend keeps*
> *asking me to have intercourse with him. When I say no, he gets angry.*

I'm upset about this because I feel if he loved me enough, he would understand and wait. I don't know whether you agree or not but, in the meantime, I don't know what to do. I want to be really sure he loves me before getting married, or else I'll call things off before it's too late. By the way I'm nearly 21.

It's not a question of testing your boyfriend and saying, 'If he loved me, he'd do so-and-so'; the real point is that you're saying no. That you refuse to have sex until you are married matters to you. I'm sure this point has arisen and been discussed before, but your boyfriend has obviously felt that once the marriage was near, you'd relent.

You say if he loved you, he'd understand and wait. He loves you all right, but in his own way, which means he feels free to disregard your expressed wishes on this subject. Anyone who has been married will tell you that no matter how sure you are, you can't be completely so. Marriage is both a risk and a responsibility for which no satisfactory insurance policies can be written.

You aren't sure enough of him to feel that he'll still want you to be his wife or respect you properly if you aren't a virgin on your wedding night. In my book that's a pretty narrow definition of love and it doesn't promise well for your future together if you're so insecure about him. I'm very sorry to sound like your old granny but you're very young, there's plenty of time. Leave the wedding bells for a bit until you know more about who you are and until you meet someone who understands you better.

She never actually states that her correspondent should go to bed with her fiancé, but that is the strong implication.

Arguably, although the lot of the ruined maid can still be tough, the confirmed spinster has fared worse in modern society. She can, of course, now earn her own living and is no longer dependent on the charity of married relatives. But her social isolation is often far greater. She now commonly lives alone, or with her parents until their death. Unlike the Victorian old maid, who at least had safety in numbers and could make friends with similarly unmarried middle-aged women, the comparative rarity of her modern counterpart means that she has no ready-made group of associates. Society, now more than ever, makes pair-bonding its norm. Those outside the two-some can be more deprived than they were a hundred years ago.

Greater attempts are made by modern society to include the divorced and unmarried mother in the community. This, I suspect, is chiefly because children are involved. Concern for children has always been a prime consideration for aunties. This is why they were so stern towards girls who seemed about to stray, yet comparatively sympathetic to the same girls when they were pregnant or mothers. No corresponding attempt has been made to incorporate the spinster into the social mix.

A published letter on loneliness brings a more rapid increase in auntie's post-bag than any other topic. It is, in many respects, the most difficult problem for an auntie to solve. She can supply a list of singles clubs, or suggest evening classes and a communal hobby. She cannot, however, make friends for her lonely readers, whether they be widows, divorced women, spinsters or unmarried mothers. For all the moral and economic changes that have affected their position, the evidence of the problem page is that isolation is as severe a difficulty for women today as it has ever been.

11

So many out of bread
SOCIAL COMMENT IN THE PROBLEM PAGE

Lust and love, hate and jealousy have been the staple ingredients of problem pages since their inception. But the stage on which these human emotions are displayed has had a whole series of backcloths. Though aunties may seem to be preoccupied with the more intimate details of human existence, they have often been required to be equally authoritative on larger matters. Law and politics, money, war and even science have regularly come within their purview.

Life, as it is seen in the pages of seventeenth century periodicals, was amusing but uncertain. There was a gaiety which would be notably lacking in the nineteenth century, but more striking is the constant insecurity. Only the goodness of God and never-ending endeavour lay, we feel, between plenty and penury. A crisis lurked in every garbage-filled gutter, and nemesis round every unlit corner. No Welfare State cosseted the failures, and friends were at best a feeble bulwark. No one could afford to lower his guard or to put his trust in strangers:

I am a barber, being lately sent for to a tavern, to comb out some gentlemen's perukes. As I was acombing 'em, one of 'em asked me whether I was willing to serve the King under Brigadier Stewart; I replied Yes, thinking to speak loyally, not knowing they were officers. They gave me a shilling, which I thought was for combing the perukes, and so stop't me, telling me I had listed myself for a soldier. We went before my Lord Mayor, where I was put on oath. I swore I did not list myself so was dismissed; it has troubled me since that I swore so rashly, therefore pray give me your opinion in the next Oracle *whether I have done ill in swearing so, not understanding their meaning, nor why they gave me the shilling? If I had gone I would have been ruined.*

If in your oath you spoke according to your intention, and as you understood them, when you received the money, we think you have not done anything amiss.

(*The Athenian Oracle*)

Enforced enlistment was only one involuntary way to travel. Another was transportation, a sentence which could be passed for offences as minor as petty theft. It raised ethical worries in the mind of one reader, who felt that the bartering in America of criminals as slaves was a sin. The editors of *The Athenian Mercury* did not share his qualms, regarding it as just punishment for the wicked. Crimes, they felt, could be mitigated by hard, productive labour. Dealing in negro slaves, however, was a different matter. This could not be justified by true Christians, being contrary to both the law of nature and the law of God. Buying them for 'Toyes and Baubles' did not lessen the offence, nor did claiming that they were prisoners of war, rightfully sold by a victorious army. Even if they were, as was sometimes argued, 'more heathens than pagans' then they still had a 'common right to those temporal blessings which an indulgent Creator had given them as well as we'.

British Law officially extended the rights of citizenship to a negro servant domiciled in England 'as soon as he can give account of the Christian faith, and desires to be baptised, any charitable, lawful minister may do it, and then he is under the same law with other Christians'.

Richard Steele, however, in 1710, published a letter in *The Tatler*, purportedly from a blackamoor page in a fashionable household, which illustrated the hollowness of the doctrine. The page might be told that he was now, as a Christian, on a par with his mistress, but he still found he was no better treated, indeed was less pampered, than the parrot she had purchased from the same ship.

Other abuses of the law also found their way into the pages of *The Athenian Oracle*:

> *A certain person on Sunday last, in the sermon time was drinking in an ale house where he dined, for which he was forced to pay 3s 6d. Yet the Justice of Peace, who caused the man to pay the said money, was the same day tippling himself in sermon time. Now I would fain know what treatment this said Justice ought to meet with, and to whom may a man safely go to inform against him; for without doubt no justice will fine or condemn a justice, but rather send the informer to prison; therefore what ought to be done in this case, that the Reformation may take its free course?*

Dunton was emphatic that a justice could, in such a case, be judged by his fellow JP's 'if the information appears to be the truth'.

When dealing with the irreligious, the magistrates of this period were not solely concerned with petty lapses of Sunday observance. They were also expected to adjudicate in witches' trials. Those held in New England are well known. Similar trials in Old England, where the outcome tended to be less disastrous for the accused, are often forgotten. One letter which appeared in *The Athenian Oracle* asked the editors' opinion of a case in Kent, in June 1692, in which three women were accused of practising witchcraft. One widow, for instance, confessed:

> ... *she had made a covenant with the devil in writing and signed it with her blood, which dropped from her nose; that she had four imps whom she called by the names of Vene, Harry, George and William; three of them were black and about the bigness of mice, they sucked her every third night; but William was like a little black man, he talked to her and had carnal copulation with her twice; and by the help of these she did mischief to beasts and men, of which she gave divers instances.*

This woman died before judgment was given, being found 'dead by her bedside in a strange posture'. One of her fellow witches was reputed to turn herself into a cat and, in this form, to pour 'black stuff' into a sleeping man's mouth, thus causing his death. These two were acquitted by the court, but others who had elected instead to prove their innocence by oath, were 'flung bound into the water three times apiece, but could not sink, though they lay a considerable time upon the water'. In order to make the experiment more convincing, a man was hired at a cost of five shillings to be similarly flung into the water. He, by contrast, sank 'and before they could get him ashore, had taken a great deal of water in his belly'.

The opinion of the editors was, first, that they would not question the decision of a court. Secondly, they were not sure whether imps existed or not, but they were sure that witches could not possibly turn themselves into cats. And, lastly, they insisted that 'such sort of examination by swimming, etc., is utterly unlawful, and a breach of the Fifth Commandment, and as subject to abuse and deceits as any other trial in nature ...'

Common sense usually triumphed. Plausible explanation were found for two-headed worms embedded in a dead man's heart, and for a corpse gushing blood when viewed by a particular mourner. Daniel Defoe, in the *Review* of 18 May 1706, showed extreme caution in interpreting a clergyman's dream which foretold the destruction of London by an earthquake. 'To give my opinion,' he wrote, 'to what I have no assurance in matter of fact, I confess, is the way to come under the lash of those people, to whom this paper is so much an eyesore that they would be glad to have so fair an advantage.' He did not automatically dismiss spirits and apparitions, but he doubted their capacity to foretell the future. As for the particular prediction, Defoe advised:

> *I would all people believed it – and live as if it would certainly come to pass; and that I think is the best can be made of the story ... what a strange alteration should we find in the countenance of the people if this were done.*

It was, however, calamity on a more personal scale that preoccupied Defoe in 1706. Still reeling from the failure of his pantile factory three years before, he devoted almost his entire correspondence column to commenting on the newly passed Bankruptcy Act. He used various letters to illustrate its shortcomings, but nonetheless in broad terms supported it since it improved a bankrupt's chance of clearing his name.

The deadly seriousness of the financial problems facing Dunton or Defoe's readers were gradually displaced as newspapers began to serve a more elevated and secure social class. It is in these smart publications that we discover the convivial, carefree atmosphere traditionally associated with the early eighteenth century. The tone is captured in a bar-maid's letter to *The Spectator*, in 1712, complaining of the 'improper discourses' with which her customers were pleased to entertain her, and of their attempts to witness her resulting blushes. The editor sympathised, and deplored the behaviour of the sort of fop who 'cannot buy a pair of gloves, but he is at the same time straining for some ingenious ribaldry to say to the young lady who helps them on'.

Apart from a capacity for friendship and for drink, 'bottom' – a cool courage in hunting, fighting and womanising – was the most prized gentlemanly quality. But duelling, initially the ultimate in 'bottom', was first frowned upon and later made illegal. The problem page, inevitably, favoured a less radical method of settling differences (preferably along the lines of consulting the editor and letting him adjudicate). Hugh Kelly was one of duelling's most scathing critics, as a stinging answer in *The Court Miscellany* of 1765 suggests:

> *In endeavouring to vindicate the character of a girl from the town, for whom I have a particular* tendre*, from some aspersions on her by a friend of mine, a quarrel ensued and he has since sent me a challenge. As I find I have not sufficient courage to meet him, (I ask) whether I ought to accept him, or go and acknowledge myself a coward, and be posted by all my acquaintances for ever after?*

> Accept the challenge undoubtedly, for if you run your antagonist through the body, or he you, 'tis three to one but the other comes to be hang'd; and then there's good riddance of two ridiculous hot-headed coxcombs, who are better out of the world than in it.

As the eighteenth century progressed women, who in 1712 had held their own in the coffee-house, were increasingly expected to confine themselves to the home. Those with pretensions to learning, or an interest in politics, were violently satirised. The contemporary wisdom was expounded on 20 April 1784 in *The New Spectator*:

> *My wife has gone mad! – What is worse, politically mad! Ever since the commencement of the Westminster election my wife has been intoxicated with politics, my servants with strong beer, and my house has resounded with nothing but 'Fox for ever!' It would have been some consolation had she confined her folly to her own house, but alas! She has been canvassing with a vengeance! And with petting one fellow, kissing another and coaxing with thousands has driven me almost horn-mad! ... Her reputation is indeed unimpeached, and I believe her present conduct arises solely from the singularity she always assumes and which is her chief, if not her only, fault. But she should remember that female reputation is of slender contexture and that*
> > *'To her belongs*
> > *The care to shun the blast of sland'rous tongues'.*
> *This, however, is impossible so long as she interferes in matters which by no means concern her or her sex ...*

The gentleman very justly calls himself a fond husband, he is indeed too fond and too indulgent in permitting his wife to disgrace herself by conduct so reprehensible ... If reasoning fails, he should hurry her into the country and, by taking her from the scene of the action, endeavour to reclaim her. It has, of late years, been too much the vogue amongst the fashionable fair to imitate in everything the other sex, particularly in modes of dress and matters of amusement ...

This, clearly fictitious, exchange was possibly designed to embarass a particular political hostess. But it underlines the trend towards restricting most activities outside the home to men. And as ladies became more 'accomplished', so their ability to work was impaired. This was not disastrous so long as they had the capital to match their idleness. But sometimes a rude shock awaited the genteel tradesman's daughter when she emerged from her smart boarding school:

> *I am 19; have had a boarding school education; speak French tolerably well; play the piano in some style; dance, draw and do ornamental*

*needle-work — My papa is a haberdasher, and wants me to stand in his
shop; and I wish to ask you whether I ought? And what is the use of an
education like mine if instead of making an advantage of it, I am to
forget it all, by mixing with shopmen and measure tape like a dowdy?
My mama says it is wrong, and as my papa can give me very little
fortune, he ought to exhibit me as much as possible with all my
accomplishments; the only chance I have of moving in my proper
sphere is by getting a rich man. Please give me your advice ...*

If your education has been sound you will not lose it by
mixing with shop women, and measuring tape; and you
will not appear like a dowdy, when, by assisting your
father, you are endeavouring to make some return for his
indulgence. I have omitted shopmen because I think a
young lady of such a mind as yours appears to be, might be
in some danger amongst them, and I am sorry to find you
can write shopmen as well as shop women. For whilst there
are few employments for females and so many out of bread
I think it will be a great shame that men are engaged at all
to do that which appears to be the peculiar province of our
sex – but for this our sex are to blame, for which I shall give
my reasons in a future paper.

(*The Lady's Magazine*, October 1817)

Quite how the female sex was responsible for its own
shrinking job opportunities the editor never, in fact,
revealed, despite this promise. But it was an ominous
foretaste of what was to become a dominant social
problem in Victorian agony columns – the unsupported
spinster or widow who had few qualifications and little
chance of establishing herself in a remunerative job. It was
not a problem that the new generation of aunties would
find easy to solve.

The re-emergence of problem pages in the 1840s did not
initially see much space devoted to female matters. For a
brief period these columns were dominated by men. As a
result, in place of the moralising over domestic virtues
found in *The Ladies' Magazine* or *The Lady's Monthly Museum*,
we now read advice for those who feared that they might
be selected by lot to be part of the militia bound for
Oregon. *The London Journal* of 31 January 1845 advised 'One
liable to be drawn' of the existence of Militia Substitute

Societies which, in return for a shilling a week and some beer money, would insure a man against selection, undertaking either to pay the fine or to find a substitute.

In general, the problem pages encouraged patriotism but discouraged involvement in other nations' fights. A 'Would-be volunteer of Garibaldi', for instance, was told by *Cassell's* on 27 October 1860:

> *We appreciate your motives and admire your spirit, but as your country has the first claim on the courage and energy of her sons, our advice to one and all of you is, stay at home.*

The American Civil War also attracted its would-be heroes. Here, too, the counsellors discouraged potential volunteers. On 17 May 1862 the inaptly named 'Cupid' was told by *The London Journal*:

> *By the time this is issued we trust you will have seen that your martial services would not be required either by the Southern or North Americans. As your money came to you at home, you should spend it at home, instead of wishing to play the amateur soldier in a cause graced by neither dignity or honesty.*

Cassell's was of much the same opinion, pointing out that to enlist in the Confederate Army was strictly illegal. The editors hoped for 'the re-establishment of peace on a solid and enduring basis' but were not disposed to depart from 'the strict neutrality marked out by the government'.

Then, as now, wars were expensive things and one parsimonious correspondent of *Cassell's* anticipated the end of the conflict in the Crimea with particular eagerness. On 29 March 1856, however, the editor was obliged to disillusion him:

> *WS asks us the following question – 'Should peace be made and the Emperor of Russia have to pay the expenses of the war, will the increased amount of income tax be returned to the different parties who have paid it? If not, what will be done with it?' Did our correspondent ever know a Chancellor of the Exchequer return anything? Such a case has never come to our knowledge. Then, 'what will be done with it?' demands WS. Devoted to the usual purposes for which other taxes are levied, of course, – spent.*

Taxes might be resented, but the tax-dodgers of the period seem to have had singularly tender consciences. On 17 January 1863 the editor of *Every Week* dealt with a letter from 'Doubt' who had evaded income tax for the past eight years. Now he had moral scruples. He was advised to send the 'conscience money' to either the Chancellor or the Inland Revenue Office, and was warned that an additional £50 fine was likely to be imposed for each unpaid year. In 1863 this would represent a hefty penalty for the average middle-class family.

Towards other sorts of dishonesty the editors were sterner. 'A London Card Sharper', for example, who wrote helpfully to *The London Journal* on 29 June 1850 to explain how to join several used postage stamps together to form one seemingly pristine specimen, was warned that 'Playing tricks with the Government is as dangerous as teasing a strange bull-dog or mastiff'. A 'Constant Reader' writing to the same magazine some three months later to reveal that he was a former arsonist who wished to turn King's evidence was given equally short shrift. He wished to know the consequences of his step. The answer was ill calculated to stiffen his resolve:

> *Why, you would be transported along with your accomplices. As an atonement to society and your Maker, it is your duty to denounce them forthwith. The law might take your repentance into consideration, and be more merciful to you than to the others.*

The mid-nineteenth century magazines reverted to the earliest Grub Street practice in their willingness to discuss such controversial matters as employment, strikes, the welfare of workers and social legislation. *Cassell's* even used its columns to prod the consciences of some Poor Law Guardians when it was felt that they were not distributing the relief fairly. One such incident occurred in 1863 when, almost overnight, the Lancashire cotton industry collapsed. The American Civil War had led to a blockade of the cotton-growing South and, with the disappearance of their industry's raw material, mill-workers found themselves unemployed:

AG has called our attention to the fact that, in many cases, the members of co-operative societies have been refused relief, both by the Poor Law Guardians and the Committee. We much regret this has been the case, but we have no power to set apart for the special benefit of members of those societies any portion our benevolent readers have placed in our hands. We shall be glad to hear that the Guardians, who have kindly undertaken the onerous duties of distributing relief, have reconsidered the principle on which they have hitherto been acting in this respect, and have felt themselves justified in adopting a different plan.

The Civil War cotton slump was, however, very much a special case and it would be misleading to imply that the popular family magazines were habitual supporters of the disgruntled working man. Practical as always, they reminded militant readers of the cost – and the probable outcome – of strikes:

A coal-whipper wishes to know if he would do right to follow the advice given him by a coal merchant at Radcliffe in the matter of striking for wages.

We are not fully acquainted with the facts, but a coal whipper ought to know that in every strike in his trade, the coal merchants have largely benefitted, while the workmen have been worse than before.

Far from being righters of wrongs, most of the late nineteenth century magazines explicitly refused to use the problem page to campaign against anything more controversial than tight-lacing. The *Girls' Own Paper* declared its 'head in the sand' policy on 16 November 1889:

AFW: We are unable to take part in the reform of existing hardships and abuses such as you name. We can only sympathise with you and all the girls working in steam laundries, or as 'packers' who have to work six days a week from 7.00 am to 11.00 pm and wish that these institutions did come under the Factory Act. But we could not take up or discuss such subjects, as they are quite out of our line.

It was left to the new mass-market magazines of the 1880s and 1890s to take a more critical stance, and to comment on recent legislation as it affected the ordinary man. Newnes' *Titbits*, for example, carried a letter in 1901 from a young shop-girl whose boss had been obliged by law to provide chairs for employees, who often spent 12 or 14 hours behind the counter. The chairs were duly provided. But anyone who was rash enough to use them would find herself looking for another job.

One solution to unemployment was to emigrate. Discussions as to whether or not to brave the unknown were so frequent that *Punch*, on 1 January 1887, devoted a whole column to parodic advice on the subject:

> *Hard Up – Professors, clerks, pianoforte-tuners, company promoters and beadles are certain to get on well in the unsettled parts of North West Manitoba. But agricultural labourers had better stay at home. They are not wanted.*

Expectations did often outstrip qualifications, and the genuine problem page (despite *Punch*'s mockery) devoted many inches each week to discouraging the obviously unsuitable. As *The Family Herald* remarked on 22 November 1902:

> *Nobody would dream of starting farming in England without experience unless he had plenty of money to lose. Yet people who see the futility of amateur work on the land at home will assume that they can take it on quite naturally in the Colonies.*

The need for white collar workers overseas grew towards the end of the nineteenth century, as did job opportunities for women – now vastly outnumbering the men in the Old Country. Increasingly, young single women went out to Canada, South Africa and Australia as servants, school teachers and office workers. Usually they found themselves husbands within the year. Problem page editors, however, discouraged their female readers from embarking unless they had arranged a job in advance. Even when this requirement had been met, the question of a long and hazardous journey remained. The *Girls' Own Paper*, as much concerned about ship-board bounders as about storms, arranged with Miss Lefroy, Hon. Secretary of the

British Women's Emigration Institute, that parties of their readers should be chaperoned by a mature matron.

Many such emigrants retained their allegiance to their English magazine, ordering it from their new colonial address. So successful was the policy of recreating British communities in microcosm that letters received from the far-flung Empire presented very much the same problems as those from Huddersfield or Harrow. But the fiction of a transplanted England, which worked so well in most places, was clearly always under stress in South Africa. In a letter to *Woman's Life*, in August 1899, a Mrs Russell who had lived in New Zealand and Australia as well as South Africa was pessimistic about the magazine's scheme to start a colonial penpal club:

> *It would answer well in New Zealand and Australia … but it would not answer here in Africa as you would not know if the correspondents were white or black to whom one was writing. The white people here seldom speak to the coloured class or make friends of them, and you cannot tell by their names, as sometimes a black girl marries an Englishman and so obtains an English name.*

> I really did not know until Mrs Russell told me that the distinction between colours in Cape Town and the neighbourhood was so severe as this. I do not wish it to be thought I am treating Mrs Russell's kind letter in any flippant spirit, but I think I must require all correspondents writing from Cape Town to state whether they are black or white.

The racial prejudice that has bedevilled South African politics ever since was clearly already rampant.

The correspondence column in *Woman's Life*, entitled 'The Five O'Clock Tea', was in many respects a final flowering of the dynamic Victorian era. A substantial number of queries dealt with commercial patents. Readers invented crafty household gadgets or new industrial processes and, with admirable business sense, wrote to *Woman's Life* to ask how they could protect the same from piracy. That this is not a topic with which our current problem pages are much concerned is, perhaps, a comment on modern British industry.

The opportunities for working women, quite apart from any innovatory talents they might have, were gradually widening. On 5 January 1901, for instance, *Titbits* advised a would-be Charley's Angel that there was no reason 'why you should not become a detective if you have the requisite ability'. There were, apparently, 'many clever lady detectives in London' although Scotland Yard would still only employ them casually and refused to have them on the staff.

But the most significant expansion came in the more prosaic world of the office, with the employment of the women who were then known, rather confusingly, as typewriters. In some offices, of course, bosses regarded their new female employees as little more than machines. But, in others, the new-fangled secretary soon learnt that fast shorthand was less necessary than fancy footwork. It came as a rude shock to some gently nurtured girls to find that, instead of the safety in numbers of a typing pool, they were expected to share an office with a man. Such girls, however, received scant sympathy from *The Lady's World* in 1907, a publication, incidentally, which had no connection with the magazine of the same name edited in the 1880s by Oscar Wilde:

> *Typist: I do not think you are quite fair to your employer in complaining of your isolated position in his office, you knew how it would be before you accepted the situation, and it is yourself or your parents who must be responsible for this. You surely could not expect he would employ you and also a chaperone to look after you! It is one of the inevitable changes that must be faced when young women go out to business – that they must be self-reliant, and trust to God and themselves for their safe-guarding just as with every lad. These attentions which your employer's son has been paying you may mean much – and an ugly 'much' – or they may mean only the outcome of a good-natured disposition ... It seems to me quite clear that somehow you must refuse these gifts, or you may soon find them the pioneers to requests for favours which you will then have more difficulty in declining, possibly to your subsequent sorrow ...*

Qualms about office propriety were further diminished by the First World War, when work became a patriotic necessity and the boss' son tended to be at the front. But war-time advisers were careful to warn working girls from becoming too mannish and ambitious in their jobs. Once the victorious heroes came back to their former posts, readers were reminded, women would have to revert to domesticity. This assumption led the auntie on *The Family Herald*, in May 1918, for instance, to discourage two female bank-clerks from taking any banking exams, on the grounds that all that was required of them was 'exactness, neatness and efficiency in the practical duties that are allotted', whereas male colleagues would be expected to 'pass through various grades and become a manager and a student of the higher branches of finance'.

The actual outbreak of war in 1914 appears to have taken most women journalists by surprise, not least those working on the aristocratic *Ladies' Field*. On 1 August 1914, as the shooting season opened, they looked forward with relish to the new sporting year:

> *Our guns are now overhauled and ready for action. Happy moment! I am sure they must be glad to come out again after their long rest …*
> *I have been asking myself what form of shooting brings most pleasure to the greatest number? Grouse shooting, coming first after a long rest, is much looked forward to, but is the sport only of the lucky few, which is a pity, as it is ideal from a woman's point of view, now that so much driving is done …*

Within a week the guns were ready for action in deadly earnest and the grouse were, for once, in less danger than the marksmen.

One auntie, however, can claim at least a degree of war-time prescience. Will Dyson's famous cartoon 'Peace and Future Cannon Fodder' appeared in 1919. It depicted the signatories of the Treaty of Versailles with, in a corner, a child whose halo reads '1940 Class'. Clemenceau remarks 'Curious! I seem to hear a child weeping!' 'Mrs Marryat' of *Woman's Weekly* didn't manage quite this degree of prophetic exactitude. But she did give at least a glimpse of the future on 7 August 1915, when she replied to a letter from a patriotic children's nurse:

... who was very anxious to leave the children she was looking after so that, as she said, she might serve 'Her King and Country'. Now it never seemed for a moment to occur to her that in helping to rear healthy children that she was serving her King and Country, and in a very important way too. The little boys of today may be the soldiers of 15 or 20 years hence. The little girls will be the mothers of the next generation.

This was the chief role of women throughout the war. Heroics were to be left to the men. However patriotic the magazine, girls were encouraged to look after their parents and other responsibilities at home, and not to lust after enlistment. Those who did volunteer, for work in the munitions industry, for example, found that their way was not exactly made smooth for them. In spite of a shortage of labour, would-be factory workers, according to the problem pages of 1916, still had to pay a premium for training at the start of their employment.

The First World War, in retrospect, is rightly seen as a great divide in social history. But for most civilians it did not bring immediate or dramatic change. Many girls' horizons actually narrowed as the men left for the front, and they remained at home with their parents. More work and less fun was the day-to-day effect of mobilisation on women. As a result the problem pages of this date are extremely 'homely', even a little dull. Though much of the advice is being given to girls whose sweethearts are at the front, the war seems thousands of miles away. There are a few letters from men about to leave for France, and some from those at the front (usually dealing with practical matters, such as how to get the banns read for a marriage on a forty-eight hour leave). But the carnage and fear of the trenches, if they appear at all, appear only obliquely.

Just as the troops anticipated returning to 'a land fit for heroes', so their womenfolk expected that they would be in some way rewarded for their war-time sacrifices. The reward never, of course, materialised. The most immediate consequence of demobilisation was unemployment, a phenomenon which would gradually worsen throughout the 1920s and early 1930s. But, despite the influx of men into the job market, not every woman automatically gave up her employment. Not every woman, after all, could now have a male breadwinner, for a whole generation of potential husbands had been decimated in Flanders. The aunties running 'The Batchelor's Letter Bag' on *The Home Mirror*, on 13 August 1921, took a practical view of the situation:

> *Old Reader (Cardiff): I don't think you should be too hard on the modern girl. To my mind, she is no worse than the girl of 30 years ago, although my memory doesn't go as far back as all that. Girls nowadays certainly have more freedom, but I don't think they are any the worse for it. Yes, it is a pity, so many of them have to earn their livings. But what are they to do? Better work and live, than stay at home and starve.*

Pre-First World War Women's magazines, when they pandered to their readers' fantasies, wrote of the glamorous life of mannequins in smart London stores or of nurses taken on long cruises by ailing employers. But for many girls in the 1920s, obliged to work at unexciting jobs, fantasy was a husband, a home to keep tidy, and children. Women's magazines (abetted by pressure from the increasingly competitive world of advertising) reflected this change, marketing a sickly sweet version of home life for their readers.

The increasing emphasis on domestic economy, knitting and home-making, owed something, also, to the disappearance of the domestic servant. Middle-class women had themselves to master child-care and vacuum cleaning. Their plight was discussed by Flora Klickman, editor of *Woman's Magazine*, in 1925:

> *If there is one woman more than another to whom my sympathies go out in the fullest degree, it is the refined and educated housewife of the middle-classes, who is struggling today with three huge burdens: high costs, inadequate means and over-work.*
>
> *It is one of the most serious of present day problems that the women who are of the most use to the nation and the most valuable to the world at large, should be crushed as they are now being crushed, with work far beyond their physical strength, and with household worries that no one, so far, seems able to relieve ...*

> ... *The women who are able to give the best training to their children, helping their intellects to develop, forming their tastes in the right direction and shaping their characters are now often compelled to do nearly everything in the way of household duties, simply because outside assistance is almost impossible to obtain, except at a prohibitive price.*
>
> ... *We all agree that training is most desirable for domestic duties; there is no work in the world that calls for a greater variety of knowledge and skill than that of a home-maker. But at the same time, there is a great deal of work to be done daily in every household that does not call upon very specialised knowledge or an elaborate course of training − work that could be very well performed by some of the present recipients of the 'dole' and thus help lessen trouble that is literally undermining the human race.*

This argument, of course, rests on the debatable premise that moral tone must come from the middle classes. But the publication of such sentiments by *Woman's Magazine* indicates that this middle-class organ, at least, was not eager to see its readers chained to the kitchen sink.

The closing of editorial eyes to so many of the social problems of the age − unemployment, the rise of fascism, the imminence of war − has led, of course, to much criticism. Cynthia White, for example, has claimed that the magazines of the 1930s 'were as comfortable and comforting as the woollies they encouraged their readers to knit'. But it is not entirely fair to suggest that women's magazines, while urging their readers to be impeccable housewives, themselves swept all metaphorical dirt under the carpet. Without leaving the domestic sphere, women's magazines of the 1930s, in their own way, became very much more adventurous.

Instead of being kept firmly in the front room or the kitchen, the reader was, for the first time, admitted to the bedroom. There, it seems, lying still and thinking of England was no longer the definition of a wife's duty. Women were suddenly expected to enjoy sex, and to many of them this may well have seemed to be a matter of more importance than the Spanish Civil War or the collapse of the League of Nations.

The first indication that popular magazines were willing

to discuss sexual problems appeared in the late 1930s, when *Woman* published a series entitled 'Psychology and Sex', and included a quiz to test frigidity. But the new openness was soon equally apparent in the problem pages. 'Evelyn Home', for instance, did not confine herself to euphemisms when she replied to the following letter in *Woman* on 1 July 1939:

> ... *My husband seems to set far too much store by the lower side of marriage. He is as ardent a lover now as he was when we were first married, and I think this is quite unnecessary.*

The phrase I object to so strongly is 'the lower side of marriage'. Marriage is a combination of many expressions – and not the least of them is the physical expression of love. It is of all shared happiness, the one thing which depends most on complete harmony between both partners. It should be a spontaneous demonstration of affection and ardour on the part of either man or wife, which is communicated from one to the other, and shared with equal joy.

According to Peggy Makins, the letters received by current aunties on this subject differ only in the vocabulary used. In 1939 a letter on frigidity would announce 'His love making does nothing to me.' Now letters say, 'I don't get an orgasm.'

The breakthrough into the bedroom was important. It opened up areas that many people find impossible to discuss with their relatives, neighbours or even spouses. It changed indeed the whole aspect of the problem page. Before, aunties had dealt principally in information available elsewhere, and in subjects which would not have been out of place at the vicar's tea-party. The frank discussion of sex, therefore, gave problem pages a new lease of life when some of their other functions were taken over by the welfare state.

The problem pages of the Second World War did take note of some public matters. One mother wrote movingly to *Glamour* of the problems she was having with her eldest daughter, who had been made an officer and brought her parade ground manner home with her. She terrorised her sister, who had remained in the ranks, as well as her parents. The auntie suggested that the mother should remind her bully of a daughter that she was supposed to be fighting against tyranny and oppression and not spreading them around her parents' lounge. War-time aunties also devoted a certain amount of space to such practical concerns as the question of who would pay for bomb damage to a house which was being bought on a mortgage, and how to cope with fear in an air-raid (deep breaths followed by singing).

But it was the new willingness to delve into the more intimate details of their correspondents' sexual lives which was the most significant development. It continued to dominate the problem pages in the 1950s and 1960s. Future generations, reading our agony columns, may be as critical of our obsession with sex as we are, for different reasons, of those of the 1920s, 1880s or 1790s. There are, however, signs that this obsession with the intimate is ending. It is, for example, becoming more common for magazines to include specialist advice columns on legal matters. Both *She* and the recently launched *Company* make use of such experts. In *She* Tricia Murray copes with anything ranging from the legal grounds for divorce to the implications of shop-lifting. In *Company*, Patricia Hewitt, Director of the National Council for Civil Liberties, draws on her expertise in woman's rights, and consumer affairs.

Modern counsellors have, however, conspicuously refused to take up the mantle of Steele, Addison or Defoe and use their problem page as a device for righting society's wrongs. When Marje Proops or Angela Willans wishes to write a campaigning article she does so, but not on her problem page. As Anna Raeburn says, 'When I give an answer, I'm responding to the dilemmas of the person who wrote to me. I'm not writing for millions.' For all its virtues, that attitude has led to a contraction of range from which the agony column is only slowly recovering.

12

THE PROBLEM PAGE TODAY

Reading problem pages is often seen as a superior form of voyeurism. We are given a peep into other people's lives without the drawbacks involved in endless chats over the garden fence or innumerable pints in the local. We eavesdrop without facing the customary moral inconvenience of that action. And our doubt about our own motives for reading these columns has affected our attitude to them.

Most modern aunties are only too aware of the lowly status of their profession. Marje Proops tells of endless dinner parties at which fellow guests dig her in the ribs, chortling, 'I bet you get a lot of juicy ones, eh?' Peggy Makins was ashamed even to admit to her friends that she was the sub-editor on *Woman*'s agony column when she began her long association with that magazine in 1937. But no auntie finds her job a source of mirth, or the equivalent of curling up with a soft-porn novel. As Marje Proops has written of these dinner party detractors, 'I wish I could invite them to read just one day's distressing mail.'

Current practioners are still fighting an image inherited from predecessors who rarely tackled anything more demanding than a wobbling bust or that 'certain question my fiancé keeps asking me'. For Peggy Makins it was the war that revitalised the problem page, obliging it to deal with genuine social problems rather than mere social froth. Since 1937 she identifies four significant changes in her postbag – a new verbal frankness, a problem of choice

rather than lack of boyfriends, an increase in the number
of letters from working women and, more surprisingly,
the growth of a correspondence with prisoners and their
dependents.

Denise Robins, better known as the author of over a
hundred and seventy books, started as an auntie the same
year as Peggy Makins, 1937. She now runs the 'Heart'
section of *She*, leaving the 'Sex' to Dr Delvin. However, the
divide is not absolute. As she herself comments, 'They
write to me asking whether it's their fault or their
girlfriend's that she doesn't have an orgasm – I can't
imagine how they expect me to know.' Marje Proops
reflecting on her twenty-six years experience as an auntie,
feels that a less repressed post-war morality has led some
of her readers to become 'hung up on sex', believing their
marriage to be doomed unless sex is perfect. 'That's
absolute nonsense, of course,' says the inimitably firm Ms
Proops.

A less repressive society has brought some benefits.
'Claire Shepherd', the auntie on *Woman's Realm* for the
past nineteen years, has found at least one heartening
change in her recent post-bag. 'I still get letters from
unmarried pregnant girls but they're slightly less frantic;
they no longer write that they're going to kill themselves.'
More permissive legislation has also been reflected in the
letters sent to Angela Willans, the Mary Grant of *Woman's
Own*. She received a spate of letters from homosexuals
after the 1967 Sexual Offences Act.

Early problem pages often pre-dated rather than
mirrored changes in social legislation. At the start of the
eighteenth century, for example, only Defoe clearly
opposed divorce, with Dunton and Browne actively
supporting it when adultery was proven. Legislators and
the church, by contrast, resolutely opposed it. As late as
the 1850s, problem page writers belonged to a liberal
vanguard, using their columns to campaign for the rights
of deserted wives. Gradually, however, the problem pages
lost their pioneering role. Possibly, as they were
increasingly aimed at women, they became more
conservative.

Alternatively, it may be that a mass readership was judged by editors to be less sympathetic towards legislation which supposedly threatened family life. Whatever the reason, it is significant, I think, that A. P. Herbert's Divorce Act of 1937 was not foreshadowed by a more tolerant attitude in the problem page. In other words the aunties condoned behaviour that the law permitted, but no longer used their columns to bring pressure to bear on Parliament.

Some modern problem pages, of course, cannot be accused of pandering to conservative opinion. *Forum* deals exclusively with sexual problems and could hardly be described as straight-laced (except perhaps as a form of deviancy). A survey by the Family Life Group, a private watch-dog on morals, actually concluded in August 1978 that agony columns in many teenage magazines 'encourage promiscuity'.

Few aunties would recognise themselves as corrupters of morals. They have, nonetheless, often led more eventful lives than one would think. Take Denise Robins for example. She's white-haired, dotes on her grandchildren, feeds sugar lumps to a small lap dog, and lives in a comfortable house in Haywards Heath with her retired-Colonel husband. But there her resemblance to the stereotype ends.

Her composer father and pretty Australian mother divorced when she was four and she spent her childhood commuting between foster parents, her mother and step-father, and a number of boarding schools. Constant financial insecurity at this age (her mother was obliged to write for her living) left its mark. Both as an adviser and as a writer of romantic fiction, Denise Robins believes that for women marriage and work are mutually exclusive. In her novels the heroines either give up a glittering career for love or are left weeping on the last page. Despite this rejection in principle of the working wife, Denise Robins herself has earned more than both her spouses (a youthful marriage at the end of the First World War broke up in the 1930s when she met her present husband, then an army lieutenant and ten years her junior).

When Denise Robins began her column for *She*, it was a truism that all good girls should be virgins at marriage. More recently she has abandoned this tenet. 'I have to change with the times; one has to, otherwise one is considered old-fashioned.' Essentially a pragmatist, even a trimmer, she has always made current social mores the starting point for her advice. In 1955 for instance, she told a Liverpool lad, in love with a girl 'with coloured blood in her veins', not to marry her. A 'small drop of black blood', she wrote, could lead to a woman giving birth to a 'totally black child'. For the sake of the child Denise Robins advised against the marriage. By 1977, however, after two decades of rapid social and demographic change, she was advising 'Coral B (Highgate)' to marry 'Henry', an Indian medical student, in the face of her parents' opposition:

> It is time your parents learned to accept people of different colour. If you really love Henry there is no reason why you shouldn't marry him. You may meet other prejudiced people who object to brown skins – but they are wrong and love can transcend all that.

Another auntie who moved almost imperceptibly with the times was Peggy Makins. When she took over the 'Evelyn Home' column, as an unmarried twenty-one year old, she was considered to have shockingly advanced opinions. By the early 1970s she was the auntie who most nearly fitted the popular view of a matronly, middle-aged and slightly out-of-touch lady. The metamorphosis was gradual. She started life in working-class London family as Peggy Carn. On leaving school she wished to be either a cook or a journalist. Her mother encouraged the latter ambition and her daughter rose from cutting newspaper clippings to being an efficient publishing secretary. Meanwhile she freelanced her work including the writing of fake problem pages for an unidentified magazine. Her first staff job was as a sub-editor on *Woman* where she stayed until her retirement.

An unwilling recruit to the agony column, she thought physical affection 'soppy' and had little sympathy for the fallibility of human nature. As a determined career girl she

despised marriage and spent her evenings in the Thames
Valley pub run by her widowed mother, helping out
presumably as a somewhat prim barmaid. There she met
Arthur Makins. She married him in 1940 and they were
almost immediately separated by the war for several years.
She therefore had some personal experience of the
loneliness facing young wives during this period.

Happily married to a man who solicits insurance, Peggy
Makins continued to offer the frank discussion of sex that
had pre-dated her marriage. Perhaps the best account of
her character came from her editor, Mary Grieves. 'I used
to think that if she had a topee on her head and was sitting
under a tropical sun, she would be a splendid district
commissioner, impartial, kind, perceptive and articulate.'
Had she indeed been a district commissioner, she might
have found the natives more biddable than her problem
page correspondents. Certainly she would not have tried
so hard to bridle a naturally autocratic nature, something
which as an auntie she consciously repressed:

> *One has to bear in mind all the time one writes anything like the*
> *Evelyn Home page that opinion is all one is dealing in, not the law of*
> *the universe. When the need for compression is paramount, one loses*
> *occasionally the space in which to remind the reader that whatever's*
> *written is 'my opinion' only. Then one begins to sound like God*
> *Almighty, and it's a horrible noise.*

As a Quaker, she believes in a loving but nonetheless stern
God, and trembles for those readers who write
'proclaiming their unshakeable trust in a good and
merciful God; because it seems to me that God is not
humanely merciful'. She occasionally prayed to God to
guide her in her reply to a problem. Apart from Anna
Raeburn, who believes in God but can't be tied down to
any particular faith, most of the other counsellors are
agnostics.

Religion and politics are supposed to be the two things
most British people are chary of discussing. But Mrs
Makins is open about both. Like most of her colleagues she
votes Labour, although she has strong leanings towards a

Conservative view of law and order ('violent criminals should be castrated so that they cannot reproduce themselves or their anti-social habits') and towards self-help.

Above all, Peggy Makins sees herself as the woman in the street (not of the street). This image is a conscious one, as is her willingness to deal again and again with humdrum problems. She explained these attitudes in an article in *The Times* in 1975.

> *People preferred to read about what might easily concern them (if it didn't concern them already) and in a woman's magazine, it should not shock the customers. Shocks are all right from the daily press, radio or television, but from a favourite weekly, the subscriber demands tranquillization, she may be moved, but not outraged.*

On the other hand, what seemed to interest her bosses was that she should be attracting a large readership 'so that the advertisements on the opposite page could be kept nicely high'. Cynically, she claimed, 'My masters did not care in the least whether I dealt responsibly with adolescent folly or the slow growing burdens of old age.'

The auntie with the public persona of cynic, however, is her colleague, Marje Proops. Tough, worldly, witty advice is Marje's trademark. Her chosen image of gap-toothed chain-smoker accords better with Nathanael West's creation 'Miss Lonelihearts' than with the stereotype of a maternal auntie. She is nevertheless a sympathetic counsellor, and a campaigning journalist for, amongst other things, an increase in widows' pensions, divorce law reform and (an old favourite) the Married Women's Property Act.

Discreet about her age, Marje must have been born around the end of the First World War into a family which ran an Islington pub. Aged sixteen, she joined a commercial art studio adjacent to Smithfield Market. There she widened her vocabulary (courtesy of the meat porters), and was taught how to make-up, dress and paint her colourless plastic framed specs with bright red nail polish by her fellow artists.

After this auspicious start in the world of bohemia, she swopped studios and became freelance. In a bad week she paid her rent by making tea. In a good week she sold fashion sketches – mostly of knitwear – to women's magazines. One day an editor asked her to write an article on the tribulations of being a young wartime mum, with a husband (by trade a building engineer) stationed miles away in the army. Marje was launched on a new career, becoming first the fashion editor and then, in 1948, the women's editor of the *Daily Herald*. Like Peggy Makins she was an unwilling recruit to the agony column, only taking over the 'Mary Marshall' column after the death of a colleague. Before answering her first batch of letters a psychologist gave her a lunch-time crash course on How to be an Advice Columnist. In 1954 she joined *Woman's Mirror*. Later she moved to the *Daily Mirror*. It was on the weekly *Woman's Mirror* that she developed an acerbic, tough-talking style somewhat akin to that of John Cassell in the mid-nineteenth century.

Like most other aunties, Marje is highly critical of doctors. She tells of lecturing to a group of them and standing in silence for some sixty seconds before barking 'Pull yourself together Mrs Jones.' Her audience laughed, but she knew she was talking to 'guilty men' – physicians who have bustled their loquacious or inarticulate female patients out of the surgery and written in their notes 'menopausal' or 'bored neurotic'.

Now almost crippled with arthritis, walking with the aid of a stick, Marje describes herself as 'pretty strong, I have to be, you can't afford a period of neurosis'. She did once temporarily give in, and was put on a course of anti-depressants. She soon, however, flushed them down the lavatory.

There is a temptation to believe that aunties must become hardened to the contents of their post-bag. Most, after all, receive between four and five hundred a week and some, like Marje, considerably more. This fear of losing the capacity to care is one reason which Anna Raeburn, formerly of *Woman*, gave for getting out. Marje, after twenty-six years in the business, seems to agonise afresh over each human dilemma. On the day I talked to her she had just received a letter from an unmarried mother who had permitted her baby to be adopted without realising the full implications of the step. No address had been included. Marje sat at her desk fretting how she could reach this desperate girl and try to comfort her.

In a review of her compilation of letters entitled *Dear Marje*, Bernard Levin raised and then answered the inevitable question:

> *Does Marje Proops do good? I cannot see how anybody reading her book can be in any doubt that she does an enormous amount, possibly – of direct, practical good, at any rate – more than any other single individual in the country. A large claim, perhaps, but, making the obvious comparison to test it, I think it unlikely that any doctor treats as many patients in a year as she treats correspondents, that any lawyer advises as many clients, that any priest even hears as many confessions.*

Her nearest rival (who may, in numerical terms, now have out-paced her) is not a doctor or a priest but a former nurse. Claire Rayner writes a problem page for Britain's biggest selling daily newspaper, *The Sun*, and contributes a weekly quasi-medical column to *Woman's Own*. Aged forty-seven, Claire is married to an artist, Des, who gave up his job in advertising when the rights to her first novel in *The Performers* saga were sold for a small fortune in America. They have three children, Mandy, Adam and Jay, and a home in North London called 'Holly Wood House' (she apologises for the conceit). On meeting her, the first impression is of immense vitality and enthusiasm – be it for lunch at Rules, her favourite restaurant, or for a current campaign on sex education for six year olds. Behind this vitality is the warmth and forthrightness which mark her counselling. Even her failings ('Am I being bitchy about her because she's much younger and prettier than me?' she asks after criticising one of her colleagues) are displayed to advantage. In common with many of her fellow aunties Claire thinks of herself as unattractive. Marje uses the word plain about herself. Peggy Makins was fat and spotty as an adolescent, and Anna Raeburn refused for years to expose her knees, wearing trousers as a cover-up.

Born into a London Jewish background somewhat similar to Marje's, Claire Rayner had a tougher time, describing her parents as feckless. As a consequence she does not share the now fashionable enthusiasm for the inner city slum – the rows of tenements with outside lavatories and filthy yards. 'I grew up in that kind of street of tenement houses,' she reveals, 'and a modern flat is a lot nicer, believe me. If you put inadequate people into a high rise block, then you are going to find that their behaviour is still inadequate. But it's the people, not the architecture.'

A busy woman, she leads a highly organised life. One day a week is spent writing her column for *The Sun*, another producing her article for *Woman's Own*. Three more days are devoted to her current book, at the rate of one chapter a day. Domesticity and socialising take care of Saturday, and personal correspondence is tackled on Sunday. It's a schedule that would exhaust most people.

Her prime objective on her problem page is to give her correspondents permission 'to be unhappy different, and to lead their lives as they wish'. They have her permission to be ill or weak. Both she and Anna Raeburn have remarked on a contemporary obsession with personal perfection. Claire runs her column on what she describes as 'situational ethics', meaning that she follows no absolute moral precepts but advocates avoiding hurt to anyone, 'including yourself'.

Apart from the general silence on homosexuality in *The Sun*, Claire Rayner is also supposed to steer clear of drugs and sexual perversion, including incest, bestiality and flagellation. Marje Proops censors only two subjects, bestiality and necrophilia (she claims her private post-bag has included letters on both). Most other aunties apply a rule of thumb self-censorship to sexual perversions and brutality. Georgette Floyd, the 'Claire Shepherd' of *Woman's Realm* for the past nineteen years, is the only one to claim that no editor has ever altered a word of her copy. 'I've dealt with practically everything,' she says 'It's the way you write about it that matters.' Responsible for the last page in the magazine, she is determined not to end on a dreary note. 'I try to put a bit of hope onto the page.'

The daughter of a printer, she was reared as a 'Sunday School girl'. Married with two children, she is a serious, yet quietly charming woman, who accords more closely to the traditional view of the auntie than many of her more famous colleagues.

Georgette finds that the most insoluble problems arise from marriage. Readers often write of twenty or thirty years of unhappy married life. 'Such women feel they've wasted their lives,' she comments, 'because they've got so little time to put things together.' She, like Claire Rayner, is concerned about the increase of alcoholism among the young. Drugs worry her less. 'A drug addict usually kills himself before he has a family. Alcoholics often have large families and don't die until they've inflicted real damage on their children.' For the last two years, in response to her large post-bag on loneliness she has initiated a Loneliness Week in conjuction with several voluntary bodies.

Arguably the most intellectual of the aunties is Angela Willans, the 'Mary Grant' of *Woman's Own*. She has a degree in English from London University, devoted five years to psychoanalysis, and is an Advisory Council member of the Humanist Society. She sees her role on *Woman's Own* as one of guiding and listening. 'You can't say do this, do that. It would be impertinent to do so.'

Her first job as an adviser was with the *Daily Herald* (though not as a contemporary of Marje) where she wrote the 'Margaret Shaw' agony column before becoming 'Mary Grant' fifteen years ago. Initially she disliked the anonymity of a pseudonym. Now she finds it 'a useful mask on occasion'. Divorced in 1974 ('We did think about mentioning it on my page, but somehow it never seemed relevant') she has two daughters, one of whom was a single parent.

Apart from her freelance work as a journalist, she has written two books, the most recent being a study of runaway girls entitled *Breakaway* which 'sold like manhole covers'. She is also a committee member of the National Council for One Parent Families, and a stalwart opponent of the Mary Whitehouse faction in the media. She suspects that our society has reached almost saturation point in terms of frankness about sex, but is fearful of the effects of a minority who wish 'to put us back into the Middle Ages' as far as individual freedom is concerned. Her personal preference is to air everything, but she does pause sometimes to consider whether her public is ready for each and every revelation.

In 1974 she started a separate column covering men's problems, in response to a post-bag in which fifteen per cent of the letters came from men. The difficulties are largely the same but men tend to see them differently:

> *They're all about finding love, losing love, and self esteem but men tend to see emotional problems as physical difficulties, whereas women talk about feelings. A woman will say 'I no longer love him.' A man will write: 'She's frigid, I'm impotent. What tablets can I (or she) take?'*

Young boys write about the size of their penises, girls about vaginal lips or breasts. 'They haven't got round to metric' is Angela Willan's brisk comment on the measurements sent to her daily.

Anna Raeburn, formerly of *Woman* is highly critical of the policy of separating the sexes, on the grounds that it creates artificial barriers. 'Men have exactly the same problems,' she argues. 'They write about being unloved, unattractive, or their partners being over or under-demanding sexually. I disapprove of luggage labels on my page.'

A former actress and secretary, Anna Raeburn first became an adviser on *Forum* and later ran a column in the feminist *Spare Rib*. At the age of thirty she joined *Woman* when Peggy Makins retired early. Apart from the highly suspect advisers on such teen magazines as *Pink*, *Valentine* and *Tina*, Anna was the auntie with the most 'alternative' reputation. Her decision to leave the sorority was partly the result of editorial friction. But it was also because 'I wanted to get out while I'm still burning, still angry.'

The new, angry school also includes Irma Kurtz of *Cosmopolitan*. Both she and Anna believe in forthright advice, and encourage their readers to do anything rather than be a victim. Irma Kurtz has described her role as that of a 'mother substitute', but her advice rarely has the motherly reassurance of a nice hot drink. An ice-cold gin and tonic would be nearer the mark.

Anna Raeburn is particularly wary of cosy comforters. Once, in desperation herself, she phoned the Samaritans. 'They kept on being so sympathetic and agreeing with everything I said. After a few minutes I just put the phone down, I couldn't stand it.' No one could accuse her of making the same mistake. On her show with Adrian Love on Capital Radio ('Don't call it counselling, it's entertainment') she reacts strongly to every call. She's pungent, argumentative, even rude – but rarely boring.

Heard with Adrian Love and Anna Raeburn on the Wednesday evening phone-in is 'Colin' a doctor who is also one of the advisers in the magazine *Company*. He shares several pages with an eminent group of specialists – Patricia Hewitt, Director of the National Council for Civil Liberties, Julia Little, training and career adviser to the Women in Management Group, and R. D. Laing, psychoanalyst, author and 1960s guru.

Laing's credentials as an agony auntie are mixed. His action-packed life has included two marriages and seven children, numerous books on medical, autobiographical and literary subjects, charges (later withdrawn) for possessing LSD, and a spell of meditation with a loin-clothed Himalayan hermit. On the other hand he has worked for the Tavistock Clinic and is a fully qualified doctor and psychoanalyst. He pointed out in an introduction to his first column in *Company* that 'For over twenty-five years I have been listening to people telling me what they are unhappy about,' and his celebrated thesis that mental problems are created by defining certain experiences as 'mental illness' when they may in fact be normal reactions to abnormal circumstances, could have a place in the problem page.

His diffidence, however, is extraordinarily pronounced.

In his introduction to *Company*'s advice column he wrote:

> *We have got to look at our problems before we can solve them. But this is not as easy as it sounds. One can be looking at something, and still not see it. It is very difficult to see oneself (and indeed to a large extent one is essentially invisible to oneself). It is very easy to deceive oneself. All we can do is to look at where it hurts, as attentively as possible ... I do not expect to be able to provide answers to most problems that are put to me. I see my function here to consist less in providing answers than in pointing the way, hopefully, to how you may work out your own answers to your own problems.*

The idea of handing the problem back to the correspondent is as old as the agony column itself. But Laing carries it to unprecedented lengths. In October 1978 (the first issue of *Company*) he told one female correspondent, 'I am not entitled to say anything about your boyfriend individually, since I have not met him.' Another reader, this time a man who wished to know why he found it so difficult to communicate with the opposite sex, was informed 'I can think of many possible answers to that question, but I am not in a position to know which is the right answer in your case.' His refusal to provide more than a background murmur from the consulting chair beside the couch may herald a new direction for the problem page of the 1980s. If so, it will be more limited than the current role of the auntie as authoritative provider of moral permission.

Overall, 'Company Counsel' is an interesting example of the use of specialists whose skills do not necessarily include those of the journalist. Their expertise is unquestionable. But the first two problem pages (based, admittedly, on problems which the counsellors had encountered in their professional lives rather than through the post-bag) are surely some of the least exciting ever to be written. There is no sense of eavesdropping, no laughter, no real tears. It is, in brief, an implicit tribute to the skills of the traditional aunties. They use experts as sources of information. They remain however, first and foremost journalists, with a duty to inform and entertain a mass audience at the same time as they answer an individual's query.

Back-up guidance is important to all the aunties I interviewed. Most either retain a doctor, lawyer or social worker or have recourse to suitably qualified friends who serve the same function in an unofficial capacity. In addition they all have a full-time office staff of from three to eight helpers. Some aides are allowed to answer letters on their own; others are only permitted to follow standard replies, showing more difficult problems to the figurehead auntie. Peggy Makins admits occasionally to consulting her husband. But her colleagues regard their menfolk as uncertain guides. Denise Robins said of her husband 'The Colonel is a gentleman, and his reaction would not necessarily be typical.' The implication was obvious.

The average weekly post-bag is between two and five hundred letters, with seasonal variations. August and December are lean months and October and January heavy (both follow holidays). In the era of the Sunday postal collection, Monday was a busy day. Now much of the mail arrives on Tuesday morning, having been written in the small hours over the week-end. Most letters include a stamped addressed envelope and are privately answered. When used for the page, letters are automatically altered to prevent identification. Dorothy Critchley, the 'Jane Dawson' of *The Manchester Evening News*, who wrote amusingly in her autobiography of the need for such subterfuge was once nearly attacked by a furious husband who believed, erroneously as it happened, that a letter she had published from an unhappy wife was written by his spouse.

Bedevilling the problem page throughout its existence has been the question of the fake letter. They do not, on the whole, worry the aunties. Marje Proops spots them by their immaculate presentation and wonderful spelling. Peggy Makins recognises two perennial subjects:

> One is that which says 'I have been engaged for twelve years to a boy I love dearly, but he never mentions marriage. Do you think he is taking me seriously?' The other makes a rather different appeal. 'My father is

in gaol, my mother's on the streets and my brother is a freak with two heads in a circus,' it begins. 'But what really bothers me is that my boyfriend has joined the Liberal Party.'

Claire Rayner is suspicious of any letter written with flowery language and no feeling, while Georgette Floyd has noticed that fake letters mimic the style and length of the (altered) letters she publishes on her page. Anna Raeburn relies on a 'gut reaction' and discards those which fail this test of authenticity. In her four years on *Woman* she has only twice received a follow-up letter which has convinced her that her initial reaction was wrong. Most of her colleagues answer fake letters as they would a real one, but sometimes slip in a sentence showing that they suspect they're being taken for a ride. All aunties regard fake letters as an occupational hazard, harmless if time consuming.

Their methods of spotting faking are not invariably foolproof. In March 1978, *Over 21*, a magazine which does not itself have an auntie conducted a consumer test of the agony columns by sending identical letters to Marje Proops, Claire Rayner, Anna Raeburn and 'Mary Grant'. The problem presented was that of a married woman, with two children and a part-time job, who had been offered new responsibilities as a fulltime manageress. Her husband feared that the quality of his home life would suffer. The replies received were marked by Tony Samstag, the journalist conducting the investigation, for speed of reply, balance, practicality, understanding and what was called 'Compassion Quotient', defined by him as 'that intangible something which conveys the warmth and sincerity of the auntie's concern and which, in my opinion is the most vital part of her service'.

Claire Rayner whose reply opened with the words 'Ye Gods, what does he want? Someone to change his nappies for him', scored highest with her advice to accept the job, and an accompanying postscript which read 'Sorry to be so tough, but you did ask me.' Anna Raeburn, who suggested a trial acceptance of the job as a compromise was deemed to have given acceptable advice. Marje

Proops, who recommended marriage guidance, and 'Mary Grant', who plumped very firmly for taking the job and letting the marriage go hang, were dismissed as unacceptable. The revelation at the end of the *Over 21* article that Tony Samstag had his own arbitrary version of the perfect reply largely, I felt, invalidated his findings.

I also wrote to the aunties, including in my sample Claire Rayner, Marje Proops, 'Mary Grant' and 'Mary Marryat' on *Woman's Weekly*. I presented myself as a married woman with three children and a depressed, unemployed and impotent husband. I had been conducting an extra-marital affair with a married man whom I fancied but did not necessarily like, and now suspected I was pregnant. What should I do?

Apart from Marje Proops, whose department – or the post – clearly lost the letter (or did she spot the fake?), the aunties responded within ten days. Claire Rayner's reply got to me in six. All agreed I should find out for certain whether I was pregnant, and Claire Rayner and Angela Willans provided leaflets from the British Pregnancy Advisory Service. The latter also included leaflets from the Family Planning Association and the Brook Advisory Centre. Despite a Liverpool address, no auntie raised the question of whether I was a Catholic. Several of them, however, recommended marriage guidance, and a retraining course for my unemployed husband. Not surprisingly 'Mary Marryat' was stern about my involvement with a married man:

> I realise that the past 18 months must have been a great strain for you, but you are most certainly not going to improve matters by getting involved with another woman's husband. No matter how attractive he may be, or how attractive he may make you feel, my advice to you is to finish that relationship.

Claire Rayner, as is her wont, gave warm-hearted, sensible advice which covered most aspects of the problem and suggested several potential sources of help.

My justification for testing aunties by writing a fake letter must be the difficulty of judging the published reply when a letter which may originally have been five, ten, or even (a Marje record?) seventy-two pages is cut to under a hundred words and answered in thirty. However expert the sub-editing, some nuances must be lost in this process. The uncondensed private replies are arguably the most important part of a contemporary auntie's work and can be sampled only by such subterfuge.

The low status of aunties compared with that of lawyers, accountants and even the much maligned social worker, rests partly on their deliberately non-specialist role. It also reflects their lack of formal qualifications – perhaps a university should start an agony auntie course alongside those on sociology and medicine? The most fatal flaw of all, however, is their willingness to give advice for free. If Claire Rayner charged, say, fifty pounds per reply she might have fewer correspondents but command more respect. Despite their low status, these secular confessors who reassure the frightened, comfort the lonely and advise the ignorant, perform a vastly useful function.

In recent years the aunties have grown more assertive in defence of the problem page. Writing in *Cosmopolitan*, in October 1978, Anna Raeburn explained how she replied to the accusation that she should be 'doing something more directly political':

> '*Listen,*' I said with the accumulated wisdom of the last 15 years, '*if it's to do with people, it's to do with politics. Nothing is more political than dealing with people's lives and that's what I do, every day of my life. You don't have to join anything or anybody to be politicalised. You have to be able to explain yourself, to communicate with other people, to fight for the right to choose and when you've made the choice, to take responsibility for having made it. You have to accept that the best things in life will stand debate, you don't have to swallow them whole. You must question the way that children are brought up, not just into sexual roles, which stifle them and deny their needs, but being fed ideals of perfection which cannot and do not exist. We teach people to want but not to strive, to envy but not to enjoy, to look for a scapegoat instead of into the mirror.*'

Looking into the mirror and catching a glimpse of one's own face, or of an era now lost, is what problem pages are about. They are still the best mirror we have got.